D0592704

Educational Innovations
in
Latin America

LA 541
.C85
1973

by
Richard L. Cummings
and
Donald A. Lemke

The Scarecrow Press, Inc.
Metuchen, N. J.   1973

INDIANA
PURDUE
LIBRARY
AUG 1974
FORT WAYNE

Library of Congress Cataloging in Publication Data

Cummings, Richard L   comp.
    Educational innovations in Latin America.

    CONTENTS: Dynamics affecting education: Cummings,
R. L. Latin America's educational heritage. Sloan, J.
Precedent and education in Latin America: the rural-
urban imbalance. Cummings, R. L. Patterns of social
and economic change since 1950. [etc.]
    1. Education--Latin America--Addresses, essays,
lectures.   I. Lemke, Donald A., joint comp.   II. Title.
LA541.C85 1973   370'.98   73-390
ISBN 0-8108-0585-5

Copyright 1973 by Richard L. Cummings
and Donald A. Lemke

Prologue [p. iii] from Hobert W. Burns, "Social
Values and Education in Latin America," Phi Delta
Kappan, vol. XLV, no. 4 (January 1964), p. 200.

PROLOGUE

"Latin America faces a paradox: To improve its
education it must change its social order; to change
its social order it must develop and distribute its
economic resources; but it does not have the educational system to provide sufficient personnel who
can do the job...."

TABLE OF CONTENTS

v

Section I

DYNAMICS AFFECTING EDUCATION

This volume is intended to provide selected examples of primary- and secondary-level educational programs and plans which grew out of the raised aspirations of Latin American nations to extend educational opportunities to their citizens during the First Development Decade of the 1960's.

Individual national targets and area-wide patterns for educational growth were set at such meetings as the Conference on Education and Economic and Social Development in Latin America, held in Santiago, Chile, on March 5-19, 1962. At that meeting general guidelines suggested that emphasis should be devoted to providing six years of primary education; extending school-related welfare programs such as meals and health services for children; dividing secondary education into two cycles, the lower cycle to provide a general background and the upper cycle consisting of specialized branches; and facilitating more scholarship support with weight given to science at the higher education level. Further recommendations concerned vocational training, rural and agricultural education, literacy campaigns and adult education, all of which were considered as essential parts of the general educational plan of each country.

The importance of education in the process of economic growth is now nearly universally recognized. Tangible evidence of the importance attached to human resources in economic development is the existence of national and regional plans for educational growth.

The editors of this volume share the conviction that two important areas of educational concern are being partially attended through the dissemination of the case histories incorporated in this text:

1) The cases selected deal mainly with primary and secondary level education including literacy campaigns and

adult education.   These levels were selected because of the
high priority importance established for these areas and of
the scarcity of reporting relative to the volume of reporting
available on higher education.   Hence, this volume is intended to contribute to ameliorating the imbalance observed
to exist in the base-line literature on education's role in
development as we begin the Second Development Decade of
the 1970's.

        2)   The second purpose is to contribute to the spe-
cific flow of educational information among all of the nations
of the Western hemisphere.   It is commonly observed that
the lines of communication in South and Central America
flow outward from the center of individual nations to the sea
and thence to Europe or North America.   Traditionally there
have been only modest levels of social, economic and cultural exchange among these neighboring nations.   The case
histories found here are primarily written by Latin American educators, about Latin American education for distribution among Latin Americans who are concerned with development trends in Latin American education.   The case histories
have been selected with the view that their innovative character and local success may recommend the more widespread
adaptation of programs of these types in other regions or
schools.

1. LATIN AMERICA'S EDUCATIONAL HERITAGE
Richard L. Cummings

Latin America's educational heritage is dominated by the intellectual traditions of Europe.[1] Threads of educational homogeneity common across the nations of Latin America today are rooted in European experience from the Medieval, Renaissance, Counter Reformation and Enlightenment periods with its variations in belief regarding the sources and tenure of knowledge. More recently, since about the time of Latin America's independence movements, Liberalism, Positivism and Marxism have been adapted from their European sources by educational leaders in Latin America.

Educational systems are, at their best, the creation of the societies whose needs and desires they serve. When societies' decision makers desired to prepare young men for professions in theology or law or medicine or teaching the liberal arts, the great medieval universities arose, comprised of precisely those faculties. In more recent times when societies wished to prepare personnel for careers in engineering, agriculture, business, and other such vocations, institutions such as the land grant universities in the United States arose and soon grew to their astounding size. Hence it is postulated that educational systems can only be understood as they are viewed against the background of their contemporary social and cultural environment.[2] The task of these systems is in great part to preserve and transmit the elements of permanent value found in the cultural heritage of the past. Yet it is as important for them to discard the obsolete as to add the timely; and they must so discard the obsolete as not to lose contact with that which has perennial worth. If the systems fail to do this transmitting, discarding, and adding in such a way that they adapt themselves to the emerging needs and interests of the men of their day, they become obsolete and then soon decay. Thus societies must find leaders of vision and initiative who are abreast or even ahead of their times, and through them found educational systems of a new character which comply with contemporary interests and needs.

A terse review of the transformation of Western World educational traditions utilizing what UNESCO definitions today term primary, secondary, and higher education will throw light on past preferences for content, organization, and structure.

When medieval boys came to the monastic and later the cathedral school[3] at the age of six or seven, the objective of their teachers was that of training them to sing in the choir and to participate in the prayers. Hence, the teachers, with the primitive means available to them in those days before printing when even writing materials were scarce, devised methods suitable to achieve these ends. They learned how to read and write Latin; nothing of widespread importance in the life of learning or culture was as yet written in vernaculars. At approximately ten years of age pupils entered upon the study of the seven liberal arts, divided into the trivium of grammar, rhetoric, and dialectic which was chiefly logic, and the quadrivium of arithmetic, geometry, theory of music, and theory of astronomy. Almost half their time was given to grammar, since Latin was then as necessary for schooling and cultural life as the vernacular is today. Consequently, the goal of most of these students was hardly the appreciation of literature. Rather, it was primarily an acquiring of the ability to speak, read, and write Latin with facility for liturgical, political, secretarial, philosophical, or theological purposes.

Latin was also used extensively in international commerce. But the medieval West never did succeed in making Latin an easily usable means of communication with the Greek-speaking world of the East.

During this later middle age universities arose. Many of the medieval universities (from the Latin universitas) functioned as corporations or guilds organized for the purpose of training and licensing teachers. Two organizational models were dominant: the University of Bologna, in Southern Europe, in which the students themselves constituted the guild or corporation and hired, promoted or fired their teachers as they saw fit; and the Northern European University of Paris which was not a guild of students but of teachers.[4] These were essentially secular institutions.

The students attending these universities quite naturally grouped themselves into "nations" according to the land of their birth.   They lived in the residence halls called "colleges. "   The lectures were given anywhere, even in nearby fields.   In time, professors rented rooms in these student halls and gave lectures in them.   (Thereby engendering the use of the terms "colégio" [Portuguese] and "colegio" [Spanish].)

The chairs or professorships in the liberal arts made up the lower (inferior) faculty, and the chairs of theology, law whether canon or civil, and medicine made up the higher (superiores) faculties.   Most of the students appear to have come to the universities to prepare themselves to practice the learned professions of law, medicine, theology, or university teaching.   The specific objective, the finis operis, of many branches of study and especially of philosophy and theology was the development of the intellectual virtues.

The parents in the home and later the teachers in the schools had as their chief ideal to form the youth into the just man pleasing to God in all respects.   Most of the students came to gain the knowledge by means of which they could win or carry on the better positions in civil or ecclesiastical society.   The students and professors alike did not deem the two objectives, the finis operis and the finis operantis, mutually exclusive.   Neither did they regard either of them as unworthy of a prudent, liberal-minded man; the traditional seven liberal arts were liberating and vocational in that time.

What was perceived as the structure of knowledge upon which this educational system had been built?

Let us turn to a systematic presentation of the philosophic questions and the medieval acceptable answers.   First, let us inquire into the nature of reality:[5]

What was the nature of the universe?
What were the origins of being?
Was there a purpose?
Was there law or system?

The preferred pre-enlightenment response to these questions was essentially Aristotelian as accepted in the Thomistic tradition.   The dualism of idea and matter was clearly dominant.   Natural law, the universal system, was derived from a supra-physical source, a creator of everything from nothing.   The Idea was: the physical universe was created and was inferior and subsidiary to the conceptual. Matter was temporal; ideas were eternal. The universe, created by a non-material being, was revealed to man as he explored its workings. Both physical and non-physical being were a priori and man did not change either of them--he could use or abuse the physical aspects of being, but he could not alter the rules of the game, and he was irrevocably subject to the requirements of the higher being. The ultimate reality was expressed in God and His ultimate law in the moral law; science could help man discover the physical law which governed the material universe, but it could not reshape it. The purpose of reality was to glorify God and reflect His greatness, to provide the stage upon which God's role could be dramatized.

Second, man, created by the same God who brought forth the universe, expressed in his very nature the duality inherent in the universe itself. He, unique in the universe, different from all other creatures brought forth by God, had a physical and nonphysical being. He had a body which expressed his physical nature; he had a soul, a spirit which expressed his nonphysical nature. Man's true and ultimate nature was expressed through his soul. The physical nature of man was governed and subordinated by his soul; his highest expression was in the spiritual realm. His destiny was in his capacity to be saved from his physical limitations and to be brought into full communion with God in a relationship which would transcend his physical being. As in the case of the question of reality, man's purpose was to glorify God, to obey His law, to achieve salvation, a state of non-physical being, external, limitless, infinite in love and understanding. No expression of man's physical being could be higher than or more desirable than the true expression of man's spiritual being and relationship to God.

Third, knowledge and the acquiring of knowledge, learning, reflected the Aristotelian dualism preserved in Thomism. Physically derived science, empirically rooted, could not refute knowledge gained by intellectual processes. The physical world could be described by science, but the higher reality could be reached, understood, and "gained" only by nonphysical processes linking the spiritual nature of man to God. At best science was the handmaiden of God, describing His works and systematizing the physical law for man's benefit; at worst it challenged the natural law, perhaps even opening the question of the existence of natural law. Since man was the only being who had a special relationship·with God, it was his knowledge which was special. The processes which animals used to adapt their environment to their purposes could not be classified as knowledge in the same way as man's conceptual processes, which abstract principles from physical experience. Two principal kinds of knowledge were possible: (1) empirical knowledge gained by and limited to physical experience, and (2) metaphysical knowledge gained only through the intellectual processes.

Finally, values, usually defined as the basis for human behavior or the criteria against which choices are made, were seen to reside in and operate from an absolute scale which had to be accepted by man. The question of values was relevant to man because of their special nature; because of the inferior nature of the physical realm, those values which derived from physical need and satisfaction were subordinated to higher values derived from the a priori moral law.

Values were not susceptible to change; they were not relative.

Man struggled to become aware of the correct values and to his utmost strove to live in accordance with the morality inherent in those correct values. Man's apparent failure to live according to the highest order of values did not prove that those values did not exist but only gave witness to man's weakness and inability to grasp the truth and live by it. 6

The traditions of Latin American educational content, methodology, administration, organization and structure were and to a great extent are rooted in these belief preferences.

In the thirteenth century, the curriculum in the arts was an Aristotelian enrichment of the trivium and quadrivium. It included grammar, philosophy, logic, rhetoric, metaphysics, moral philosophy, mathematics, and natural philosophy such as Aristotelian physics, astronomy, or biology. Comparatively little attention was given to ancient literature as such. The curriculum of the arts lasted for from four to seven years. Consequently, a student frequently partook of this curricular offering from the age of twelve to sixteen, at the completion of which he might receive a degree of Bachelor of Arts. This curriculum served to maintain early medieval or feudal society which had been essentially agricultural. It contained three classes: first, the clergy;

second, the nobility of princes, barons, knights, and squires;
and third, the peasantry, comprised of serfs bound to the
soil, free <u>villeins</u> or renters, and slaves.

Feudalism had reached the height of its development
in the tenth century and had then began to decay. The decline was already noticeable in France and Italy by the end
of the twelfth century. The system continued longer in Germany and England, but by 1500 it was almost extinct in all
countries of western Europe. Many relics of it, of course,
survived until much later--some until the middle of the
nineteenth century in central and eastern Europe. One needs
not seek far for the causes of the decline of the feudal regime. Many of them were closely associated with the revolutionary economic changes of the eleventh and succeeding
centuries. The revival of trade with the Near East and the
growth of cities led to an increased demand for products of
the farms. Prices rose, and as a consequence some peasants were able to buy their freedom. Moreover, the expansion of commerce and industry created new opportunities
for employment and tempted many serfs to flee to the towns.
Once they had made good their escape, it was almost impossible to bring them back. Still another economic cause
was the opening of new lands to agricultural production,
mainly on account of the higher prices for products of the
soil. In order to get peasants to clear forests and drain
swamps, it was frequently necessary to promise them their
freedom. The Black Death, which swept over Europe in the
fourteenth century, while not exactly an economic factor, had
results similar to those of the causes already mentioned. It
produced a scarcity of labor and thereby enabled the serfs
who survived to enforce their demands for freedom. With
the peasant a free man, the manorial system was practically impossible to operate and one of the chief props of the
feudal regime had been broken.

The political causes of the downfall of feudalism were
also of major significance. One was the establishment of
professional armies and the inducements offered to the
peasants to become mercenary soldiers. A second was the
increasing complexity of equal relationships; a single vassal
could owe allegiance to several lords, and in some cases
lords became vassals to their own vassals. Another was
the adoption of new methods of warfare which rendered the
knights somewhat less indispensable as a military class. A
fourth was the condition of chaos produced by the Hundred
Years' War and the peasant insurrections resulting therefrom.

A fifth was the influence of the Crusades in eliminating powerful nobles, in promoting the adoption of direct taxations, and in compelling the sale of privileges to communities of serfs as a means of raising money to equip armies. But probably the most important political cause was the rise of strong national monarchies, especially in France and England. By various means the ambitious kings of these countries in the later Middle Ages gradually deprived the nobles of their political authority.

Thus, while the Middle Ages were passing away and then while the Ranaissance was blossoming, the political and social orders were changing.

Many men felt that scholastic writings were addressed too exclusively to man's intellect; they wanted something which appealed to all of man's faculties: his intellect, his will, his emotions, his aesthetic sensitivities, his imagination, and the powers of his body. [7]

The shift in interest was largely to a Christian humanism, which became increasingly rationalistic. Men were turning their attention from the scholastics' preeminently intellectualistic and speculative science of God to a more keenly experienced and emotionally warm science of man. They did not exclude the life to come, but concentrated more and more on the living of a rich, full life on earth. Schools were constrained to conform to the interests of their age. Through the height of the Renaissance from 1453 to 1527, there was an extraordinary enthusiasm for antiquity. Many educators devised a training almost exclusively in classical literature.

One of the most important phases in this movement was the revival of the ancient ideal of liberal education as formulated by Plato and Aristotle and adapted to the Romans by Cicero and Quintilian. It was the ideal of leading the free man to train all his powers of body and soul to excellence, that he might become the good citizen and benefit his fellow man.

The Renaissance was a highly complex movement of forces and factors. Men expanded in spirit through the invention of printing, geographical discoveries (which included the Americas), a growing interest in experimental science, and a many-sided interest in the satisfactions of life. One of the causes of this new life of the Renaissance was the

fact that little by little the men of the Middle Ages had
brought about an improved standard of living.

During this period dialectics and disputation had become important subjects of study.   The teachers of one generation after another were prone to do quite the same things
which their predecessors had done, without examining the
relevance of their subject matter to the newer demands of
their contemporary life.

Hence, after the scholastic philosophers and theolo-
gians had become lost in contentious details and were teaching more for the sake of mental discipline rather than for
the worthwhileness of their subject matter; and after the
ergoists had, by distinguishing and subdistinguishing, turned
their words so completely into technical terms that no one
else felt confident of grasping their meanings, a reaction to
this procedure arose.

In the medieval period, spiritual values had held the
highest place.   Service to God, the care of one's soul, justice and charity towards fellow men were universally deemed
to be man's chief duties, and the model of life was the saint.
In place of these ideals, many humanists, shifting their interests more to man and his worldly concerns, revived and
substituted ideals drawn from classical literature.   One of
these was what they named "Humanitas. " By this term they
meant an ensemble of qualities--intellectual force, literary
excellence, artistic taste, polished manners, and elegant
bearing--all intended to enhance that being who was their
ideal: man considered as a citizen.   The subjects deemed
likely to produce such a man came to be known as "the humanities (litterae humaniores). "

Particularly in Aristotle does one find clear distinction between the training in the arts which were deemed especially characteristic of the free men possessing leisure for
contemplation and the training in the useful arts then thought
to be suitable particularly and almost exclusively for the
slaves.   But the European social economic reality of the
1500's differed from the two-part context of just the master-
and-the-slave.   By the time of the early sixteenth century,
western society was commonly composed of three classes:
a landed aristocracy born to this class, a commercial aristocracy or bourgeoisie of merchants and artisans, and the
large numbers of peasants in the country and poor laborers
in the cities.   Old loyalties to a single Christian Church

were divided by the Protestant Reformation.   National consciousness was on the rise.   The Catholic or Counter Reformation was initiated to strengthen the Church. 8

The Catholic Reformation was greatly aided and abetted
by the Society of Jesus (Jesuits), the most militant of the
religious orders fostered by the spiritual zeal of the sixteenth
century.   Founded by a Spanish nobleman from the Basque
country, Ignatius Loyola, in 1534 the Jesuits became increasingly more influential defenders of the true religion and
teachers in the Hispanic world until by the time the Society
was suppressed by the Pope in 1773 it had a veritable monopoly on education in Spain and her empire. 9

Religious historians point out that St. Ignatius Loyola
made innovations in the form of religious life, in order to
adapt it to the new needs of his time.   In the early centuries
of monasticism in the West, the person who wanted to live
for God would enter a monastery or convent in order to
serve Him by a recollected life within its enclosure, especially by reciting the office in choir and by working.   In
time, lay persons settled near the monasteries and the
monks or nuns ministered to their needs.   Thus, an aposto-
late was added to their religious life, but it had not been
the primary concern of their founders.   In the early thirteenth century, when men were living more in cities for
commercial pursuits and not going to the monasteries for
spiritual help, St. Dominic and St. Francis added something
to meet the new needs.   They intended their friars or canons
regularly not merely to recite the office in choir within their
monasteries and convents, but also to go out to minister to
the people who would not come of their own accord.

Ignatius Loyola led the Society of Jesus to undertake
active works such as foreign missions and instruction of the
ignorant and poor in both sacred and secular subjects.   He
eliminated the obligation of reciting the office in choir and
of wearing a monastic habit which would have alienated many
of the students his order aspired to reach.

By these innovations Ignatious Loyola incurred suspi-
cion and criticism.   Some even said that he was dropping
part of the essence of religious life.   But he courageously
held to his resolution of devising measures likely to be edu-
cationally more effective in his time.   Eventually the Holy
See itself settled the controversies by giving fullest approval
to the form of religious life which Ignatius initiated.

Ignatius' spirit of innovation, cautiously carried on
through experimentation, is prominent in his work and writing in the field of education.   First, Ignatius preserved what
was of perennial value in the preceding education, especially
the philosophy and theology which found its best expression
in theistic Thomism rooted in Platonic-Aristotelian idealism.
Second, he discarded much that had become obsolete, especially the exclusively intellectual character of much of the
late medieval education which caused so many men of the
Renaissance to react against it; and third, he added many of
the literary and artistic graces and the attention to form
which the men of the sixteenth century esteemed so much.

When the liberal education of the earlier Renaissance
was in transition to the more narrow humanistic education of
the later Renaissance, Ignatius was synthesizing his educational preferences.   He did not overemphasize Ciceronian
style nor deem it the only worthy medium to communicate
the truths of theology.   Ignatius was aware of the growing
importance of the vernacular languages.   Some indication of
his awareness is the fact that he wrote his Constitutions in
Spanish. 10

Ignatius Loyola advocated that students first prepare
themselves well in grammar and humane letters.   Thereafter they might involve themselves with other approved
curricula--poetry, rhetoric, logic, natural philosophy, moral
philosophy, metaphysics, or mathematics.   Languages were
necessary tools for the study of Scripture and Loyola wanted
Jesuits and their students to be capable Latinists.   Ancient
writers--e.g., Jerome and Augustine--had studied humanities in both Greek and Latin.

There were various reasons for building a good foundation in the humanities.   First, to penetrate to realities and
substantial thought such as that found in scholastic philosophy
and theology, the mind had to be habituated to labor.   By
working in easier matters within their capacity, namely, the
humanities, pupils not yet habituated became able to work
upon matters of greater importance.   Second, time was well
spent in learning humane letters, for if the young man
reached the age where his interests were caught by more
important matters, for example the substantial thought, only
with greatest difficulty would he come to know languages
well.   An intellect once accustomed to the more important
and nobler mental operations would not bend itself down to
those most lowly.   And languages were useful for under-

standing Scripture. Third, languages, especially Latin, were useful not only for learning but also for adding some lustre to the communication of thought to others. Fourth, it was an era which was highly fastidious and those who did not know languages had little prestige. Fifth, knowledge of language was especially necessary in the Society of Jesus for dealing by word of mouth or by correspondence with so many differing language groups. Sixth, it was highly important completely to master the language once and for all, in order to keep it afterwards and be able to use it with full competence.

Thus the basic value Loyola saw in the study of Latin and Greek in the mid-sixteenth century was their usefulness in learning and using theology. He recognized the importance of Ciceronian Latin, but as a means helpful for expounding theology in his own day, and therefore as something to be adopted. He did not deem it an end in itself, nor regard it as a means as perennially useful as the theology itself. His end was a scientifically established Catholic outlook, and the literary graces fashionable during the Renaissance were a means especially suited to make the truths of theology more readily accepted in that period. While he saw the value of artistic graces, he did not commit himself forever to the ephemeral fancies of the early sixteenth century. For Loyola, the literary graces were means and should be adapted to the ever changing tastes of men.

Loyola's educational scheme if taken in its entirety of prescriptions for both higher and secondary education was formalized in the Jesuit plan for general education, the Ratio Studiorum. General education here was the Christian paideia, the preparation of a young male so that he might come to be a cultured man competent to play an active role in the social and cultural life of his era. Ignatius proceeded by practical means towards a concrete objective, that of forming Christian men who would be equipped and eager to influence for good the men of their own era in the social, cultural, political, and religious environment about them at the moment. He wanted to train, not the whole man in the abstract, but the whole man for participation in his concrete environment and era.

The best known edition of the Ratio Studiorum, officially approved in 1599, appeared at a most fortunate moment in history. Neither the rise in importance of vernacular writings nor the antipathies which were to later spring

from the nascent spirit of nationalism in so many newly unified nations had at that time disrupted the unity of loyalty in
Southern and Central Europe, primarily directed to the Ro-
man Catholic community. Europe was still a res publica
litterarum Latinarum. Hence the Ratio Studiorum could and
did produce a unity of procedure throughout the farflung hundreds of Jesuit colleges which were springing up in more
and more cities, many of which had few or no other schools.
Indeed, many of these schools were the first free public
secondary schools founded by their cities. The Ratio was
the instrument through which Ignatius' ideals in education
were effectively achieved on an unprecedentedly wide scale
in Europe and the colonies in the Americas until the Society
of Jesus was expelled from Brazil in 1759 and the Spanish
colonies in 1767.[11] The departure of the Jesuits was a
staggering blow to education in the Americas.

Absolutism, characterized by a mood which preferred
order and security more than liberty, had arisen in Europe
out of the chaos of the Black Death, decay of the manorial
system, the Hundred Year's War. The economic policy of
mercantilism and the wedding of church and state authority
had gone hand in hand with the theories of absolute rule.
However, the intellectual revolution of the seventeenth and
eighteenth centuries significantly modified political and educational preference in Europe and in the New World.

The Enlightenment, led by René Descartes, Isaac
Newton and John Locke, reached Latin America in the latter
half of the seventeenth century but did not gain momentum
until the eighteenth century after the Bourbon monarchs
sought to open Spain to Europe and the world. In essence
the Enlightenment represented a skeptical revolt against
traditional dogma and was an attempt to replace undisputed
and traditional authority by a desire to verify by investigation and experiment.

Jesuit humanism, with its interest in natural history
and pragmatic learning, was illustrated in the Americas in
the Enlightenment period by Father José Gumilla's The Enlightened Orenoco, Father Vincente Maldonado's Chart of the
Ecuadorean Territory and Juan de Velasio's History of the
Kingdom of Quito.[12] And, Father Andrés de Guevarra y
Basodzábal placed nationalism and experimentalism against
authority and tradition as did many of his fellow Jesuits.[13]

Disgruntled, upper-class Creoles in the Americas

were attracted to this set of ideas which coincided with their economic and sociological frustrations with the Spanish Crown and its colonial administrative system. A rise in valuing sensory-based ways of knowing derived from nature first challenged and later was incorporated into New World educational systems. The Enlightenment did not reach Latin America only through nefarious and risky smuggling; the texts of the Enlightenment were read by many reputable teachers with, at first, a mild caution but not fear. The Recreación Filosófica (1751-52) of Teodoro Almeida, advocating the physics growing out of subjecting ideas to nature, was an eighteenth century textbook in the University of San Carlos of Guatemala. In Chuquisaca, Canon Tarrazas housed the library in which Mariano Moreno read natural law in the metropolitan palace itself. The Portuguese educator Luis Antonio Verney (1713-1792), making use of Locke, was gospel in Caracas. The censorship of the Inquisition, well established though it was in law, was essentially bureaucratic and ineffectual. [14]

The chief educational handicap to a wider-ranging exploration into the secrets of nature in the Americas was the shortage of instruments. Yet von Humboldt was impressed at the ingenuity and skill with which José Caldos, for example, contrived to measure the altitudes of mountains by the parsimonious process of taking the temperature of water at its boiling point.

Independence brought few changes; Simón Bolívar's revolution left a political vacuum similar to the educational vacuum created by the earlier expulsion of the Jesuits from the Spanish and Portuguese colonies in the Americas. No continent-wide focus of regionalism or political solidarity came to replace past loyalties to Spain or Portugal and no new dominant educational philosophy arose to serve the new nations created in the Western Hemisphere.

Many of the intelligentsia continued to look to Europe for intellectual leadership. In literature, for example, the vogue of Paris continued to be emulated in Latin America during the nineteenth and early twentieth centuries. [15] Liberalism and romanticism influenced Latin American education in the late 1700's and the early 1800's. Liberalism placed great stress on written codes and constitutions, assuming that if the law of the land abolished tyranny and injustice, then some approximation to earthly paradise would follow. But laissez faire economics and government did not

work well in the Americas and gave way to "new liberalism"
or "Positivism" in the late 1800's.   Positivists postulated
that scientific laws governed the functioning of society and
that once such laws had been discovered it was the duty of
governments to intervene, whether asked to or not, to enforce these laws on society for its own good.

Positivism
implied that there would be an oligarchy of scientifically
educated investigators who would determine what were the
basic laws governing the satisfactory functioning of society
and then persuade or force society to adopt appropriate
mores and behaviors.   This interventionistic mode, quite
different from the old classical laissez faire neutral or non-
participating posture for government placed great emphasis
upon planning and implementation as a means of social and
economic development.   Marxist thought is also interventionistic but calls for the restructuring of the society prior to
or concomitant with the restructuring of the school.

During the more than four centuries of educational
effort in the Americas, there developed a tradition of experimentation with changing educational ideas and ideals.
The contemporary efforts documented in the chapters to
follow thus represent an extension of the long standing commitment to educational innovation in the Americas.

Notes

1.   Leopoldo Zea, "Is There an American Philosophy?" in
     Panorama, Washington, D. C.:   Pan American Union,
     November 1944, p. 12.

2.   Isaac Kandel, "Problems and Trends of Education in
     the Latin American Republics" in Intellectual Trends
     in Latin America, Austin, Texas: University of
     Texas Press, Institute of Latin American Studies
     proceedings, April 13 and 14, 1945, p. 89.

3.   Edward M. Burns, Western Civilizations, 7th ed.,
     New York: W. W. Norton and Co., 1968, p. 378.

4.   Burns, Ibid., p. 379.

5.   See Michael Chiappetta, "Philosophy of Education in
     Latin America" in Phi Delta Kappan, Vol. XLV, No.
     4, January 1964, pp. 241ff.   The following five
     paragraphs are for the most part taken from

Chiappetta as found on p. 215.

6. This pattern of preference is long lasting. See Don Miguel Antonio Caro's nineteenth century Hispanic commitment to pre-existent law when from "what is we rise to what ought to be ... we leave chaos and enter into order ..." in Mariano Picón Salas, A Cultural History of Spanish America, Berkeley: University of California Press, 1962, p. 41.

7. Chiappetta cites the pattern of de facto urbanization and modernization in Latin America today as not being compatible with philosopher kings and thus mandating a shift in basic educational philosophy. His view is that Thomistic-Aristotelianism is still dominant, op. cit., p. 216.

8. Edward Burns, op. cit., p. 481.

9. Burns, op. cit., p. 484.

10. Loyola's Constitutions deal with every aspect of the life of the Society of Jesus from recruitment of candidates to means of preserving the Society and insuring its growth. See Joseph de Guibert, S. J., The Jesuits, Their Spiritual Doctrine and Practice, translated by William J. Young, S. J., Chicago: Loyola University Press, 1964, pp. 139-151.

11. Margus Mörner (ed.), The Expulsion of the Jesuits from Latin America, New York: Alfred A. Knopf, 1967. See sections III and IV, pp. 117-172.

12. Picón-Salas, A Cultural History ... [see note 6], p. 131.

13. Ibid., p. 140.

14. Arthur P. Whitaker (ed.), Latin America and the Enlightenment, New York: Appleton-Century Co., 1942, pp. 34-49, 72-73.

15. Murdo MacLeod, "Area Essay: Latin America," in Carlton Beck Perspective on World Education, Dubuque, Iowa: William C. Brown Co., 1970, p. 314.

2. PRECEDENT AND EDUCATION IN LATIN AMERICA: THE RURAL-URBAN IMBALANCE

John Sloan

For those of us who are concerned with the politics of development in the Third World, the past decade has been a sobering experience. A period filled with violence, rioting, civil wars, coups, military revolts, and corruption, it is now likely to be spoken of as a decade of political decay rather than the "Decade of Development" envisioned by the United Nations.[1] We are now painfully aware of the failure of present strategies of modernization to overcome the vicious circles of underdevelopment. The Mexican economist, Miguel Wionczek, reflects the present pessimistic mood toward programs of modernization by estimating that, out of the 100 underdeveloped nations in the world (containing two-thirds of mankind), only fifteen have a reasonable opportunity to achieve significant development in the near future.[2]

The experiences of the 1960's make obvious the need in the future for a much greater mobilization of resources and institutions in the underdeveloped nations. But perhaps the most essential requirement of development is innovative thinking concerning the process of modernization. Social scientists in both the developed and the underdeveloped worlds should propose new policies that are not carbon copies of practices that were successful for Europe and the United States; the past decade has taught us that models of behavior imported from the highly developed Western countries frequently do not work in the dissimilar environments of the Third World. New policy proposals must be cognizant of the unique characteristics of both the obstacles to development most likely to be confronted and the strategies of development most likely to be successful in a particular nation.

This essay will examine the need for educational reforms in the rural areas of Latin America. Such reforms in rural education would overcome several obstacles to modernization if they had as two of their goals the reduction of rural-urban migration and the education of the bulk of the

24

rural population to a level where they could increase the political pressure for successful agrarian reform programs.
Thus, we shall examine first the characteristics of the developmental process in Latin America and then, the present
education system, and finally we will outline a few reform
proposals.

Characteristics of Latin American Development

Latin America is the most developed region of the
Third World. Since the end of World War II, most Latin
American nations have pursued policies of import-substitution
which have resulted in a duplicative, light industrial development in most of the countries. The pursuance of state-
directed strategies of industrialization by nations which had
been basically agrarian until World War II has resulted in a
unique form of capitalism based on state-encouraged monopoly rather than laissez faire competition. The resultant
economic system has produced a multitude of economic, social and political changes, but has not had the dynamic effects throughout the society which were hoped for by middle-
class reformers.

Protected from internal and external competition by
controls of the nation-states, Latin American capitalism is
characterized by poor management techniques, poor quality
control, and high costs of production. Import-substitution
policies have brought about a situation where the nations of
Latin America produce about 86 percent of their manufactured
goods for domestic consumption;[3] but the duplicative nature
of this development, the high cost of production, and the high
protective tariff in each of these countries has meant that
only 7 percent of Latin America's exports are manufactured
goods. Despite the impressive gains of industrialization
from 1940 to 1960, Latin America still suffers from a colonial economy in that most of her foreign exchange is still
earned, as in the nineteenth century, through the sale of
primary goods to the developed world, primarily the United
States.

A second unique feature of the Latin American economy is its pathological concentration in a few industrial metropolitan areas. The Economic Commission of Latin America (ECLA) estimates:

that the area of less than 5, 000 square kilometers

represented by the metropolitan areas of Buenos
Aires, the Municipality of São Paulo, and Mexico
City accounts for over a third of the total value of
Latin American production, although it contains
only about 8 or 9 percent of the region's population. Within each country the two main industrial
centers usually constitute a very high proportion
of the nation's industry: 66 percent for the metropolitan area and Rosario in Argentina; about 40
percent for the municipalities of São Paulo and
Guanabara in Brazil; 66 percent for the economic
areas of Santiago and Valparaiso in Chile; over
45 percent for Mexico City and Monterrey in Mexico; 56 percent for the Lima-Callao area in Peru;
and about 75 percent for the single city of Montevideo in Uruguay. [4]

One important social consequence associated with
these characteristics of the present Latin American economic
system is rural-urban migration. This migration is caused
both by "push" factors, such as the lack of opportunities in
the countryside, and by "pull" factors, such as the lure of
jobs, education, and a better life in the city. In recent
decades this migration has reached massive proportions in
almost every Latin American country with the exception of
Cuba. Table I estimates the urban and rural population
trends in seven Latin American countries from 1950 to 1970.

The industrialization process has shown a disappointing incapacity to employ the swelling populations of the cities.
Part of this incapacity can be explained in terms of the
changing needs of technology. For example, Claudio Velez
points out that

In the 1870's Britain was the first industrial power
on earth and was producing her first million tons
of steel. To achieve this over 370,000 workers
were employed. In Latin America today, Argentina, Brazil and Mexico are well over the million-
ton mark ... and a rough estimate shows that
only seven or eight thousand workers are needed
to produce each million tons of steel.... Such
examples abound and they all point to a fairly obvious development: industrial technology has
changed; it is now more capital than labor intensive. [5]

TABLE I. Estimated Urban and Rural Population Trends in ICAD Study Countries, 1950-1970.

Country	Thousands of people			Percent	
	Urban	Rural	Total	Urban	Rural
Argentina					
1950	11, 199. 1	5, 893. 9	17, 093. 0	65. 6	34. 4
1960	15, 001. 9	5, 664. 1	20, 666. 0	72. 6	27. 4
1970	18, 200. 8	6, 260. 2	24, 461. 0	74. 4	25. 6
Brazil					
1950	18, 783. 0	33, 161. 0	51, 944. 0	36. 2	63. 8
1960	31, 991. 0	38, 976. 0	70, 967. 0	45. 1	54. 9
1970	51, 000. 0	44, 300. 0	95, 300. 0	53. 5	46. 5
Chile					
1950	3, 389. 7	2, 364. 2	5, 753. 9	58. 9	41. 1
1960	5, 028. 0	2, 346. 0	7, 374. 0	68. 2	31. 8
1970	6, 925. 0	2, 467. 0	9, 392. 0	73. 7	26. 3
Colombia*					
1950	3, 160. 7	8, 107. 5	11, 268. 2	28. 0	72. 0
1960	5, 353. 0	8, 961. 0	14, 314. 0	37. 4	62. 6
1970	8, 394. 0	9, 897. 0	18, 291. 0	45. 9	54. 1
Ecuador					
1950	944. 0	2, 289. 0	3, 203. 0	28. 5	71. 5
1960	1, 422. 0	2, 787. 0	4, 209. 0	33. 8	66. 2
1970	2, 235. 0	3, 395. 0	5, 630. 0	39. 7	60. 3
Guatemala					
1950	701. 0	2, 101. 0	2, 802. 0	25. 1	74. 9
1960	963. 0	2, 579. 0	3, 542. 0	27. 2	72. 8
1970	1, 353. 0	3, 172. 0	4, 525. 0	29. 9	70. 1
Peru					
1950	3, 058. 6	4, 773. 4	7, 832. 0	39. 0	61. 0
1960	4, 607. 0	5, 542. 0	10, 149. 0	45. 4	54. 6
1970	7, 229. 0	6, 433. 0	13, 662. 0	52. 9	47. 1

*Meta, Chocó, Comisarías e Intendencias are not included.

Source: ICAD studies.

The indiscriminate importation of labor-saving, capi-
tal-intensive technology from industrialized countries, in
which labor is scarce, expensive and well-educated and capital is relatively plentiful, to underdeveloped nations where
the opposite conditions prevail, is not likely to have positive
consequences. Such a situation guarantees the "marginaliza-
tion" of a large part of the urban labor force. Only a small
proportion of the growing urban population is absorbed by the
industrialization process; the bulk of the population is
channelled into a service sector which, though segments of
it are often well-organized and politically active, remains
economically marginal. ECLA estimates that in many of the
Latin American countries underemployment--marginal jobs
such as selling newspapers, hawking lottery tickets, shining
shoes, etc.--affects between 20 and 30 percent of the whole
labor force.[6] In brief, urbanization is increasing more
rapidly than industrialization.

Despite the cities' incapacity to absorb rural migrants
into a productive economic system, the migrants continue to
come. They usually end up living in self-built slums surrounding major cities. A good description of such slums is
provided by Andre Frank:

> The self-built settlements are almost by definition
> unplanned. As such, they usually are almost de-
> void of any urban services. They generally lack
> running water, forcing their usually female and/or
> minor inhabitants to fetch water in cans from near-
> by or even from outside communal sources. Some-
> times the water is trucked in and sold at a con-
> siderable price. Electricity is either unavailable
> or clandestinely tapped from nearby wires. Sewage
> systems and often even cesspools are unknown.
> Garbage collection is non-existent--on the other
> hand, the settlement is often built on the garbage
> dump itself.... Schools are far away and crowded
> or simply inaccessible. Many self-built settlements
> are far from the center of town, from employment
> opportunities, and transportation is inadequate and
> costly in time and money.[7]

Given the particular characteristics of urbanization in
Latin America, the growth of cities should not be viewed as
an indicator of modernization. To a great extent, urbanization in Latin America indicates misery and lack of opportunity in the countryside and misery and surplus labor in the

cities. The growth of the cities thus serves as an obstacle
to development, because urban groups pressure and receive
from governments urban services which consume the resources necessary for the modernization of the countryside.
The urban migration contributes to a vicious cycle whereby
the rural victims of urban colonialism migrate to the city
and contribute to the further exploitation of their rural
brethren.

A second important social consequence associated
with the present Latin American economic situation is the
rise of the urban middle class, the major beneficiary of
post World War II social and economic changes in Latin
America. It is estimated that the middle class represents
from about one-half the population in the most highly urbanized countries (Argentina and Uruguay) to one-tenth of the
population in the most rural countries (Guatemala and Paraguay). The middle class now exercises the dominant influence over the political, economic and educational systems
of Latin America.

The rise of the middle class in the Western world
was generally beneficial to the political and economic development of the nation-state; but in Latin America it has
proven to be a mixed blessing. While great faith was
placed in the rising Latin American middle class by such
scholars as John J. Johnson[8] in the late 1950's, today
many social scientists argue that

> the growing middle strata of the Latin American
> cities constitute a phenomenon quite different from
> that of the frugal, enterprising middle classes
> which were supposed to have impelled the develop-
> ment of nineteenth century Europe. The Latin
> American middle strata is accused of aping the
> ostentacious consumption patterns of the upper
> classes, of relying on clientele relationships, gov-
> ernment protection against competition and expan-
> sion of public employment to the neglect of much-
> needed entrepreneurial activity; and of failure to
> provide political leadership capable of more than a
> superficial modernization of the traditional struc-
> tures. [9]

It is particularly significant that the three countries
with perhaps the strongest middle classes--Argentina, Chile
and Uruguay--have had the greatest amount of economic dif-

ficulty.

In politics the middle class has supported governmental efforts to create political reforms, industrialization, massive public works, and welfare and educational programs.
These policies have benefitted the urban middle class in
terms of employment, wealth, consumption, security and
power, but they have not benefitted either the urban slum
dweller or the bulk of the rural population. The efforts of
the urban and rural poor in collaboration with leftist segments of the middle class to attain fundamental reforms have
sometimes served only to frighten the middle class into the
arms of the military.[10]

Thus, the rise of the middle class has produced economic development in the cities but little development in the
rural areas. In rural Latin America, a very small proportion of the population still controls most of the land--es-
pecially the good land--while the bulk of the population continues to be subject to the kinds of exploitation initiated by
the Spanish colonizers.

The sociologist T. Lynn Smith estimates, "Probably
more than half of all the people in Latin America today are
gaining their livelihood through a system of agricultural techniques or a system of farming that is more primitive than
the Egyptians were using at the dawn of history."[11] It is
not surprising, therefore, that agricultural productivity in
Latin America actually fell 11 percent per capita between
1938-39 and 1963-64. Per capita annual peasant incomes in
Brazil, Chile, Colombia, Ecuador, Guatemala and Peru
average between $40 and a little over $180.[12]

So far the Alliance for Progress has not been able to
change these conditions. A special investigating subcommit-
tee of the Committee on Government Operations studied U.S.
aid operations affecting agrarian reform and reported that:

> Agrarian reform is moving only glacially. Gene-
> rally speaking, the wealthy landowners still con-
> trol the soil. The campesinos still live the never-
> ending cycle of borrowing on the future to exist
> today. Now the cities of Latin America are over-
> flowing with millions of squatters who see greater
> hope in the squalor of city slums than they did in
> the furrows of land owned by some other man.[13]

The basic characteristics of the developmental process in Latin America can now be summarized. In the
words of William Glade, the middle class has succeeded in
"the grafting on of a species of state sponsored industrial
capitalism to the trunk of an agrarian anachronism which
had previously been modified only enough to permit the ex-
port sector to sprout."[14] Instead of the expected conflict
between the rising middle class and the landowning class,
as happened in the West, there was reconciliation and compromise at the expense of the rural population. The com-
promises allowed the landowning classes to maintain their
control in the countryside. The changes wrought by the
rising middle class, therefore, were effectively limited to
urban enclaves. Consequently, the incidence of economic
dualism--twentieth century cities and eighteenth century
countrysides--is more pronounced in Latin America than in
any other continent.

The Present Education System

In the nineteenth century most Latin American nations
adopted French and Iberian models of education, and the
structure of Latin American school systems have changed
very little since that time. Primary education begins at age
6 or 7 and lasts for 6 years; secondary school also has a
6-year program. Most secondary schools prepare students
for university training by the granting of the bachillerato
(bachelor's degree). There are also secondary schools which
provide vocational education and special education for those
planning to become primary teachers (escuelas normales).
Almost half the students attending secondary school are in
private schools; most of these are church schools which receive public subsidies. At the university, a beginning student enters a particular faculty of the university, depending
upon which profession he intends to pursue--medicine, law,
engineering, or the humanities.

The Latin American governments, under the influence
of the middle class, have broadened the scope of the traditional educational system, but have not changed its function.
According to ECLA,

> In quantitative terms, education in Latin America
> has maintained more sustained and consistent rates
> of expansion over a long period than the other sec-
> tors of public social action or the economies them-

selves.   Between 1956 and 1965, the percentage of
the total regional population enrolled in schools of
some kind rose from 13. 3 to 17. 1.   This gain required an average annual rate of 7. 2%, about two-
and-a-half times the regional rate of population
growth.   During the same period, enrollment at
the primary level rose by 57. 6%, enrollment at the
middle level by 110. 6%, and enrollment at the
higher level by 92. 3%. [15]

Unfortunately, the significance of the great increases in enrollment figures in considerably reduced when one takes into
account the rapid population increase.   Out of the 108 million
children between the ages of 5 and 20 in 1965, 65 million
were not enrolled in schools.

    Confronted with the dilemma of an exploding popula-
tion and limited resources, Latin American governments have
concentrated their educational resources in the urban areas.
For example, a 1966 study of the rural-urban dichotomy in
Mexico (a nation which experienced an agrarian revolution!)
reveals the figures shown in Table II.

Table II.   Rural and Urban Students in Mexico, by Grade[16]

Grade	No. of Rural Students	No. of Urban Students
1st	1, 277, 002	1, 122, 310
2nd	701, 561	835, 264
3rd	412, 227	754, 699
4th	220, 985	652, 515
5th	124, 041	559, 111
6th	81, 647	469, 542
	Teachers	Teachers
Titled	27, 493	64, 649
Untitled	21, 895	22, 404

    Figures similar to those in Table II are available
for Brazil.   Southern Brazil contains four states, the most
urbanized and developed of the nation.   Recent studies show
the gross disparities in education expenditure per capita between the South (containing 36 percent of the population) and
the rest of the nation.   The South spends 59 percent of the

educational budget. The major state of this region, São
Paulo, has an educational per capita expenditure seven times
larger than the states of the Northeast, which contain 22
percent of Brazil's population. In John Saunders' words,

> There is, indeed, a myriad of indices that reflect
> not only the greater modernization of the South,
> but also an increasing differential especially be-
> tween it and the North and Northeast regions of
> the nation. To the extent that the latter are prob-
> lem areas because of these differentials rather
> than because of their actual levels of development,
> those areas will tend to become more rather than
> less problematic with the passage of time as a re-
> sult of the increase of these differentials. [17]

The problems of Latin American education are not
confined to the fact that not enough money is being spent in
the rural areas. Given the present characteristics of the
educational systems--for instance, their curricula--massive
increases in rural expenditures would not relieve the dual
nature of Latin American societies, and would increase the
urban migration rates.

The most frequent criticisms levelled against the
curricula used in Latin American educational systems are
conveniently summarized by Oscar Vera. In his words,
they fail to serve the needs of the uneducated masses in that

> they are encyclopedic, overladen with material, ex-
> cessively ambitious and rigid; that, quite remote
> from the daily lives and experiences of the pupils,
> they tend to lose sight of the basic aims of general
> education and encourage memorization, verbalism
> and intellectualism rather than the development of
> personality, initiative, powers of observation, the
> acquisition of the habit of scientific inquiry and the
> application of skills and knowledge to the problems
> met in everyday life; and finally, that they include
> topics of doubtful value and exclude others which
> would be of greater use and efficiency educational-
> ly.... [18]

These same characteristics dominated the educational systems decades ago when access to schools--particularly
secondary schools--was limited almost exclusively to the
upper classes. Oscar Vera's study concludes:

> The structure contents and tendencies of education
> at all levels are derived in the main from the con-
> ception of educational needs implicitly maintained
> by small sectors of the population, rather than
> from a careful and well-balanced analysis of the
> universal demands of culture and present-day life,
> and the characteristics and requirements peculiar
> to the country and its different areas, as seen
> from the point of view of economic, social and
> political development.[19]

The "small sectors" referred to are essentially alliances or
cultural mergers of values between the upper and middle
classes. According to the anthropologist Richard Adams,

> While it is possible to distinguish a growing middle-
> income sector, the older and basic dual structure
> of prestige and value system has not changed as
> much as has been supposed. Rather, the apparent-
> ly new middle group is only an extension of the
> traditional upper class, both in terms of economic
> position and of basic values.[20]

The middle class achieved full integration into the
partially developed societies of Latin America by 1950.
Through a process that has not yet been adequately explained,
the middle class acquired an interest in maintaining that partially developed society, and it has used the educational system as a means of excluding the rural and marginal urban
populace from sharing its newly acquired power and privilege. In the words of one observer, a look at the educational system "reveals that this school system has built a
narrow bridge across a widening social gap. As the only
legitimate passage to the middle class, the school restricts
all unconventional crossings, and leaves the underachiever
to bear the blame for his marginality."[21]

Evidence supporting the stratification function performed by the educational system is supplied by ECLA.[22]

> During the recent years of expansion, the internal
> efficiency of the school systems, assessed by their
> ability to retain pupils until the completion of a
> course, improved hardly at all. In 1957, 41 per-
> cent of the primary enrollment in the region as a
> whole was concentrated in the first grade and only
> 7 percent in the highest primary grade. In 1965,

the percentages were 38 and 8.

In Brazil, of each 1,000 students who begin primary schools, 66 finish in the fifth year, 16 graduate from high school, and seven finish the university.

The present educational system mis-educates the established elites and non-educates the bulk of the rural population. In terms of developmental needs, the present system mis-educates by promoting a disdain for manual labor, an attraction toward urban centers, a reluctance to work in rural areas, and an acceptance of a highly stratified society. Furthermore, it orients students into occupations which are not related to the human resource requirements of development. For example, although 46 percent of the Latin American labor force is in agriculture, the school system has produced only 20,000 professional agriculturists for all of that region.

The school system non-educates through a process whereby,

> The school selects and rejects; it encourages dropouts. The social situation of most students is such as to promote high absenteeism, early school desertion, early frustration and discouragement through incapacity to meet the rigid demands of examination.... It is where ... problems are most grave that the school's deficiencies are most pronounced. It is in the rural areas that there are the fewest schools, the greatest proportion of incomplete schools, the most poorly paid and least trained teachers, the greatest shortage of teaching materials, the least adequate provision for helping the student with books and materials, food, clothes, and health problems.[23]

In conclusion, the disparities in the distribution of education continue to parallel and reinforce the disparities in the distribution of income and status. The static functions of Latin American educational systems prevail over the dynamic functions; that is, the systems are preserving most of the values and attitudes which have hindered the self-sustaining development of the continent rather than acting as a spearhead of social change in bringing about the creation of values more congenial to a fully modern society. "In education, as in the economic and political systems," according

to ECLA, "the previous structures have shown surprising
resilience and adaptability in absorbing the imported models,
and in changing without arriving at the fundamental transformations that now seem to be requisites for dynamic development. "[24] Thus, the present educational systems are not
solving the basic developmental problems of Latin America,
but are, instead, part of the problem.

Need for a New Rural Educational System

As has been pointed out, two of the most difficult
problems in Latin America are the low productivity of labor
in agriculture and the massive flow of migrants to the cities.
Therefore, I would emphasize rural over urban educational
reforms, first, because the rural population has the greater
need, and, second, because urban reforms are likely to become counter-productive due to increasing internal migration.

Most social scientists agree that agrarian reform is
one of the essential solutions to the problems of low agricultural productivity and rural emigration. Defined broadly,
agrarian reform means, on the one hand, an increase in the
number of economically viable family farms and, on the
other hand, the modernization of large farms, whether under
private ownership or other forms of tenure. Both trends
will necessitate rural labor capable of operating machinery
and ready to absorb new techniques from the printed page,
radio and demonstrations. The present educational system
is not laying this foundation; obviously new educational policies are required for the countryside.

According to a UNESCO observer of Latin American
education, a new

> education policy compatible with human dignity--
> and economic needs-- ... can only be evolved by
> giving up any idea of doing it in a classical style.
> It has to be something completely new and to a
> very large extent self-financing.... The problem
> for Latin America is not to produce geniuses cap-
> able of extending the frontiers of knowledge ...;
> it is rather to have an education system capable
> of inculcating people's minds with the simple knowl-
> edge of agriculture and biology of 1910! You
> could then double, treble and quadruple agricultur-
> al output. [25]

Democratic reformers in Latin America have attempted, usually unsuccessfully, to break the vicious cycle of rural poverty by agrarian reform proposals. Following any successful implementation of an agrarian reform program, reformers emphasize the necessity for rural education to insure that the distributed lands will be put to good use. The proposal here presented is to reform rural education systems without waiting for the successful implementation of a land distribution program. Hopefully this would create an inducement mechanism and multiply the pressures for agrarian reform.

Presently, the peasants are for the most part unorganized and intellectually and politically unarmed to pressure for reform. Reform-minded urban politicians who support agrarian reform are often assuaged by symbolic responses in the form of laws passed but never implemented. Furthermore, under the present political systems, the conflicts among the military, the middle class, the landowners and the unions are usually settled at the expense of the peasants. Given the personalismo of the Latin American culture, along with its societal consequence of a lack of social consciousness, it is imperative that the rural people develop their own indigenous leaders and organizations--in essence, their own sources of power--to look after their interests.

A second goal of rural educational reform should be to create a population that is both capable and willing to enjoy life in the countryside. Rural education should teach not only farming, but a whole host of other occupations needed to improve the quality of life and opportunity structures in the countryside. The achievement of such a goal would stop, or at least slow down, the internal migration which has now become a depressing multiplier of the costs of economic development in most Latin American countries. In answer to those who say this is impossible, such a policy has already been undertaken in Cuba with some success. Given modern technology and communications, it may be less costly to improve the quality of life in small rural towns than in large cities.

However, the basic problem of identifying the kinds of rural educational reforms necessary to promote the development of the countryside remains. Here one is reminded of George Bereday's assertion that "those who seek remedies [to social problems] in the reform of school systems deal with the tail end of change rather than with its

sources. " Bereday stresses that the static features of school
systems outweigh their dynamic features. History suggests,
according to Bereday, "that successful rapid reforms of
schools are extremely unlikely. Historically, successful rebuilding or refurbishing of educational structures has been
possible only through war or as a result of war or similar
cataclysms. "26

Given the present educational institutions in Latin
America and the middle-class values of most of the teachers,
one cannot be optimistic about reforming rural education
quickly. The fact that such reforms will be difficult does
not mean they are impossible, however. The first important
step is to widely publicize the vital need for rural educational reform so that appropriate resources can be allocated to
confront the problem. The second step should be innovative
thinking and creative experimentation. A variety of rural
educational experiments could be supported by the Inter-
American Development Bank, private U.S. foundations,
church groups, Latin American and United States universities, the Peace Corps, the United States Agency for International Development, and Latin American governmental
agencies. Here, we can list only a few of the possible experiments in reform.

First, it might be worthwhile for Latin American
governments to require all university students to spend at
least one year teaching in the rural primary schools. Such
a program might reduce the urban-rural dichotomy while
increasing the literacy rates and educational opportunities in
the countryside. Somewhat similar policies have been attempted in the past: by Mexico in the 1930's, Guatemala
in the late 1940's, and Cuba in the early 1960's.

Second, it might be useful to experiment with educating rural populations on special farms rather than in formal
schools. These farms could be run by the state, the municipio, the church, or local peasant cooperatives. They could
function as boarding schools for the children of migratory
workers, as day schools for the children who live nearby,
and as adult educational facilities. Such educational farms
could offer a number of advantages. One of the great problems of vocational education is that it is more expensive
than general education. An educational farm employing
modern techniques, however, could eventually become self-
financing. Furthermore, while serving as a rapid dissemi-
nator of agricultural information, it could also offer instruc-

tion in a variety of semi-skilled trades such as carpentry, brick-laying, etc.

Finally, Latin American school administrators might try building a series of central schools in the rural areas and have teachers based in these schools fan out into the countryside to meet with students. The manpower for such an ambitious project would have to be supplied by university students who would be compelled to devote one year to such service to the nation as part of the requirements for a degree. Students in the vicinity of the central school could attend classes there; children in more distant and isolated places could be taught by the traveling teachers several times a week.

Obviously, there is no assurance that any of these experiments in reform will work. But if we recognize the weaknesses of the present educational systems in the rural areas, we can then begin devising new programs, some of which may help to overcome the urban-rural disparities by improving the life of the bulk of the population in the Latin American countryside.

Conclusion

In the words of David Abernathy and Trevor Coombe, "Education and politics are inextricably linked. A government's educational policy reflects, and sometimes betrays, its view of society or political creed."27 The educational policies of most Latin American governments reflect the merged interests of the upper and middle classes. The rise of the middle class to political and economic power has brought modernization to the cities but has not yet significantly modernized the rural areas of Latin America. Modern cities are still living off the labor and production of the poverty-stricken countryside. It is particularly disturbing that the educational systems of Latin America, rather than attempting to overcome this situation, are actually a contributing factor to the rural-urban dichotomy.

We have called for fundamental rural educational reform so that the rural population can organize and share in the benefits provided by development. Such reform will not be easy. When one witnesses the difficulty the United States is having in devising educational policies to integrate the 13 percent of its population which is black to American society,

one can appreciate the problem of the financially poorer
Latin American educators in trying to integrate much higher
proportions of peasants and Indians into their national societies. The effort is essential to Latin America's development, however, and deserves considerable study and innovative application.

Notes

1. Samuel P. Huntington, Political Order in Changing Societies, New Haven, Conn.: Yale University Press,
   1968.

2. Miguel S. Wionczek, "Introduction, " in, Economic Cooperation in Latin America, Africa and Asia, edited
   by Miguel S. Wionczek, Cambridge, Mass.: The
   MIT Press, pp. 1-24.

3. ECLA, The Process of Industrial Development in Latin
   America, New York: United Nations, 1966, p. 115.

4. Ibid., p. 89.

5. Claudio Veliz, "Centralism and Nationalism in Latin
   America, " Vol. 47 (Oct. 1968), p. 70.

6. ECLA, Education, Human Resources and Development
   in Latin America, New York: United Nations, 1968,
   p. 44.

7. Andre Frank, "Urban Poverty in Latin America, " in:
   Masses in Latin America, edited by Irving Louis
   Horowitz, New York: Oxford University Press, 1970,
   p. 221.

8. John J. Johnson, Political Change in Latin America:
   The Emergence of the Middle Sectors, Stanford,
   California: Stanford University Press, 1958.

9. Andrew Pearse, "Introduction: Sociologists and Education, " International Social Science Journal, Vol. XIX
   (1967), p. 320.

10. Jose Nun, "The Middle Class Military Coup, " in: The
    Politics of Conformity in Latin America, edited by
    Claudio Veliz, New York: Oxford University Press,

1967, pp. 66-119.

11. T. Lynn Smith, Studies of Latin American Societies,
     Garden City, N.Y.: Doubleday, 1970, p. 254.

12. Solon L. Barraclough, "Agricultural Policy and Strate-
     gies of Land Reform, " in: Masses in Latin America,
     [see note 7], p. 128.

13. "U.S. AID Operations in Latin America Under The
     Alliance For Progress, " Thirty-Sixth Report by the
     Committee on Government Operations, 90th Congress,
     2nd Session, p. 24.

14. William Glade, The Latin American Economics, New
     York: American Book, 1969, p. 459.

15. ECLA, Education, Human Resources ... [see note 6],
     p. 9.

16. Vision, Vol. 33 (Sept. 15, 1967), p. 41.

17. John V. D. Saunders, "Education and Modernization in
     Brazil, " in: The Shaping of Modern Brazil, edited
     by Eric Baklanoff, Baton Rouge, La.: Louisiana
     State University, 1969, p. 122.

18. Oscar Vera, "The Educational Situation and Require-
     ments in Latin America, " in: Government and Poli-
     tics in Latin America, edited by Peter G. Snow,
     New York: Holt, Rinehart and Winston, 1967, p. 108.

19. Ibid., p. 111.

20. Richard N. Adams, "Political Power and Social Struc-
     tures, " in: The Politics of Conformity ... [see note
     10], p. 16.

21. Ivan Illich, "The Futility of Schooling in Latin Ameri-
     ca, " Saturday Review (April 20, 1968), p. 57.

22. ECLA, Education, Human Resources ... [see note 6],
     p. 10.

23. Frank Bonilla, "Brazil, " in: Education and Political
     Development, edited by James S. Coleman, Princeton,
     N.J.: Princeton University Press, 1965.

24. ECLA, Education, Human Resources ... [see note 6],
     p. 10.

25. Thomas Balogh, "Land Tenure, Education and Develop-
     ment in Latin America, " in: Problems and Strategies
     of Educational Planning, Unesco: International Insti-
     tute for Educational Planning, 1965, p. 70.

26. George Z. F. Bereday, "School Systems and the En-
     rollment Crisis: A Comparative Overview, " Compara-
     tive Education Review, Vol. XII (June 1968), p. 126.

27. David Abernathy and Trevor Coombe, "Education and
     Politics in Developing Countries, " Harvard Education
     Review, Vol. 35 (Summer 1965), p. 287.

3. PATTERNS OF SOCIAL AND ECONOMIC CHANGE
    SINCE 1950
    Richard L. Cummings

        Latin American countries are now in a dynamic stage
of population growth and technological transition characterized by rapid rates of urbanization, alienation, and conflict
which contribute to rising levels of frustration. During the
1950-1964 period, the growth of the urban population was
some 25 million in 16 Latin American countries where two
censuses were taken.

        The Centro Latino Americano de Demografia (CELADE)
estimates that the population of the region as a whole was
25 percent urban 75 percent rural in 1950, that these ratios
had changed to 33 percent urban and 67 percent rural in
1960, to nearly an equal 50-50 split in the late 1960's.
Table I demonstrates the current percentage distribution of
urban population in 19 Latin American nations. By 1975
some 56 percent of the population will be urban, says the
center, and more than 60 percent of some 358 million inhabitants will be living in urban areas by 1980.

        At the time of the last census, generally 1960, there
were nine Latin American cities--Buenos Aires, Rio de
Janeiro, São Paulo, Mexico City, Santiago, Lima, Caracas,
Bogotá and Montevideo--with populations in excess of one
million inhabitants. By the end of 1970, it is estimated
that eight more--Recife, Belo Horizonte, Salvador, Porto
Alegre, Medelin, Cali, Guadalajara and Monterrey--have
grown to more than one million, and that by 1980 there will
be a total of 27 cities with more than a million inhabitants
each.

        Both "push" as well as "pull" factors operate to draw
large numbers of people from the countryside to the cities.
Among the "push" factors are the inadequate size of agricultural holdings, the fragmentation of farms as small plots
are subdivided with each passing generation, the lack of
clear title to the land, the employment of agricultural

Table I. Latin American Urban Population, Literacy, and Government Investment*

Country	% Population Urban	% Literacy	% National Government Investment in Education
Argentina	78.9 (1970)	91.5 (1960)	4.2 (1969)
Bolivia	29.3 (1967)	39.8 (1968)	16.6 (1969)
Brazil	47.6 (1970)	71.0 (1969)	8.7 (1969)
Chile	74.2 (1969)	89.6 (1968)	11.8 (1969)
Colombia	57.7 (1970)	72.9 (1964)	12.7 (1969)
Costa Rica	49.0 (1969)	84.4 (1963)	27.8 (1969)
Dominican Republic	40.0 (1970)	53.1 (1968)	12.9 (1969)
Ecuador	45.7 (1970)	69.7 (1969)	21.6 (1969)
El Salvador	38.8 (1968)	49.0 (1961)	23.4 (1969)
Guatemala	30.8 (1970)	37.9 (1964)	16.5 (1969)
Haiti	17.3 (1970)	22.0 (1967)	14.1 (1970-71)
Honduras	32.2 (1969)	47.3 (1961)	20.6 (1969)
Mexico	58.7 (1969)	83.7 (1969)	26.7 (1970)
Nicaragua	39.7 (1969)	49.8 (1963)	21.6 (1969)
Panama	47.1 (1969)	76.7 (1960)	18.3 (1969)
Paraguay	36.0 (1970)	74.4 (1962)	13.2 (1969)
Peru	51.9 (1969)	61.1 (1961)	21.5 (1969)
Uruguay	79.9 (1970)	90.5 (1963)	29.9 (1969)
Venezuela	74.9 (1969)	73.9 (1969)	15.2 (1969)

*Data from Inter-American Development Bank, Social Progress Trust Fund Report for 1970, Socio-Economic Progress in Latin America (Washington, D.C., IADB, 1971), various pages.

laborers at extremely low wage levels and the use of primitive methods for crop and livestock production.

Professor Sloan has pointed out in the preceding chapter that the cities act as magnetic forces "pulling" the rural population with their attraction. The success of one rural migrant who finds employment in urban industry or some tertiary sector activity may be sufficient to draw several of his friends and relatives to the area, where their fate is not so happy. Overall a population growth rate of over 3 percent per year and rural emigration to the cities combine to swell the overall rate of urban growth in Latin America beyond that experienced by the more urbanized world. The map attached here demonstrates the rates of overall population growth and overall urban growth rates. Western Europe and the United States took more time for this vital transformation than Latin America is taking and therefore had more opportunities to adapt themselves to changing conditions.

Between 1925 and 1960, the economically active population of Latin America swelled by nearly 36 million people, growing 110 percent from 32.5 million to 68.2 million. Of the total recorded increase, the farm sector absorbed 12 million. This left 24 million workers to be incorporated into other activities. Looking back at the development of today's advanced countries, we find that urbanization was accompanied by a rapid rate of manufacturing expansion. In virtually all cases, service occupations--including trade and government jobs--occupied a much lower proportion of the labor force than manufacturing.

In Latin America, it is significant that the share of manufacturing in total employment grew in the region by less than 1 percent between 1925 and 1960, while urban non-manufacturing activities increased their share by 14 percent. Moreover, the value added per capita in Latin American manufacturing is less than half the yield recorded in Western Europe. Thus, while Latin America approaches the degree of urbanization found in the economically developed regions, it lags far behind them in employment opportunities in productive urban activities and thus in the standards of living afforded by these activities.

The societies in which industrialization started two centuries ago were largely free from the pressures under which Latin American leaders must operate today. The

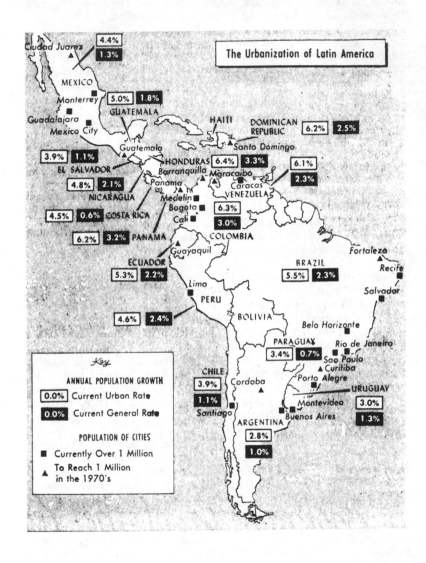

The Urbanization of Latin America

Key

ANNUAL POPULATION GROWTH

0.0% Current Urban Rate

0.0% Current General Rate

POPULATION OF CITIES

■ Currently Over 1 Million

▲ To Reach 1 Million in the 1970's

This map is reprinted by permission of the Milwaukee Journal, from their April 12, 1970, article "Latin American Cities Grow Too Fast" (Accent section, page 3).

welfare state had not come into existence, knowledge of higher standards of living in other regions had not set into motion the "revolution of rising expectations" and the pressure to live up to the standards and obligations of an affluent circle of modern nations was nonexistent. In Latin America, as a result of all these factors, the rate of urbanization has exceeded the region's capacity to provide sufficient employment, housing, education and other social facilities to meet an ever growing demand.

Education is one of the aspirations of the growing urban population which exerts pressure on enrollments at all levels. In the 1956-1965 decade, the enrollment increased at an average annual rate of 7.2 percent, a rate that is double the growth rate of the total population. High rates of increase of intermediate and higher school enrollments are an index of the growth of the middle classes with the rapid urbanization. Quantitative advances, however, are not commonly accompanied by equal improvements in the qualitative aspects of education. Not all of the nations have undertaken the structural reforms and orientation and modernization of content and methods of the national systems necessary to adapt the educational process to the unique characteristics of the urban environment and the needs of economic growth.

The magnitude of the urbanization process and the diversity of demands created by living in the urban context--urbanism--appears to mandate a faster rate of capital formation than has been observed in the past; a concomitant raising of levels of agricultural productivity for domestic consumption; expanded secondary sector production; educational reforms more closely related to economic objectives and contemporary urbanism, and research and development of technologies adapted to this contemporary environment. These observations are not intended as a strategy for development; they simply represent an attempt to focus upon and draw conclusions flowing from an analysis of the phenomenon of the rapid rate of urbanization taking place in Latin America and to present these conclusions as the generalized context within which the specific examples of educational innovation must demonstrate their viability or perish.

Section II

CATALYSTS FOR CHANGE

Changes in educational systems are often the result of the thinking of one person or a small group. Most frequently they take the form of a particular instrument, innovation or process. These catalysts are designed to be used in a way that the entire educational system will be renovated, from teacher training to utilization of materials, from building construction to curriculum plans. In Latin America during the 1960's a series of these catalysts were in evidence.

Considered in a social-historical setting, changes in the 60's were a necessity for Latin America. Bulging school enrollments were viewed by liberal politicians as one of the fundamental challenges which had to be met. Thus, whenever traditional systems lacked some of the resources or flexibility needed to meet this challenge, educational leaders turned to educational innovations of the day to help them complete necessary educational reforms. Results however, have been mixed. On the one hand, some of the changes were innovative and successful. On the other, some were unsuccessful redraftings of already antiquated systems and approaches.

The articles which follow are early analyses of some of the more innovative changes which have taken place, changes which are almost certain to exert a heavy hand of influence in the decade of the 1970's. The section might be conviently sub-divided into two groups. The first six articles analyze special elements which were used to bring about the change while the last five articles stress system-wide reforms.

The necessity for a proper setting for change is shown in the Costa Rican article (number 4). Then, the use of a lab school, television and textbooks is analyzed

49

in the next four articles as to their role in precipating larger changes.   Finally, a Minister of Education shows (article
9) what his country needed to do to change a secondary
school system from private to public.

An adult literacy program for Latin America starts
off the second sub-section (article 10).   Then, the process
of revolutionary educational change is described by analysts
in articles 11 and 12.   And finally, two approaches to the
development of rural education in Paraguay and Guatemala
are analyzed (articles 13 and 14) by the men who worked on
the inside during the early phases of these projects.

There are many more innovations occuring in Latin
America.   Almost every country has initiated some type of
reform.   Increased international contact at seminars and
meetings has helped spread information of neighboring educational systems.   Internal demands for educational improvement are in keeping with the rising expectation levels in the
region.   How individual nations might profit from the experiences of others to meet their own needs, and how countries might cooperate on regional projects which will benefit them all could very well be the result of these early
catalytic changes.   The later 1970's will almost certainly
see an expansion and a development of these processes now
in motion.

4. STRUCTURAL EDUCATIONAL CHANGES NEEDED IN COSTA RICA
Peter Tobia

This study is devoted to recording some thoughts which may in part explain why Costa Rica is considered to have developed and progressed further than other countries in the Central American region, not only in social and economic matters generally, but specifically in developing a more productive educational system. Probably the most succinct explanation of why Costa Rica is considered to have developed and progressed further than any other country in Central America is found in the words of Herring:

> Costa Rica is unique among the Central American states in the whiteness of her population, the honesty and constitutional orderliness of her political life, and the intelligence of her citizenry. Presidents serve out their appointed terms, handle the nation's business frugally and honestly.... Costa Ricans boast more school teachers than soldiers. It is a country of moderate size farms. [1]

Herring is supported by Clark, who describes Costa Rica as "clean and refreshing, a Switzerland in an alien sea, " having "inherited none of the racial complexities of its bigger cousins to the South, "[2] or to the north.

The whiteness of Costa Ricans is attributed to two facts: first, that there were fewer Indians in Costa Rica when the Spaniards arrived; and, second, that these Indians were nearly all eliminated in the wars of conquest. The population of Costa Rica is 97 percent Caucasian, the highest in the region. Mauro indicates that the people of Costa Rica are "more completely European in blood than any other Latin American country, except Uruguay and Argentina. "[3]

The economy of colonial Costa Rica was based on agriculture. Lacking a supply of Indians or slaves to de-

velop their farms, the Spaniards who settled in Costa Rica
had to do the work themselves. This lack of a labor supply
made Costa Rica less attractive to colonists than to some of
the other Spanish colonies. Mauro states that the immi-
grants who did come to Costa Rica "were hardy farmers
whose descendants today are an industrious people."[4] Ri-
cardo Castro editor of the Costa Rican newspaper, La Nación,
in attempting to explain to Clark why Costa Rica was different from the other countries, stated, "The conquistadores
knew that El Dorado was not to be found here and they
moved on. The Spaniards who colonized Costa Rica thought
of it as a future home, not a fortune chest to be smashed
open."[5]

        Stewart substantiates the fact that the early Spanish
settlers who remained in Costa Rica had to work their own
farms due to the lack of a labor supply. He holds as evidence for the foregoing the striking "absence of those great
land holdings which were the rule in other parts of Spain's
American dominions."[6] This explanation helps clarify Herring's statement that Costa Rica is a country of moderate
size farms. Costa Rica has not had the socio-economic
problem of land reform characteristic of the other Central
American countries. Stewart concludes, "The Costa Rican
was from necessity self-sufficient."[7] This also helps to
explain, "the development of a democratic spirit among the
Costa Ricans."[8]

        The characteristic of self-sufficiency of the colonial
Costa Rican, which Stewart points out is comparable to that
developed by the North American colonists, is unique to
Costa Rica. No other Central American colonists had this
attribute. Mauro maintains that Costa Rica attained a truly
republic government earlier than most of the other Latin
republics for two reasons: the people are concentrated in
one small area in the central plateau; and, because of their
geographical position, they remained aloof from the continual
conflicts between the other states.[9] Colonial governors re-
sided in Guatemala. What control they might have exercised
over the province of Costa Rica, therefore, was greatly
limited because of its physical location with respect to
Guatemala, lack of communications and great difficulty of
travel. This lack of direct control gave Costa Rica an opportunity to develop her self-determination, which has been
instrumental in her development, stability and enlightenment.

        The military has been a dominant and viable force in

the political life of many Latin American countries.   Clark
describes it as a force "which makes and unmakes governments."[10]   Banks and Textor indicate that for many years
there has been an "uneasy alliance between arms and politics
in Latin America."[11]   In some countries this force has led
to instability and has retarded democratic progress.   Costa
Rica, according to Clark, "dissolved its army because it
interfered with a civilian mandate of the 1948 vote."[12]   It
is interesting to note that after the army was dissolved, its
headquarters in the capital city, San José, was converted
into a museum and cultural center.   The studies of Fitzgib-
bon and the Feierabends, the former on democratic progress
and the latter on political stability and level of coercion,
rank Costa Rica very highly not only in comparison with
Central and other Latin American countries but with other
countries of the world.   These are further contemporary in-
dications of Costa Rica's development and progress.

Costa Rica's educational situation was given little attention during the colonial period.   However, after independence in 1821 the concern for education increased.   The
constitution of 1844 and 1847 contained specific provisions
for the development of education.   The former placed the
responsibility on the government to provide education for its
citizens and the latter contained detailed guarantees that the
State would establish necessary schools so that the rights of
the citizens to be educated might be fulfilled.

The Constitution of 1869 contained provisions which
established free, compulsory and public supported primary
education.   The Public Education Bill of 1866 established
the formal educational system, principles of administration,
and the method of organization.   The role of the teacher in
Costa Rica was enhanced by the law of 1899, which accorded
professional status to teachers.   These constitutional provisions and laws concerning education and others which followed, were for the most part, the most profound in Central
America and appear to have served as prototypes for other
countries in the region.   They established the important role
education would play in the development of Costa Rica's
democratic way of life.

Several structural factors seem to have influenced
the educational production of Costa Rica.   It may be well
for the other Latin American countries to study these factors
and possible to adopt them as a means to help improve their
own educational production.

First--the role of the Superior Education Council, and
its relationship to the Ministry of Education, are unique in
Central America and are comparable to that of the State
Board of Education with the State Department of Education in
the United States.   The lay council is on a level above the
Ministry of Education.   It establishes policy and provides
guidelines for the Ministry to follow.   In the other countries
educational councils have an advisory function only and are
generally a part of the Ministry of Education.

Second--boards and committees of education are found
throughout the Latin American region.   In general these
boards and committees are charged with the responsibility of
promoting relationships between the school and the community and fostering their integration.   However, in sophisticated Costa Rican organization, there is a school board in
each school district as well as an administrative board in
each secondary school.   These boards have certain rights
and can contract obligations for the realization of the aims
of the school.   Thus in Costa Rica these boards and committees have a role similar to a board of education in the
United States.

Third--the role of the Minister of Education in his
relations with the University of Costa Rica: in that country
the Minister of Education is a member of the university assembly, the highest governing body of the university.   In
Nicaragua the Ministry of Education has a representative on
a similar body which governs the University of Nicaragua.
In the other countries there is no representation of the Ministry of Education on the governing boards of the national
universities.   This unique position which the Minister of
Education in Costa Rica holds with the University of Costa
Rica appears to be one in which the University can be more
responsible to the needs of the country than in the other
countries.   In the other countries the relationship between
the Ministry of Education and the university is generally
strained.   The concerns and needs of one or the other frequently are neither discussed nor considered, thus limiting
the role of the university in development and progress.

Kandel sees that "a nation seeks through education to
mold the character of its citizens and so reflect its aims--
political, social, economic and cultural."[13] Without question this study identifies Costa Rica as an example of a
country which has proven the soundness of Kandel's concept.
In her we see the role of education in nation building in

which the stability of the nation rests on the character of its people--a people who have not allowed a dichotomy to exist between the ideals of their personal life and the ideals of their country. Through the integration of both they have become strong.

Notes

1. Hubert Herring, Good Neighbors, New Haven, Conn.: Yale University Press, 1941, p. 302.

2. Gerald Clark, The Coming Explosion in Latin America, New York: David McKay Company, 1962, p. 38.

3. Dana G. Mauro, The Latin American Republics, 3d ed., New York: Appleton-Century-Crofts, 1960, p. 405.

4. Ibid.

5. Clark, The Coming Explosion in Latin America, p. 38.

6. Matt Stewart, Keith in Costa Rica, Albuquerque: The University of New Mexico Press, 1964, p. 3.

7. Ibid.

8. Ibid.

9. Mauro, The Latin American Republics, p. 405.

10. Clark, The Coming Explosion in Latin America, p. 158.

11. Arthur S. Banks and Robert B. Textor, A Cross-Polity Survey, Cambridge, Mass.: The M.I.T. Press, 1963, pp. 113-114.

12. Clark, The Coming Explosion in Latin America, p. 158.

13. I. L. Kandel, The New Era in Education, Boston: Houghton Mifflin, 1955, p. 13.

5. A LABORATORY SCHOOL IN GUATEMALA
Herbert G. Vaughan

Throughout many localities in Latin America there exists a unique educational institution: the bi-national school. Initiated during the Second World War they brought together diverse cultural groups and differing curricular orientations. And as a result of more than two decades of experience, linkage between these institutions and the national system of education has been established. This chapter describes one particular bi-national school, the American School of Guatemala, and its contributions to the national system of education.

There are several types of private schools to be found throughout Latin America. Church related schools have been founded by various churches or church related institutions. Family or individual enterprises, wholly owned and operated by individuals or families, quite often operate on a profit making basis. Company owned schools are established by companies for their employees' children in foreign based operations. Bi-national schools are "community-owned," private non-sectarian schools operating on a non-profit basis and offer both American and national curricula.

The historical antecedents help define the setting within which the present day Guatemalan society and its centralized educational system evolved. Educational ideas emanating from colonial times continued their influence when nationhood was achieved. Private or church related schools continued to predominate and have hindered the development of a strong public school system. Social class structure from colonial times influenced educational patterns. The coming of independence did not basically alter educational patterns or thought, nor did succeeding authoritarian governments. Until the social revolution of 1945 Guatemala's educational system was strongly influenced by its Hispanic past.

While not part of Guatemala's long term development, the American School has been affected by the Hispanic past.

Being private, the school has tuition fees as its primary
support. The secondary curriculum includes the official
<u>Bachillerato</u> program which emphasizes university prepara-
tion so that the student body comes from that part of the
population where children expect and parents can afford university study. The School's curriculum follows the one
drawn up by the centralized Ministry of Education. Its calendar is identical to the one used in the public schools.
And uniforms, a custom in Guatemala, are still used for
special occasions.

Yet, the American School is a hybrid institution with
many unique innovations. Its founding in 1945 came during
an auspicious period when the country began to explore new
ways to break with the past. The school is non-sectarian
and the student body comes from diverse religious, national
and socio-economic backgrounds. This is novel in Guatemala for most private schools are oriented to a particular
clientele and are not concerned with the community-at-large.
The school pioneered co-education and built a strong program of co-curricula activities. It is organized on a non-
profit basis with its board serving without compensation.

Unfortunately, the original statutes did not permit
the school enough latitude to develop and expand its program.
It requested, and was granted in 1948, "laboratory school"
status by the President of Guatemala. This meant that the
school, in addition to its regular duties, could undertake
educational experimentation--modify curriculum, hire foreign
personnel and change examinations. Since then the laboratory status has been renewed, further elaborated, and am-
plified by numerous ministerial and presidential decrees.

Its laboratory status has been evaluated by outside
consultants on different occasions. One such report listed
criteria by which the school has successfully met its challenge:

1. faculties which include men and women who have
    special training, and who are committed to re-
    search;
2. laboratory school is freed from normal restric-
    tions that apply to other schools;
3. laboratory school has access to additional funds
    for its research;
4. laboratory school develops relationships with
    other institutions of learning;

5. special permission for the development of materials or other methods used for teacher training;
6. its program must be superior, and its methods of administration, supervision and curriculum development subjected to constant evaluation and improvement.[1]

This article will highlight various relationships that it has established with the Ministry and other institutions. These relations have enabled the school to undertake curriculum reform and develop program materials; to expand the knowledge of child growth and development and its relation to classroom learning; to construct tests and related evaluative instruments used in measurement; and to introduce the concept of in-service teacher training programs.

Curriculum--Program Materials

When the school undertakes activities in curriculum development it consults with the Ministry and its technical council. Many times other organizations assisted in projects, conferences and workshops: the former ICA (now AID) and the educational servicio SCIDE (now ACEN); individual private and public schools; private foundations, such as Kellogg; and regional organizations like the Institute of Nutrition of Central America and Panama (INCAP). The school draws up preliminary curriculum drafts when working with the Ministry; these are turned over to the Ministry and its technical council for their approval and modification, and become the property and responsibility of the Ministry.

> Whatever has been adopted by the Ministry of Education has been concluded on the basis of their criteria alone. The American School makes its original suggestions, but has not tried to influence any other school in any way in retraining or removing certain parts of the program.[2]

After the political crisis of 1954, the Ministry inaugurated the National Teachers Congresses of 1955 and 1956. The American School actively participated in one of its commissions, the commission to reorganize secondary education. An outgrowth of this activity was the Ministry's reorganization plan for the secondary schools to be completed by 1961. The school requested and was granted permission to implement the first three years of the new bachillerato curriculum

before the public schools; later requests were granted for
the fourth and fifth years. Thus, the school experimented
and initiated the national college preparatory curriculum
three years before it was made official in the public schools.

Primary curriculum needed attention, too, and in
1956 the Ministry and SCIDE asked the American School if
it would develop curriculum and materials and assist with
in-service teacher training programs. The school accepted
this responsibility on the condition that its work was preliminary and did not constitute official representation of the
Ministry. In 1957 the school gave the new programs to the
Ministry. For the next three years under the Ministry's
supervision these programs were tried out at several selected schools. Meanwhile, the American School adopted
the program in its own primary schedule, modifying it at
the end of each year.

> When it became evident in 1960 that the Ministry
> of Education would probably adopt the programs,
> one large public school took the initiative in pre-
> paring the final drafts for the Ministry of Educa-
> tion. During the first two weeks of vacation in
> November 1969, the teachers of the public school
> met daily to discuss the programs and make neces-
> sary revisions. A representative from the Ameri-
> can School was invited to attend their meetings.
> In this way the improvements that had been made
> by the American School were incorporated. The
> final drafts were prepared and turned over to the
> Ministry of Education by the public school. In
> November the new programs were made official
> for all urban elementary schools. [3]

While not part of the above official curriculum, the
school developed over the years inexpensive program materials for the six grades. Up to 1967, materials had been
sent to 12 Latin American countries and 22 institutions in
the United States. In Guatemala materials have been requested from 16 schools, private and public, three universities, one regional organization and two commercial banks. [4]

Since the school began it has offered two college preparatory curricula: the American High School diploma and
the Bachillerato. In 1966, with permission from the Ministry, the School offered a third curriculum, the fused, which
combined the former two. When a student completes the

fused curriculum he receives both the Bachillerato and high
school diplomas simultaneously, without excessive duplication
of courses.   Mathematics, science and English are taught in
English, while social studies and Spanish are taught in Spanish, and physical education, industrial arts, home economics,
art and music are taught in both languages.   To date results
continue to be most promising. [5]

Child Growth and Development

When the Laboratory School program began in 1949
no basic longitudinal study of child growth and development
existed anywhere in Latin America.   Prevailing generalizations concerning Latin American children were based, usually,
on simple assumptions, individual experiences or analogous
reasoning from studies done in Europe or the United States,
not on empirical evidence.   It was clear from the start,
then, that this area would be an integral part of the Laboratory School program.

Development signifies change and differentiation; the
evolutionary process that operates in children modifies their
size, structure and organic functions, as well as their growth
and maturity.   A progressive and dynamic differentiation pre-
disposes the individual to attain a superior level which permits new forces of conduct; and this is only possible when a
given individual has reached those full potentialities which
had previously lain in latent form.

Since 1954 measurements have been made of the pupil's
height, weight, number of erupted permanent teeth, strength
of wrist grip, skeletal growth and academic achievement.
The physical measurements were translated into growth stages
by months.   The result was a group of growth ages; height
age, weight age, dental age, carpal age and a group of educational achievement ages.   By measuring and testing the
same pupils annually, longitudinal records were established.
While the School has not been able to make extensive use of
the data in other public schools, the School staff has used
the data on individuals and groups within the School.   "In
case studies of learning and behavior problems, the longitudinal records have provided objective data as a firm basis for
the discussion of teacher observations, impressions and
opinions. "[6]

Test Construction

Traditionally, testing has held an important place in Guatemalan education, especially in the development of courses and teaching materials. In fact it has occupied a position of exaggerated importance because the central government determined promotion on the basis of tests made up by the Ministry and administered by it. The character of the tests dictated even more the program and what kind of teaching took place because the teacher soon realized what the final tests would require and taught accordingly. If the tests required memorization of isolated facts and points of information (which was often the case) then the teacher would emphasize these in her teaching. Meanwhile the student learned what was expected of him, and on examination day he geared his previous "learning experience" to pass those finals.

From 1945 to 1949 the School followed exactly the official program and examinations; upon its designation as a Laboratory School it was able to develop and administer its own examinations. The objective of its testing program, carefully outlined to the Ministry in 1949, is still in effect: "the objective of teaching is understanding, and if we do teach for understanding we must test for understanding."[7]

Contemporary educational practices take for granted that the teacher has available a reliable appraisal of the ability and achievement of her students: the standard intelligence and achievement tests. But prior to 1949 none of these were available to the teachers at the School or any other school. Furthermore, there were no tests for the Spanish speaking student that took into consideration his cultural environment. While published tests could be bought and imported from the United States at great cost, they had little practical value when applied to the Guatemalan educational setting. The School has developed and is standardizing the following tests and received permission from various publishing concerns to print and distribute them at cost to various educational institutions throughout the country and Latin America.

Intelligence Tests

Pintner-Cunningham, Form A (including norms for the
    Guatemalan child)
Pintner Non-Verbal, Intermediate, Form A

Otis Alfa AS
Otis Gamma EM, Rapid Evaluation
Otis Intermediate, Form A
Otis Superior, Form A
Stanford Binnet, Verbal Form L and E, Primary to
    Higher
Wechsler Bellevue, Adult Scale, Form 1 Verbal (WAIS)
Wechsler Intelligence Scale for Children (WISC), Verbal

Interest Schedule

Thurstone Interest Scale

Reading Readiness Tests

Pre-Reading Test
Basic Reading Test
Intermediate Reading Test (the first of a series to
    cover all elementary and secondary grades)

Aptitude Tests

Differential Aptitude Tests Form AM
    a) Numerical Ability
    b) Speed and Accuracy
    c) Verbal Reasoning
    d) Abstract Reasoning
    e) Spatial Relations
California Aptitude Tests, Battery
Holzinger-Crowder Uni-factor test, Battery
Crawford Test of Manual Dexterity
Bennet Test of Manual Dexterity

Teacher Education and In-Service Training

In-service training is another essential and continuing
part of the Laboratory School program, as it assists both
the American and Guatemalan staffs. However, in a more
specific sense the in-service program has become more
specialized since 1955. The basic purpose of the in-service
program is to help teachers improve their methods and their
understanding of methods of teaching and principles of learning. In addition the program attempts

to help develop the professional teaching and administrative personnel; to give help to the profes-

sional in education when there are problems; and
to correct deficiencies in the preparation of the
teacher in reference to the teaching materials, to
the methods of teaching and to general knowledge. 8

The School initiated its cadet teacher program in 1955.
Trainees are selected from graduates of the normal school.
They receive beginning teachers' salaries and are assigned
to regular classroom teachers of the elementary staff for
three months' experience at each of three different grade
levels. The secondary school cadets work in the various
subject matter classes for ten months. The relationship between the regular grade teacher and that of the in-service
trainee is similar to that between a critic teacher and a
cadet teacher (trainee) in a teacher's college in the United
States. The critic teacher comes from either the Guatemalan or American staffs, and the administrative personnel of
the elementary and secondary sections coordinate the program.

Whenever the School has a vacancy in its regular
teaching staff, it is often filled by one of the cadets. If
the School has no need for their services, they take jobs in
various private and public schools or with the Ministry after
their one year of training. The School believes that it
should have several cadet teachers in training at all times.
Since the School started this program more than 15 years
ago more than 46 teachers have participated; 13 have become regular members of the staff. While the total number
is small compared to the country's overall needs, these cadet teachers are greatly valued by the Ministry. Many of
them now occupy important positions within the Ministry,
various schools and with different technical assistance
agencies.

Relations with the University of San Carlos

The School maintains a close, cooperative relationship with the country's national university, the University of
San Carlos. In 1954 the School suggested that "cooperation
between both institutions could beneficially result in solving
the ever present problems ... that originate from the inter-
dependence of secondary and higher education. "9

The reciprocal relationship has allowed both institutions to share facilities, materials and staffs. The School

has had the University's assistance in the use of the Faculty
of Humanities library facilities and in the help of different
university specialists in the development of special programs.
At the University's request the School developed the University's admissions program, conducted a seminar in university teaching and hosted a regional conference in testing and
admissions programs.

In 1962 the University's Medical Science Faculty wanted
to develop a program in methods of test evaluation. Members
of this faculty and the American School began preliminary
discussions covering the following: problems and theory of
evaluation, theoretical and practical learning, objective examinations, norms and statistical methods.

The results of the above became known throughout
the University and other faculties wanted information. The
Faculty of Medical Science asked the Faculty of Humanities
for help in developing a program of admissions for its incoming students in 1963.   The faculties of chemical science,
pharmacy and dentistry also requested the School's assistance
via the Faculty of Humanities. The School accepted the responsibility and developed and administered the following
tests to the incoming students: general ability, language,
mathematics, natural science and foreign languages.   In
1963 the University created the Department of Basic Studies
which comprised the first two years of study for all students
enrolled. The Faculty of Humanities asked the School's assistance in the preparation of materials, and the organization
and development of the admissions program. By 1965 a
complete battery of tests was developed and an admissions
program was operative.

The University of Valle

The University of Valle is an outgrowth of the educational experiences of the American School as a Laboratory
School.   While the school provides elementary and secondary
programs for more than a thousand students, the school has
carefully established relationships with the Ministry, University of San Carlos and other institutions. [10]

Over the years the problems of higher education and
secondary education have become more closely related. The
trustees of the School became convinced that an independent,
non-denominational university could make a significant contri-

bution to higher education as the School has made to elementary and secondary education. Therefore, the University of Valle represents the logical outgrowth of the American School's laboratory experience.

In 1965 interested persons connected with the School explored the idea of establishing a small, private university to be sponsored by the American School Association (ASA), and there was favorable reaction. Later the same year, the ASA requested such a university of San Carlos, which, at that time, had the authority to authorize Valle's establishment. The Superior Council of the University of San Carlos granted authorization on January 29, 1966 and classes began on March 1. Valle shares the School's 52-acre site and buildings.

Valle was founded by the board of trustees of the ASA. As a legal entity under the civil code of Guatemala the ASA possessed the requisite legal characteristics to sponsor the University. Furthermore, the Association's tradition of a non-profit, non-political, and non-religious operation made a desirable organizational base for the development of such a university. Valle is an experimental university, and does not duplicate the existing universities found in Guatemala or Central America. Traditional faculties such as law, medicine, engineering and dentistry are not a part of Valle. Rather, it emphasizes general studies, preparation of professional specialists in education and social sciences, and furthering educational research and development programs. The new university's over-all goal is to produce people who are able and willing to assume responsibility promoting progress in the economic, political, educational and cultural development of Central America. So that this goal may be achieved the following long range goals have been established:

The University will direct its attention so that it promotes understanding of regional problems, especially those of Central America and the hemisphere. This will be important for secondary teachers, equipping them to introduce insights and perspectives of the social scientists into Central American classrooms. Another objective is to further develop Guatemalan and Central American education. The School's 20 years of experience has already contributed to the development of education. Now the School's laboratory emphasis will be to design organizational frameworks, methods and procedures through which education may be

improved in efficiency and quality with the hope that when
Guatemala doubles its expenditures for education, more than
double the present educational output will result.

In connection with the School, the University has established the Institute for Educational Research which develops and demonstrates new models of classroom organization, curriculum, teaching procedures and teaching materials
at all levels of education. It is hoped that Valle will influence other institutions of higher learning by providing similar models.

The third objective is to conduct long range research
and to train research workers. The Institute will be the
vehicle in which research is conducted in the following areas:
curriculum teaching materials and educational materials;
preparing research oriented teachers and workers; developing techniques of evaluation and test development; continuing
study of child growth and development; consultant services to
other institutions and painting publications. So that these
goals may find application in order to improve education,
experimental programs are developed and demonstrated by
the Institute through the School and the University.

The fourth objective is to produce a person with a
liberal education. It is believed that such a person possesses
qualities of intellect and character that are important no
matter which vocation he enters or in which region of the
world he resides. The last and perhaps most important objective is to develop highly trained teachers. The program
is designed to produce a limited number of very qualified
elementary and secondary teachers who will provide leadership in the educational development of Guatemala and the
region.

The Academic Program. The University provides
studies, training programs and research projects not offered
in other institutions in Guatemala. And the emphasis is
placed on those activities that contribute to the development
of education. The sequence of the general studies program
is gradually being changed from two to four years, combining the last two years of secondary education and the first
two years of university. The acute problem of the lack of
articulation between the two levels of education, the inefficiency due to overlapping programs and the absence of sequence for serious academically-minded students have promoted development of this four-year program. Courses are

taught by university professors and secondary teachers in a
team teaching arrangement.

Presently, a special four-year curriculum project is
in process under controlled conditions, attempting to improve
the curriculum, teaching and testing of social sciences, natural sciences and humanities, both for the secondary and at
the University level. The four-year basic studies program
is being patterned after the results of this study. By giving
answers to numerous problems faced by Central American
universities in their liberal arts general studies program,
this project, when completed, should have at least a small
effect on the secondary schools and universities throughout
the region.

Because Valle is small it can be selective in the
choice of faculty. Many come from the University of San
Carlos; others, from the United States as visiting scholars
to conduct research under cooperative agreements. The student body represents a cross-section as a revolving scholarship loan fund encouraging a wider representation has been
established. The maximum number for the student body is
300 students.

While the University has no departments, as they are
known in the States, three faculties, or divisions, were established in 1969: Science and Humanities, Social Sciences,
and Education. The three faculties are authorized to grant
the licanciature based on five years of study. Later, post-
graduate studies leading to the doctorate will be established.
All students take the two years of general studies or its
equivalent. Non-degree candidates will be granted sub-pro-
fessional diplomas with areas covered by the three faculties.

The Preparation of Teachers. Quality and quantity
are acute in Guatemala in terms of teacher training. The
University's emphasis in teacher education of a limited number of very qualified persons with leadership potential is
based first on the need for educational change in addition
to educational expansion. The great demand for teachers
is so acute that the Ministry and the University of San Carlos must develop teacher training programs on a mass production basis. As there is great change in the economy and
society, there should be similar changes within education,
but such changes are not often provided for.

For change to occur in education, individuals, insti-

tutions and organizations must be prepared to produce this
change.   The key is the teacher and every emphasis must
be put on improving his training.   Therefore, the most
promising candidates must be singled out for specialization
so that their leadership potential is realized.   These "specialists" must not only have technical training in their areas but
they must also have the kind of education that will make
them effective leaders.

The Institute of Educational Research.   As the Laboratory School is an integral part of the University of Valle,
so is the Institute, one of the few establishments of its kind
in Central America.   The Institute's purpose is to put research at the service of educational planning and development.   In view of this commitment the following are important functions of its long range program: the training of
teachers and educational research workers; evaluation of
production of tools for the profession; and, dissemination of
information via various means.   Several projects are now
underway, some of them having their origin in the Laboratory School: longitudinal study of child growth and development; program of test development; research and development of curriculum, teaching materials and educational
methods; publications; and, school service.

Institutional Development.   While the ASA was an appropriate body to found the University, it was decided to
transform it to a university foundation; on July 28, 1967
this decision was reached.   The statutes for the new foundation were approved by the ASA on February 9, 1968, and
the government is expected to approve them in 1970, thus
legally constituting the founding of the University.

The trustees of the foundation are responsible for
general policy and fiscal operation.   They appoint two boards
of five members each, one for the operation and management of the University and one for the School.   The boards
have the policy and financial guidelines set by the Foundation which provides a responsible framework from which to
work.   The ASA's members become trustees of the foundation with additional members being nominated periodically.

The University's administration is kept as simple as
possible.   The Directive Council, composed of a rector,
vice-rector, secretary-general and director of general
studies, is the responsible administrative group of the University.   It delegates the execution of administrative deci-

sions to an executive secretary.   The academic and administrative heads of the various divisions of the University, as
members of the Directive Council, are most often under the
chairmanship of the vice-rector.   Emphasis is on coordination among all departments and divisions, maintaining maximum unity of academic relationships.

     Relations with other institutions.   Close relationships
have been established with other institutions: Memphis Public Schools, Colby College (Maine), Kalamazoo College,
Michigan State University, the University of Pennsylvania
and Harvard University.   Staff members from the universities of Michigan and Pennsylvania cooperate in the longitudinal study in child development.   Several universities have
sent students to take part in the regular classroom activities in the laboratory school.   These relations continue and
will be expanded in the near future.

     Valle maintains relations with various Central Ameri-
can and Guatemalan institutions: the Regional Office for
Central America and Panama (ROCAP); the Superior Council
of Central American Universities (CSUCA); the Federation of
Private Universities of Central America (FUPAC); the Inter-
American Program in Communications Research (PIIP); the
Institute of Nutrition of Central America and Panama (INCAP);
and the two private universities in Guatemala, Dr. Mariano
Galvaz and Rafael Landivar.   The Laboratory School has
been accredited by the Southern Association of Secondary
Schools and Colleges for more than ten years.   In 1967 the
National Education Association named the Laboratory School
as one of its demonstration schools, thus giving official
recognition to the quality of the University's teacher training
program.   The NEA has offered to work closely with the
University providing equipment, materials and staff consultants.

     The University's institute has been working closely
with the Educational Testing Service, Princeton, New Jersey,
carrying out the test development program.   Several of the
Institute staff have received training at ETS workshops in
the states and ETS consultants have provided advice and
training to the program in Guatemala.

Conclusions and Implications

     The American School is unique.   In one sense it is

traditional in that it maintains the college preparatory curriculum; the student body comes from that segment of the
population where children expect and parents can afford university training; its calendar is identical to the one used in
the public schools; and it is a private institution getting support from tuition. And in another sense the school is new
because of its laboratory status and subsequent activities.
Therefore, the School is a hybrid institution, one that is
neither Guatemalan nor American but a blend of the two.

The School is Guatemala's first laboratory school,
and perhaps the first one of its kind in all of Latin America.
The growth of the School took place during the most turbulent period of Guatemala's modern history. At no time,
however, were the School's requests or actions ever challenged by the various administrations or by the Ministry of
Education, although many technical assistance projects and
programs were altered or discontinued; the School's activities continued without interruption throughout its entire history.

The national curriculum currently used in public
schools throughout the country was first developed at the
School. Prior to 1955 public school curriculum reflected
traditional values and was composed of long lists of unrelated subjects. The School requested permission to experiment with a new curriculum before the public schools. After a period of adaptive experimentation at the School, the
Ministry of Education adopted the programs and incorporated
them in the public schools. By 1961 both primary and
secondary curriculum reflected the preliminary work done
at the American School.

Prior to 1949 no testing in the public schools was
based on psychological measures. The School introduced the
concept and use of objective testing for measuring student
performance, which in turn led to the development of standard I. Q., achievement and aptitude tests. In two decades
the School standardized more than 20 tests to fit the Guatemalan students and developed and severally administered
locally constructed tests.

Through its research in testing, the School has been
able to help the University develop a selection process based
on adequate and equitable testing. Since 1958 the School has
assisted various faculties in developing and administering
admission tests. Now the University has its own admissions

program and administers its own tests. In addition, a De-
partment of Vocational Guidance has been established at the
University which utilizes various tests developed at the
School.

Realizing that most teachers are products of the normal school, lack university training, and many times do not
possess proper teacher certification, the School has developed the awareness for in-service training. Through
numerous conferences, workshops and visitations, the School
has introduced modern methods of teaching, program materials and curriculum guides to many Guatemalan teachers.
The Ministry has recognized this service and in 1961 recommended that the School expand its program of in-service education.

Many of the School's contributions are now being
transferred to the University of Valle, Guatemala's only private and experimental University. With recognition from
the Guatemalan Government and its national university, San
Carlos, Valle has a firm foundation in which to broaden the
preliminary efforts started by the laboratory school.

Implications for Further Study. The bi-national,
community-type, non-profit American Schools have two basic
functions. One is to provide the children of United States
dependants with a quality education, enabling them to enter
United States universities. And to a great extent this has
been proven: the schools periodically receive grants in aid
from the State Department; many are accredited by regional
accrediting associations; and many have established consultant relationships with stateside universities. Another primary function of these American Schools is to assist with
the national system of education. Since the majority of students are nationals this has further implications. The curricular choice will be the bachillerato as the vast majority
of graduates will attend private or public universities within
the country and they will earn their livelihood there.

As suggested by the Guatemalan example other bi-
national schools might benefit by laboratory school designation. This need not occur at one time but could be achieved
over a number of years. Below are listed several ways in
which these schools could make further contributions to the
national systems of education; undertaking or expanding such
activities would make laboratory status easier to achieve.

A bi-national school is, in a sense, a guest in the host country. Rather than just existing for a foreign clientele apart from the national system of education, it is part of the community-at-large. Laboratory status would give the institution greater permanency as part of the community. The more the bi-national school is perceived by others as part of the community-at-large the greater and more lasting its contributions can be.

Generally curricula in these schools tend to be dual, one national and one American. A fused curriculum, like that of Guatemala, would bring the two philosophies closer together, and, in turn, would serve a unified student body. As Ministries of Education periodically change their curricula, they could draw from the experiences which the bi-national schools have had. The concept and use of texts and program materials are not evenly advanced throughout the schools in most countries. If the bi-national schools could produce inexpensive up-to-date materials this might assist the Ministries of Education in their curricular reforms.

Teacher training and in-service teacher education present a unique area in which many contributions can be made. The average teacher at the bi-national school has had more preparation than one at a national school. Informal conferences, workshops and the like can be easily organized. These not only afford an exchange of views between the American teachers and nationals but assist the communication flow between the various educational institutions. Since many of the bi-national schools have had stateside consultants assisting the American staffs, these could be easily extended to include the national teachers.

The relationship between the School and Guatemalan education has been established and described in some detail; it is implicit from this discussion that the School has had a definite effect on Guatemalan education, which in turn suggests that the School has influenced the Ministry's course of action at several points. These effects and influences might now be evaluated and interpreted. This article has not sought to prove the precise effects nor evaluate the degree of influence that the school has had on the Ministry and its programs; hopefully they may be evaluated in the future by empirical studies undertaken by social scientists.

Likewise there exists a similar relation with other bi-national schools and national systems of education. Even though it is probably to a lesser extent than the Guatemalan, nonetheless there is some degree of linkage as no institution exists in isolation. Whether bi-national schools have directly influenced various Ministries of Education is problematical. Certainly, laboratory status would increase the influence.

Finally, since the Guatemalan and other bi-national schools have produced several graduating classes a study of the long range contributions to the national systems of education is possible. Where the School's graduates go, employment opportunities they find and the significant leadership roles they have to play in their respective societies-- these represent some of the areas of potential investigation. Certainly the role of the bi-national Schools in Latin America is significant.

Notes

1. Clair J. Butterfield, Stephan A. Corey and Kenneth J. Rehage, An Appraisal of the Laboratory School Activities of the American School Activities of the American School of Guatemala, Guatemala: The American School, 1954, p. 4-5.

2. First Bi-Annual Report to the Inter-American Schools Service, Washington, D. C., 1961, Guatemala: The American School, 1961, p. 32.

3. Second Bi-Annual Report to the IASS, 1962, p. 2-3.

4. El Colegio Americano de Guatemala como Escuela de Ensayo, 1967, Guatemala: Colegio Americano de Guatemala, 1967, p. 43-46.

5. ... Como Escuela de Ensayo 1967 [see note 4], p. 12.

6. Warren A. Ketcham, as quoted in First Bi-Annual Report to IASS, 1963, p. 14.

7. August-November Report to the IASS, 1949 [see note 2], p. 3.

8. Ministerio de Educación Pública y SCIDE, Cuatro Experiencias del Colegio Americano de Guatemala como Escuela de Ensayo. Primer Seminario Nacional

sobre Problemas de la Educación Guatemalteca.
Guatemala: The American School, 1961, p. 36.

9.   ... Como Escuela de Ensayo, 1954, p. 32.

10.   This section is adapted from the following mimeographed publications of the American School: "A
Brief Description of the Universidad del Valle, "
January 9, 1968; "The Universidad del Valle de
Guatemala: A Brief Description of Present Activities, " March 1969; and "A Description of the Universidad del Valle de Guatemala, " March, 1970.

6. MY TEACHER, THE TV SET*
Charles Marden Fitch

Television is one of the scarce dynamic methods for educating people, which are so often sought but seldom found. Only within the last ten years has the truly revolutionary tool of television been put at the service of millions. To a teacher educational television can be a catalyst, a sparker of student interest. The same exciting medium can mean to the industrialist a steady supply of better trained workers. To you and me educational television fosters a deeper understanding of our culture and provides an entertaining reference work to the world.

I recall with tenderness my first visit to a cold drab neighborhood school on the outskirts of Bogotá, Colombia. The occasion was a visit to watch the children receive one of the natural science programs I had produced for Colombian national television. The classroom teacher and I stood silently at the back of the dimly lit room. Off in one corner, on a carefully constructed wooden stand, was a television receiver recently installed by Colombian technicians and Peace Corps volunteers.

With the first notes of a Mozart horn concerto, our theme for the program series, the children became somewhat anxious yet attentive, but as the program progressed their mood changed to animated participation. They answered questions, looked sad or laughed, but constantly reacted to the talented presentation of the television teacher. Immediately after the broadcast the classroom teacher began a planned follow-up lesson based on suggestions made in a teacher's guide previously supplied by the office of educational television within the Ministry of Education.

---

*Reprinted by permission from the March 1969 Americas, a monthly magazine published by the General Secretariat of the Organization of American States in English, Spanish, and Portuguese.

Here for us to appreciate was a living example to
demonstrate that television with a live classroom lesson is
especially powerful with students in the primary through the
secondary grades. A specific lesson is taught dynamically
by combining the talents of two teachers: one on television
and the other with the students. There are some who insist
that television produced for in-school use be termed "instructional." Actually after more than ten years of challenging
and exciting creative work in the field of television I still
find the term "educational" to be more indicative of television's broader important value in a classroom, the community center or in one's home. I have seen television serve
as a superior aid to those who wish to teach. We have also
used television programs both as part of a classroom lesson
and as an entertainment aimed at a home audience. In the
two cases our program content helped the viewers toward an
appreciative understanding of life.

In Colombia, recently, we were mainly concerned with
helping teachers to do a better job of teaching the established
traditional curriculum as supervised by the Ministry of Education. Television, though, is a captivating visual medium
when used creatively, so we found that, as a result of our
programs, the teachers were more apt to apply explorative
or action teaching as contrasted with the classical lecture
methods. The students, of course, found learning more
meaningful in this explorative atmosphere. Social studies
and the sciences, especially, are areas in which television
is encouraging the classroom use of charts, actual specimen
examples, field trips to study local industries, habitat observations in adjacent forested locations and a host of other
teach-by-doing techniques. Students and their teachers in
the classrooms, inspired by exciting television programs,
are eager to try new procedures of exploring the standard
subject courses.

Peru has had success in teaching basic literacy
through the coordinated use of educational television and local community guides or lesson leaders. In 1964 I had the
pleasure of talking with a Peruvian education official who
explained to me her projected plans for using educational
television (ETV) in Peru. Colombian friends of mine in the
national television system were invited to Peru where they
exchanged ideas that aided in the expansion of the Peruvian
ETV project. A 1968 conference in Peru provided further
opportunities for educators to explore innovative ideas in the
field of educational broadcasting. The Peace Corps, in

September of 1968, began an experimental ETV project with
the Imperial Ethiopian Government, while in Nigeria ETV
has been in use several years, both for adult and lower
school education.   Italy's Telescuola achieved great success
with adult education in a plan that uses group viewing and a
classroom tutor.

The same sort of system is now being used in Colombia, where adults meet together in evening classes, supervised by a resident teacher.   The adult education classes
utilize the same television receivers that are used by their
children during the school day.   Another practical method
requires the establishment of community viewing salons, often located in a quiet government building or a local health
center.

In all of these applications it is of paramount importance to include a teacher in each classroom.   Professionally produced ETV programs are powerful, yet it is necessary
to have a live teacher working with the students if the maximum benefits are to occur.   The local teachers, however,
need not be regular elementary classroom teachers.   In
adult health education, for example, it is sometimes desirable to use a doctor, a trained nutritionist or a similar professional as a guide for adult students who receive instruction via television broadcasts.   With responsible coordination
it is usually possible to involve already established teams of
educators in the new project of extending education with
television.

Government teams in agriculture, public health, technical training and nutrition, for example, and Peace Corps
volunteers are all potential organizers of community study
groups.   These locally inspired classes meet in viewing
salons or classrooms, as mentioned earlier, but the responsibility for coordination is left to the cooperating volunteer or government agency.   The educational TV department
supplies the programs, always at the correct hour, and perhaps study guides.

The educational television programs I have studied,
including those of Italy, Japan, England, Germany, Canada,
Puerto Rico, Nigeria and various other countries, all illustrate that the use of television to help teach a specific
school curriculum now receives major support around the
world.   Such programs, for actual in-class instruction,
must be produced by teams that are in close communication

with the teachers who will utilize the television broadcasts.
Printed guides, cumulative serial texts, visiting coordinators
from the Ministry of Education, anf frequent conferences in
various parts of the country between representatives of the
production teams and the teachers themselves are all means
of fostering valuable communication between, as it were, the
studio and the set.

In special teacher education programs I produced for
the Colombian ETV project we always featured new techniques in various areas of education.   Most countries that
utilize television for instruction realize that active production
units, especially concerned with teacher training, are an important part of the educational system.   These production
teams, sometimes the regular staff members who normally
produce programs for student viewing, consult experts in all
fields of education.   It is the job of the teacher education
production team to produce meaningful programs that will
help the local teachers in their own professional growth.

In the United States, open broadcast educational television often provides general enrichment rather than specific
instruction for classroom viewing.   A series of natural
science program segments, which I presented on WNDT-13
TV for two years, is a good example of this approach.   My
aim was to provide a basic understanding of our environment and the complex ecology of nature's world.   Each program featured living plants, original films, live animals and
other illustrative examples.   The varied elements were fused
by narration and music to create an unusually effective presentation.   Many adults wrote to say how much they appre-
ciated the programs even though the presentations were designed for younger people.

Currently a number of educational programs are produced as specials on our commercial networks.   The spon-
sors often furnish advance study guides to interested teachers.
In my own high school biology classes I have found such programs quite useful.   The students enjoy using ETV and
learning becomes the pleasure it always should be.

This article is an introduction to open broadcast ETV
but similar applications of television in education or instruction are also being made through closed circuits.   The
limited systems broadcast only to those locations that have
a cable connection or a specific frequency receiver.   Where
the cost of cables is not prohibitive, cable broadcasting

offers advantages of very clear reception, multiple channels, multi-language audio possibilities and a full control of schedules.   In rough terrain, however, where no telephone lines have penetrated the jungle, and in most national plans to use ETV, the open broadcast is usually the most satisfactory method to employ.   All of the programs, in open broadcast, can be viewed anywhere that a signal travels.

The assignment of channels for the exclusive use of educational broadcasting is practically obligatory in applications of ETV where schools or community viewing salons are involved.   If only limited broadcast time is available, between entertainment programs on commercial television, the problems of production and of reception scheduling can be excessively complex.   Reliable financing is also an important step in the establishment of a sound national plan to utilize the potential of television for education.

In this limited space I can but touch upon the details of how television is being used as an educational medium in Latin America.   Aside from productions within the United States, my own professional experience has been primarily in Colombia and El Salvador so the examples here are based upon the pioneer television projects in these countries.

The applications of educational television, still only partially discovered, will of course prove valuable the world over, especially in developing countries.   Some of the most effective uses of television are seen when the broadcast is an integral part of a carefully structured educational plan that joins face-to-face teacher-student relationships with professionally produced television programs.   In the most constructive sense, however, one need not limit educational television productions to those offering some form of instruction.   Programs produced especially to create prideful cultural understanding and general appreciation, or to explore the meaning of our lives, have an important part in the broadcast plan for any country.

In the New York metropolitan area we now have the opportunity of viewing, on an educational television station, a program devoted entirely to the black community.   Similar programs of a broad ethnocultural nature are available in Spanish and some other languages.   Within the developing countries, where practical primary education is of great immediate concern, there is an urgent need to incorporate the common culture into any television produced for educating the local populace.

The standard curriculum areas of social studies and
natural science contain a wealth of local material ready to
be captured and constructively used in educational programs.
First, of course, one must train television producer-directors
in the specialized techniques required to translate abstract
ideas such as educational concepts into powerful, arresting
audio-visual presentations. Quite simply this means that the
successful director-producer must be much more than a man-
ipulator of mechanical devices; he must understand the goals
of a country, he must appreciate the dreams and the obligations of the individual. A smooth relationship of respect and
cooperation must develop between the television talent (teacher) and the director-producer.

A technique that has yielded superior results involves
the use of a television teacher in film segments that are
custom produced for the program at hand. In Colombia, for
example, biologist-telemaestra Ines Triana Garay appears in
film segments within her natural science programs. The
film sections, skillfully integrated into the studio portions of
her program, illustrate ideas, show material and capture
phenomena that are impossible or very difficult to present
in the television studio.

By putting the television teacher in these film segments the director achieves three important goals:

1. The television teacher develops a deep understanding of the material being presented since she has seen
and researched her subject in a variety of locations around
the country.
2. The prestige and believability of the telemaestra
is greatly increased when the student audience recognizes
her in direct experienced contact with the subject matter.
3. Finally but of equal importance the classroom
teacher develops respect and admiration for the television
teacher. It is visually evident within the films that the
teacher chosen to present her subject on a national broadcast is uniquely qualified for such a large responsibility.

The use of film segments produced for national television programs has an added advantage in that interest is
created wherever films are shot. Residents of even the
smallest town are thrilled to assist in films that will later
appear on television. Segments of motion pictures originally

created for one subject area will frequently prove to be of
value in other areas. A carefully indexed library of cine
and still photographs will, after several years, be an in-
credibly rich source of local examples to be used on television as superior teaching tools. Identification between the
viewers and the program content is immediate. The audience
sees Juan or Lola working in their own nation rather than a
remote country populated by persons who do not resemble
anyone they know. Although these considerations may not
seem important to those with international educations they
are very important indeed when one is striving to educate a
largely provincial audience.

Television is unsurpassed as a medium to be employed for the close study of material and procedures. On
television every school in the country can see a single careful dissection of an animal done beside a chart of its internal organs, followed by a segment of motion picture illustrating heart action and blood flow. Finally we may use a
talented, well-trained teacher to present carefully researched
material interspersed with interest-sparking questions. To
produce all of these illustrative examples "live" in each
classroom throughout the nation would be impossible, even
in the most developed of countries, yet through television
a single cine projector, one dissected creature, one professionally created chart and a single talented teacher are
made instantly available to thousands. The result: better
education at lower financial costs than alternative methods.

The teachers in a nation's schools, who are sometimes forced to teach at a level beyond their training, are
helped to do their best by the inclusion of superior educational television programs in their daily lesson plans. The
classroom teacher will learn from good ETV programs along
with the students. One may actually broadcast teacher education programs before, between, or after the classroom
hours, of course, but even without this extra production effort the school teachers will grow through two methods:

1. Classroom guides, well coordinated with the televised segments of a lesson, are printed and distributed to
all of the schools where television is used. These guides
are clear, concise outlines, a page or two, listing what will
be covered in the television program and a few suggestions
for classroom activity before, during, and after a broadcast.
The printed, sometimes illustrated, guides may well be accompanied by sections of an expanded curriculum guide that

will accumulate to create a text by the end of the school
term.

    2.   Watching the television programs a classroom
teacher is often exposed to more ideas than during his period of teacher training. It is undeniably stimulating to watch
an especially talented telemaestra present well-illustrated
ideas or to see a perceptively produced professional film of
an activity never before witnessed.

7. INSTRUCTIONAL TELEVISION IN EL SALVADOR*
Eugene Nuss

The use of television in El Salvador's broad educational development program is deserving of special note for several reasons. Most important of these is that within the education venture in El Salvador, television has become more than a medium of instruction. It also functions as a powerful catalytic agent, a role that promises to influence human learning and development even more than do the lessons it imparts each day to the secondary schools of the country.

Very early in the project, program planners adopted a broad perspective of instructional television--one that is probably unique among projects of this type and magnitude. As a result, priorities set by the planners showed clearly that they saw ITV as something more than a relatively inexpensive substitute for well-trained teachers. In effect Salvadorean leaders and their North American advisors recognized that television, regardless of its quality, could not by itself effect educational reform. The directional signal of instructional television in El Salvador was not "locked" on technological hardware. Television is, and will continue to be, one of the major components of the educational reform program in El Salvador. The fact that it is one of the major components rather than the major component, makes the tale worth telling. Even though, at this time, it is not possible to completely evaluate results insofar as gains in student learning are concerned, it is already clear that TV has made an indirect, though none the less telling, impact on every phase and aspect of the Salvadorean adventure in education. To understand the adventure and the impact it is necessary to know something of Salvadorean society and its earlier level of educational development.

*Published as "The Role of Instructional Television in the Education Reform Program of El Salvador," Educational Broadcasting Review, April 1971. Reprinted with permission.

Small Country, Large Problem

Relative to its neighbors, Guatemala and Honduras, indeed to most countries of the world, El Salvador is a very small nation. It is the smallest mainland country of the Western Hemisphere; it also has the dubious distinction of being one of the most densely populated societies in the hemisphere (389 inhabitants per square mile). Only 150 miles East to West and 75 miles North to South, El Salvador faces the Pacific Ocean to the south from its niche in the Central American isthmus.

With a rapidly expanding population (nearly three and a half million people as of 1960 census), a severely limited supply of natural resources; and 95 percent of its land area already under cultivation, El Salvador has two alternatives. It must develop its technology, its industry, and its level of productivity or abandon the hope of first-class nationhood. These imperatives can be met only if the human resources of the society are developed and utilized in a more fruitful manner than has been true of the past. It is apparent that El Salvador cannot continue to rely almost exclusively on an agrarian economy (coffee as its main cash crop) if it is to progress as a modern society.

The present Salvadorean administration has recognized education as an important key to social and economic growth. It is also aware that the traditional education system has not adequately served the national interests. As recently as 1964 (latest data available) El Salvador reported an illiteracy rate of 56 percent of the adult population; in 1967, 30 percent of the school age population had never been enrolled in a school; only 50 percent of all children who did enroll got through the second grade; approximately 15 percent of all students who entered the first grade reached the seventh grade; and only about 1 percent reached the level of higher education.

These data show clearly the inadequacy of the traditional education system to carry out the mandate of the National Constitution, which demands the "universal" and "democratic" education of the Salvadorean people. Further, beyond the basic or general education level there was a great void where vocational training should have been, and an over-emphasis on preparation for the university and, consequently, professions already crowded. Until the present reform, teacher training was fragmented into a number of very small training programs, each shackled by a "classics" curriculum and a methodology based largely upon concepts of rote learning and mental discipline.   The traditional Salvadorean system of education could only preserve the Salvadorean status quo.

        The present government, under President Sánchez Hernández, is serious about educational reform.   In 1969, 27 percent of the national budget went for education.   The $22,864,000 allocated to the Ministry of Education for 1968 was about double the budget of any other government agency. The 1970 commitment to education was approximately 30 percent of the national budget.   However, the financial resources of El Salvador are not unlimited.   The government had tried, without notable success, to combine economic efficiency with educational improvement--an impossible goal where human resources are underdeveloped and technology is in an early stage of development.   The Punta del Este Conference of April 1967 seemed to offer the Salvadoreans an opportunity to accomplish this much sought after combination.   At the Punta del Este Conference, President Johnson invited a Central American country to participate in an educational reform program with the U.S. in which educational television would be a major component.   Further, President Johnson suggested that this project might serve as a model for other Latin nations.   Salvadorean leaders showed immediate interest in this idea, and it was then that instructional television became an integral part of the broad education reform project.

Preparations for Educational Reform

        In July, 1967, President Sánchez Hernández appointed a new Minister of Education, Mr. Walter Béneke.   A former diplomat, businessman and world traveler, Mr. Béneke launched into a five-year educational reform program by proposing the reorganization of nearly every educational function beginning with the Ministry of Education.   Under the motto "Efficiency, Quality, Sufficiency," program objectives were spelled out, phases of program development were identified and arranged in a timetable.   Top priorities were: 1) the reorganization of the Ministry of Education; 2) the centralization of teacher training; and, 3) the creation of a Division of Instructional Television within the Ministry. These three major projects were to form the base from which the educational reform program was to proceed, and

were scheduled for completion before the end of 1968. The
new Minister had set for himself a very demanding time-
table.

Regarding the reorganization of the Ministry, the plan
brought together into one relatively well-equipped building
the various administrative offices of the Ministry which were
previously located in a variety of places throughout the capital city of San Salvador. A management consultant firm was
hired to study the organizational structure of the Ministry
and make recommendations. These focused on the decentralization of administrative responsibility and set forth a
more efficient assignment and description of tasks primarily
in the interest of avoiding duplication. The creation of an
Administrative and Personnel Office within the Ministry was
a major provision of the reorganization.

Prior to 1968 the teacher-training responsibility in
El Salvador was shared among seven official normal schools
and an indeterminate number of small private schools. Program coordination and development in these normal schools
was seriously hampered by both their physical separateness
in various parts of the country and by the absence of a central director of the teacher-training program at the institutional level. Under the reorganization plan, a teacher-
training center was created and assigned the exclusive responsibility for government sponsored teacher education in
El Salvador. In addition to training teachers, the new "Normal School" was designed to train administrators and supervisors, and to serve as an in-service training facility.
Further, the rather extensive campus of the Normal School
had room to house a center for production of the television
programs as well as for training all personnel, including
teachers, to be involved with television.

The third major part of this phase of development
was the creation of a Department of Educational (Instructional) Television as an integral part of the Ministry of Education. The Department became operative early in 1968 and
at that time assumed responsibility for all aspects of the
ITV component. This department has gradually grown from
its early nucleus of some 20 persons until reaching its
present strength of 124 in early 1970. The functions of this
group include the production of classroom TV programs in
all major subject areas; at the Plan Basico level, the writing and distribution of teacher guides and student workbooks;
the training of classroom teachers to utilize ITV programs;

and the management of all matters related to the organization and implementation of the medium. Moreover, the location of the ITV group on the same site as the Normal School made possible a close articulation between ITV and teacher-education.

The ITV system adopted in El Salvador will provide the core material of the curriculum to all Plan Basico Schools (grades 7-9). The typical TV class contains three parts: 10 minutes of review and motivation by the classroom teacher; 20 minutes of televised instruction; and 20 minutes of follow-up in which the classroom teacher expands on the material presented, initiates learning activities and answers questions. The teacher is provided with a printed guide containing not only a lesson plan with objectives and a summary of the lesson but suggested activities and projects for the students. Students receive printed workbooks with summaries of the TV lesson and questions to be answered on the material as a reinforcement of the concepts learned.

During 1969, there were 15 televised lessons per week in all five of the first year Plan Basico subjects according to the following proportion of TV classes to total classes: math: 3/4, general science: 4/5, Spanish: 2/5, social studies: 3/5, English: 3/3. In 1970, guidance, music and art are to be added to the televised courses for the second year. In 1969 the first-year courses were tested in 32 schools with 1,100 students. In February 1970, 80 percent of all public Plan Basico schools began using the first year ITV system (110 schools and 11,000 students). The same pilot group of 32 schools will test the second year (eighth grade) courses. This method will follow through 1972 when all public Plan Basico schools will have ITV with an expected enrollment of more than 50,000 pupils. Private schools, which presently constitute about 40 percent of the secondary schools in El Salvador are encouraged but not forced to participate in ITV, although they must follow the national curriculum, and some have joined the system by purchase of a TV receiver.

Effects of ITV Technology on Education

In the history of technology, there are many chapters about the impact of a single technological change on the societies of the world. Educational technology, like its predecessors, has created expectations among the general public

for radical and far-reaching changes. Moreover, when new
technology is applied to highly traditional school systems, the
expectations for important changes increase. The history of
recent applications of the new technology in developing and
developed areas has not confirmed such sanguine expectations.
The use of television in many school systems in both advanced and developing countries has failed to yield results
equal to expectations in so far as learning increments are
concerned, although the evidence is positive in most cases
[see Schrammet et al., New Educational Media in Action,
Unesco: Paris, 1967].

One of the problems, almost certainly, has been that
the technology was applied in a superficial manner, and that
as a consequence, the traditional educational system was
left largely intact. In the case of El Salvador, it is too
early to say that television has revolutionized the educational
system, but there is evidence of considerable change in important sectors of this system. The following sections will
attempt to trace the short term changes in the educational
system of El Salvador that instructional television has brought
about and, on the basis of these short term changes, to make
some predictions about long-range effects of this innovation.

The most immediate effect that instructional television
has on the secondary student in El Salvador is to alter and
expand the information system by which he learns. In the
traditional rote learning system prevalent throughout much of
the developing (and developed) world, the teacher is the chief,
often the single, source from which all new information flows.
The pattern begins with information dictated by the teacher
and the precise words of the dictation are copied into notebooks to be memorized so that at a later date a question
from the teacher (provided the proper words are used) acts
as a stimulus for the response of the student from the appropriate section of the workbook now transferred into memory. This process is defined as education and the student's
efforts are called learning.

The use of television has altered this system by increasing the number of sources of information from which
the student learns. For example, the student will typically
receive 20 minutes of many class periods from the television
teacher. He also has a workbook which gives a summary of
the matter covered and obviates the necessity of laboriously
copying this into a notebook. The classroom teacher is encouraged to provide additional reference books referred to in

the workbooks. Common class projects also allow the students to learn from one another as they cooperate in carrying out the construction of a relief map, or the display of
local Mayan artifacts, for example. In science classes the
television teacher uses simple experiments to encourage students to learn from observation of the physical world around
them. Thus the environment itself becomes an important
source of information and knowledge. The use of more
audio-visual aids by the classroom teacher also tends to
break down the single, verbal information source of the rote
system.

The expansion from the number of sources from
which a student is expected to gather information changes the
task of the learner considerably. In the rote system, it is
the teacher who structures the information and dictates it to
the student in a form already processed for memorization
and recall. Learning in this system consists of the memorization of the verbal strings uttered by the teacher. In the
new system, the student faces a double problem: the amount
of information is expanded so greatly that he can no longer
easily memorize it all; and the information comes to him in
a variety of forms so that he is forced to learn how to process this information himself in a way that will be useful
for storage and recall. These two changes make the student necessarily more active in the process of learning.

Thus, ITV, which is sometimes accused of encouraging passivity among students, would appear in the Salvadorean
project to create exactly the opposite reaction among its
audience.

Evaluation

The system of evaluation for a rote learning system
must obviously stress memorization. Where few books or
libraries exist, students are expected to carry around large
stores of information in their heads. Such has been the
case in El Salvador. The emphasis on memory is mirrored
in the type of testing common in the schools where a great
deal of weight is given tests that call for memorized definitions and the verbatim recall of isolated facts. Traditionally, teachers in El Salvador have been left to create
their own tests, since no national testing program existed.
Student evaluation has been based almost entirely on a few
teacher-made tests with quarterly and final tests counting

most heavily for promotion.

Instructional television has focused attention on a
number of problems in the area of evaluation which might
not otherwise have been considered had the educational reform only stressed teacher training and curriculum change.
Among these problems are the following: (1) The need to
evaluate how the curriculum and television are succeeding
in the classroom means that student achievement must be
measured differently. The rote-type test is not a valid
measure of a type of learning that does not depend solely
on memorized notes from workbook, but, rather on a much
broader spectrum of information sources. (2) Two reasons
suggest the need for the development of common tests:
teachers have had no training in test development and can
not be expected to create adequate tests on their own, and
no group comparisons of how television classes are doing
can be made without common examinations. (3) As a general consequence of the previous considerations, Salvadorean
officials began to realize the need to create some kind of
permanent national testing program to expand with the
growth of curriculum change and televised classes. A similar need for training classroom teachers to better evaluate
their students in the light of new learning goals was a concomitant realization. This has resulted in the initiation of
specialized training for a few Salvadoreans who in turn can
both help create a testing group within the Ministry and an
evaluation staff for teacher training.

Teachers

Perhaps the most distinctive characteristic of the impact ITV is making on the Education Reform Project of El
Salvador is in the area of teacher training. In the original
thinking and planning for the project it was felt that teacher
training could be confined to courses designed to teach the
teacher how to best utilize the ITV program he would receive in his classroom. This type of training program is
typical of other ITV projects, where teacher preparation
has been limited to brief workshops, or instructions via TV
and/or supervisory personnel--sufficient, no doubt, where
teaching is considered the exclusive domain of the television
teacher and where the classroom teacher is more monitor
than teacher.

However, once the planner adopted the broader view

of Education Reform, with ITV seen as a major, but not necessarily dominant component, it became apparent that the classroom teacher needed to know a lot more than how to to act (react) when the television tube was on. An analysis of what the classroom teacher needed to know in order to teach effectively in the Reform Program showed clearly that his professional requirements were no less than, and very little different from, the skills, knowledge, and attitudes required of teachers who are expected to teach effectively without television. Based upon this conclusion, a teacher training program was planned which must be considered unique in a variety of aspects when compared with other education projects where ITV is used.

Project leaders decided that all teachers who would teach in the new program must be re-trained at the National Teacher Training Center. The length of training for these teachers was set at nine months of full-time study (except for a relatively small group of teachers, felt to be superior because of prior training and experience, for whom only a two-month summer session was required). The significance of this decision can hardly be overemphasized in view of the following implications: 1) all teachers to be retrained would have to be replaced in their classrooms during the training program, 2) a broad-based teacher training program would have to be organized and implemented, 3) teachers in training would have to be paid their regular salaries since they are largely family heads or at least major financial contributors to their families, and 4) given a nine-month training program, the possibility existed to make basic changes in teacher attitudes toward the nature of teaching and learning. All of this is to say that the opportunity now existed to change the traditional concept of education in the thinking of those who must carry forward any change to be realized-- namely the teacher.

In the area of teacher training, as was the case with the expanding information system, ITV served as a powerful motivator. It brought attention to bear on the role of the classroom teacher, indeed it challenged the education planners to train their teachers not only to utilize TV programs, but to become better teachers in their own right. An over-simplified psychological analysis of how this pressure for up-grading teachers manifested itself is as follows: the mere existence of an education reform movement is threatening to many teachers, especially to those who feel they have been trained to teach and who feel they are effective in the

classroom. (It should be noted here that virtually all Salvadorean teachers have received at least two years of training
beyond the nine-year general education level, and that a fair
number are graduates of the normal schools.) Further, it
is a repugnant thought to most teachers that they could be
replaced by a television set, regardless of the quality of the
TV lessons transmitted.

With these considerations and their implications regarding teacher attitudes in mind, the Project planners
recognized that it was necessary to train the classroom
teacher in effective teaching methodology and modern curriculum content and thus cast the teacher in the role of effective
teacher able to utilize educational television as a valuable
resource. The alternative most typically found in ITV projects is to cast the television teacher in the role of effective teacher with the classroom teacher as helper, monitor,
etc. The overwhelming acceptance of ITV by the teachers
of El Salvador suggests the wisdom of the choice made by
the planners.

Yet another important psychological impact is the
interaction between the television teacher and the classroom
teacher. While it is certain that the TV teacher should provide a model to the classroom teacher, he may also provide
a challenge, one which says "Can you teach as well as I
can?" when the classroom teacher generally has good rap-
port with the TV teacher, the response is more likely to be
constructive than merely defensive. That is, the classroom
teacher is more often motivated to improve his teaching
rather than to attack the TV teacher--all this to the good of
teaching and learning.

It is apparent that a psychological climate has been
created in which the principal figures, TV and classroom
teacher, can work in team-like fashion. Thus, teacher
training, seen originally as preparation for ITV utilization,
has become for El Salvador a bona fide re-training program
with the potential to upgrade the professional level of all
public school teachers in the country. This commitment by
the Minister of Education and A.I.D. project planners, must
be considered a factor of major significance in the Reform
Project.

Curriculum Development

In no sector of the Education Reform Program is the role of ITV as catalytic agent seen more clearly than in the area of curriculum development. At the outset it was recognized by Program planners (Salvadorean, North American, and a UNESCO advisor to the Ministry of Education) that curriculum revision was a fundamental prerequisite to educational reform. Plans were laid that called for USAID-employed curriculum experts to work with Salvadorean experts and the UNESCO advisor to review and revise the entire national curriculum, grades 1-9. What was not agreed upon in the beginning was the extent to which the old curriculum would have to be examined, and perhaps changed.

As a result the examination of the curriculum began as a rather superficial study of content areas. There was no effort made to evaluate the traditional offerings in light of national goals; no concern for teaching methodology; teaching and learning activities, or materials of instruction. The curriculum was narrowly conceived (much to the frustration of North American advisors) as an outline of the content to be taught in each subject matter area of the curriculum. This modus operandi continued through the production and public telecasting of the first of the ITV programs for the seventh grade. Then serious questions were raised about the "new" curriculum. It was apparent that what instructional television was transmitting to the schools of El Salvador was not a new curriculum at all, but simply the old curriculum "cleaned up a bit, " but with the same old methodology; perhaps a wider and better array of audio visual aids, but with little that could be termed "new" in the sense of a more promising approach to teaching and learning.

This public exposure of outmoded curriculum content and ineffective teaching methodology was one of the more important services rendered by the television medium as a part of the Salvadorean Reform Project. Curriculum study and development have not been the same since. For out of the great dissatisfaction with what ITV was projecting came a basic change in attitude toward the matter of curriculum construction, indeed toward the very nature of curriculum. These new attitudes are manifested through attention to curricular objectives stated in terms of behavioral goals for students; an increased effort to provide for the articulation of behavioral goals and individual and national needs; and a serious attempt to make teaching methodology consistent with stated goals.

Without instructional television, curriculum reform in
El Salvador may have come, one day, to recognize the relationship of curriculum content and methodology to the development of individual behavior, and the realization of national goals. With instructional television, that day of insight undoubtedly came sooner.

New Supervisors for a New Program

It is a matter of record that from the outset the Reform Program recognized the need for supervisors trained
in the methods of modern supervision. Historically, school
supervisors in the Salvadorean schools were untrained, inefficient and ineffective with regard to helping teachers to
teach better. The school supervisor in El Salvador, as in
much of Latin America, has been thought of traditionally as
an inspector, one who checks on the teacher to see that he
is present when he should be, that the floors in the classroom are clean, that reports are submitted on time, etc.
While it was agreed early in the Program that a new type
of supervision was needed to carry forward the plans of the
Program, considerable confusion existed as to the exact role
of the new supervisor, his title, and job description. It
was thought by some that there should be two sets of supervisors; ITV Supervisors, and general School Supervisors.
Early planning suggested that the ITV supervisor and the
school supervisor should work in close cooperation, but that
their respective areas of responsibility should remain essentially distinctive.

This dichotomous arrangement in the field of supervision may serve well in an education system where ITV is
used but not fully integrated as a part of the total program
of education. Planners of the El Salvador program decided
that this type of organization in the area of supervision
would not work well for them. Their commitment was to a
system of education in which the classroom was a learning
center which must receive and coordinate all resources
available. They came to see that the separation of supervision into ITV and non-ITV segments could not contribute to
the function of such a learning center.

As the respective roles of the ITV teacher (telemaes-
tro) and the classroom teacher emerged, the role of the

supervisor also became clearer. It was recognized that the
"traditional" classroom teacher would cease to exist under
the new program only in his "traditional" sense, and that in
his "modern" role as teacher he would need greatly improved
teaching skills, including, but not limited to, techniques of
television utilization. With this realization, the type and
quality of supervision needed became apparent. It was in
this manner that the program of school supervision emerged--
not as a specialized service designed to enhance the effectiveness of the telecasts, only, but as a service to the teacher as a utilizer of instructional television, and as a classroom teacher in his own right. The system of school supervision being developed in El Salvador is modern in every
sense of the word. Supervisors are being trained to assist
teachers in every aspect of their work; the organization of
the system is designed to reach all teachers in ITV and non-
ITV classrooms. Once again it is clear that ITV has
served as a catalytic force to promote educational changes
outside of, and possibly of greater long-range importance
than the television activity itself.

Conclusions

        In the five areas of change discussed above are sug-
gested implications for the future development of the education system and those most directly involved in it--students
and teachers. Assuming that the Education Reform proceeds in its present orientation, and that the role of instructional television continues to be directed by this orientation,
certain predictions can be made with reasonable certainty.

        (1) Students who learn to use the expanded informa-
tion system will develop mental abilities not previously encouraged by the traditional education system of El Salvador.
Skills in finding, analyzing, and coordinating information
will contribute to greater problem solving ability. The
capacity to think divergently will increase greatly, thus
making possible greater productivity wherever creative effort is required. Reading books and other materials as a
means of acquiring problem-solving information will tend to
create appreciation for literature and scientific data. The
future school graduate of El Salvador will be a much better
informed person: he will be more keenly aware of his world
and better able to make decisions about it.

        (2) The new system of evaluation will place empha-

sis on behavioral objectives. It will give teachers and administrators a realistic rationale upon which to make decisions about curriculum, including teaching methodology. Tradition and inertia will yield as prime movers in the area of educational development to evaluative data which suggest the relationship between educational objectives and education programs.

(3) The nature of teacher-training now developing in El Salvador will contribute to an increased professionalization of the teacher group. Courses for teachers now offer for the first time academic credits and quality points. With this base, a system of teacher certification may be expected to emerge. Teachers are also learning for the first time a variety of teaching techniques, each based in a teaching methodology, which in turn rests upon a psychology of learning. The future teacher in El Salvador will enjoy both a material and psychological advantage over his predecessor. His self-esteem as a professional person will be higher; his self confidence in the classroom will be greater; his position in the academic and social community more secure.

(4) Curriculum has come to be seen as a developing entity in contrast with the old notion that it was a static body of knowledge to be transmitted to each generation of scholars. The future curricula of El Salvador will adapt better to the changing needs of Salvadorean society and to new information about boys and girls and how they learn. This newly-acquired flexibility will give to the school system a viability and integrity it has neither earned nor received in the recent past. Increased public confidence in the public schools of El Salvador will be manifested through a continuing commitment to quality education by the Salvadorean public.

(5) The new system of school supervision will better insure the continuous improvement of classroom teaching. It will make possible a vastly improved network of communication among the various levels of the education establishment. Supervisors will give to teachers an increased sense of professional pride and security that will contribute to the upgrading of the profession. Supervision in El Salvador will encourage the involvement of teachers in the process of educational development. Above all, this involvement will promote the well-being of the teacher group, and, in a sense, guarantee the future quality of teaching and learning in the classrooms of El Salvador.

As part of the new technology making its impact in education, instructional television holds great promise for many, especially to educators in emerging nations. To some it is a panacea for all the ills associated with an antiquated teaching-learning enterprise. To others it is a means of enrichment; a supplement to the basic fare, that extra "something" badly needed in unimaginative programs of studies found not uncommonly in emerging and emerged nations. Still others see television as an inexpensive medium of instruction that can replace untrained teachers and costly books, and at the same time bring to the classrooms a high-quality diet of instruction. To date, empirical studies of the use of instructional television fail to suggest that any of the abovementioned aspirations are being universally satisfied where television is in use.

It will remain for the empirical researcher to detail the changes in student learning which can be associated with the use of instructional television in El Salvador--he will have tough going; the variables are multiple and interrelated. On the other hand it may not be terribly important that all the variables be identified, isolated, and correlated. What may be more important is that television as a major component of the Education Reform Program be recognized as being more than a medium of instruction. It must also be understood as a catalytic force that gave impetus and direction to educational change.

8. THE CENTRAL AMERICAN TEXTBOOK PROJECT*
    Manuel A. Arce

    It is true today, and it was much more so in 1962
and before, that elementary public school children of Central
America have few textbooks and teaching materials to work
with.   The lack of books and teaching materials was so
acute before 1962, that Central American educators showed
concern about that problem.   They recommended, in several
seminars in education organized and carried out at different
times and in different locations by the Cultural and Educative Council of the Organization of Central American States
(ODECA), the necessity to study and to take some action
related to the preparation and printing of children's books
to be distributed freely to the students of the elementary
public schools of the region.

    Casual surveys proved that very few children of
Guatemala, El Salvador, Honduras, Nicaragua, Costa Rica
and Panama, the six countries which occupy the 197, 775
square miles of the Central American Isthmus, had books
of their own or, if they had some in a certain classroom,
they were so different that it was almost impossible to use
them as textbooks.   The need of books can be further explained in the following data and information published in
ANDE (National Education Association) of Costa Rica. [1]

> Central America and Panama, with a population of
> more than thirteen million inhabitants and a gross
> national product per capita annual income which
> fluctuates between $217. 00 in Honduras and $435. 00
> in Panama, had, in 1964, about 1, 500, 000 pupils
> enrolled in the first through six grades of the

---
*This article is a résumé of "An Experiment in Regionalism:
The Central American Textbook Project, " by Manuel A. Arce
and Donald A. Lemke, published by the Language and Area
Center for Latin America, the University of Wisconsin - Mil-
waukee, 1970.

public elementary schools [in 1968, public and private: 2, 261, 000]. About nine out of ten do not have textbooks specifically written for them in the "fundamental" subjects which are being taught. A casual observer can prove this assertion by visiting public schools, especially in the rural areas.

In order to help in the solution of the problem related to the lack of textbooks for children, the Regional Office for Central America-Panama (ROCAP), a regional unit of the Agency for International Development (AID) of the United States set the basis for the organization of the Regional Textbook Program for Central America and Panama as early as 1962.

The Beginning of the Textbook Program

Since the organization of the Textbook Program in Guatemala City in 1962, its general goal has been to prepare common basic textbooks for children from first through sixth grade for free distribution. The program was backed and approved by ODECA from the beginning, in spite of its different locations. Now it is located in El Salvador.

Another very important purpose of the Program was to try to integrate, in part, education in this area. With economic integration in the region developing at a fast pace (Central American Common Market), it was imperative that the educational systems, curriculums, plans of study, basic teaching materials, etc., be integrated. The Regional Textbook Program was the first serious and operational effort to integrate the elementary education of the Isthmus. Conscious of the problem to be solved and the general goals to be achieved, the Textbook Program set up the following objectives:

1. To develop a series of basic textbooks for the first through sixth grades in reading, language, mathematics, science, and social studies.
2. To include in the books for children and guides for teachers, content and methods based on the most recent educational research, in order to attain an improvement of the teaching-learning process in the Central American elementary schools, including Panama.
3. To advise the personnel in charge of writing the manuscripts in such a way that they produce

books which could help develop the spirit of a
big country: Central America.

4.   To supervise the actual writing and printing of
books.

5.   To help the Ministries of Education in the orientation of key personnel, as far as content,
methodology and use of textbooks are concerned,
in order to enable them to orient principals and
school teachers of their respective countries.

6.   To help the development of private enterprise in
each country, giving opportunities to the Central
American printing industry to publish the books
written at the Center.

The Program started with the adaptation of readers
for first- and second-grade children.   These books were
first written by Guatemalan teachers as a project of the
Inter-American Cooperative Service of Education in Guatemala, [2] directed to help rural teachers with the teaching of
reading.   They were adapted, with the cooperation of the
five Ministries of Education, but the adaptation was limited
to vocabulary changes; the illustrations, typically Guatemalan,
were not changed because of lack of time.

These books were distributed the next year by President Kennedy at the time he met with the Presidents of Central America in Costa Rica.   On that occasion he stated the
following in "El Bosque, " San Jose, March 19, 1963:

The textbooks that we have distributed today symbo-
lize the program of great scale that will bring to
Central America and Panama more than two million books for elementary schools.   With these
books, millions of children will make use, for the
first time, of the necessary instruments in order
to overcome ignorance, which constitutes one of
the most difficult obstacles for the development of
their countries. [3]

Even though the Textbook Program was already organized and operating with the economic help of the Government of the United States and the backing of the Ministries
of Education, through ODECA, at the time of the President's
visit, most of the long-range plans and ideas were still on
paper, ready to be put into practice in the future.   By dis-
tributing books to children, President Kennedy made it clear
that the Government of the United States was aware of the

need of textbooks for children in Central America and that
it was willing to support economically and technically, much
more than in the past, a program of this type. After the
preliminary accomplishments and hopes for a bright future,
the program was ready to strive in meeting the long-range
objectives it had set before.

Organization and Dynamics of the Program

In a project of this nature, if it is to achieve the objectives it has set off, it must be the outcome of a cooperative effort. In a broader perspective, this cooperative enterprise is made of the Ministries of Education--by themselves or throughout ODECA--which select the "writers, "
and help shape the educational policy of the Center; ROCAP,
which provides financial support and part of the technical
help needed. The AID Missions in each country pay the cost
of the printing of books and help the Ministries with their
responsibility to orient the teachers in the proper use of the
books.

As far as the work that must be accomplished within
the "four walls" of the Center, the idea of a team work activity is always present. In order to produce textbooks in
the five curricular areas previously mentioned, there are
five teams of "writers. " Each team is made up of six persons, since in each group every one of the six countries is
represented. Thus, there are 30 "writers, " all Central
Americans.

Each team is helped by a specific advisor, whose
main responsibility is to be chairman in the discussion and
research sessions and to serve as a human resource person
in technical and educational matters, especially in curriculum and methodology. It is intended that the specific advisor represent as many Central American countries as possible
in order to balance the expression of the interests and needs
of the nations. There is also a Central American technical
advisor. He molds the five curricular areas of the program
into a unit, following the same general philosophy and principles. In this sense, he is in charge of the technical phase
of the writing process.

The Center utilizes two- to four-week visits of consultants for the five subject areas. The consultants come
from the United States and different countries of Central and

South America. They are well-known educators and writers with international prestige. The consultants help the "writers" by working through the specific advisors. They express their points of view on the content subject matter, context and methodology which should be included in the books, and also give lectures. However, it is up to the "writers" and the specific advisors to accept or reject these points of view, because they know their environment and are responsible for what is included in the books.

The Ministry delegates are not professional writers. They are usually good school teachers, most of them elementary, who have shown interest in the subject matter to which they have been assigned, and/or teachers who have written something for children. For that reason, they are called author-teachers or "writers." The author-teachers are selected by the Ministries of Education of the different countries, who pay their salaries and assign them to the Regional Textbook Center in El Salvador. They are regular employees of their respective Ministries. This is very important, because by paying the salaries to the author-teachers, the Ministries are assuming direct responsibility for the Center and are involved in the process. In that way, the program is their program.

When the author-teachers arrive at the Center they learn to work in teams and although they are experienced teachers they are trained in their new jobs. By working together, they learn a great deal from each other, from the specific advisors and from the consultants. In a way, the Center is an in-service textbook writing experiment. When the author-teachers go back to their own countries, they usually hold better positions, often related to the kind of work they were doing at the Center.

The internal administration of the Center is in the hands of a director and an administrator. Of course, as it has been shown before, the Regional Textbook Center is a part of ODECA. Therefore, the Center must follow the administrative rules and procedures of that organization. As it can be seen, Central Americans are in charge of all aspects of the administration. The director is the official responsible for making the final decisions concerning technical matters, after taking into consideration the points of view of the technical and specific advisors, and the heads of the editorial and production departments. As director of the Center, he contacts the Ministers of Education periodically to know their opinions about this organization. Knowing, judging, and balancing the different points of view, he is in a better position to arrive at wise decisions.

Common Basic Textbook for Children

If one of the purposes of the Regional Textbook Program is to help integrate elementary education in Central America, it is obvious that the books to be written have to be common basic textbooks to be used in the region. According to the purpose expressed, there are two concepts which should be explained, common textbooks and basic textbooks.

Common Textbooks. The idea of common books in the region should not be interpreted as having just one book in each subject matter for a certain grade, as was said by some critics. The good educators believe in providing as many books as possible to children in order to enable them to be in contact with different information and points of view. In this way, they can draw their own conclusions. The idea of having common basic textbooks means that third-grade children of Central America will have the same basic textbooks in science, for instance, as well as other books and materials. Because of the circumstances, the fact was that the only textbooks children of most rural regions had were the basic textbooks provided by the Regional Textbook Program through the Ministries of Education.

To prepare common basic textbooks for one country is not an easy task. However, if that country has a fairly well-conceived and organized curriculum (called Program of Studies in Central America), with subject matter graduation and sequence, the job is made easier to the writer, even though a textbook is not the systematic development of the Program of Studies. Unfortunately, the Programs of Study of the different countries of Central America were anachronistic at the time the Center was planning to write common textbooks. This is important, because a writer cannot write a good textbook--as far as the content is concerned--when, as Jerome Bruner states, "the school programs, in almost all countries, follow the scientific progress with a backwardness approaching disaster."[4]

Even if the Programs of Study had been up to date, the Textbook Project faced a serious problem. The plan was to write common textbooks for six countries, and there was not a common program of studies (curriculum) for the region. So, it was decided to prepare a document which could serve as a common program. Each Ministry of Education sent a top educator to work for six months at the Center. Taking the six Programs of Study as the basic material, and improving the sequence and graduation of content in the different subject areas, they wrote the Modelo de Curriculum[5] (curriculum model) which is, in fact, a content guide. This curriculum model, under constant revision, has helped the writers to decide what content they should include in a certain textbook. The process of how to teach the subject matter through the book is another problem.

Basic Textbooks. It is imperative to explain here the meaning of the term "basic," as it is understood at the Center, and now in the elementary educational circle of Central America. The term is new, because basic textbooks, as they have been written, are new in the region. Basic textbooks are conceived as series of books for first through sixth grade designed to help children learn concepts and develop skills, abilities, habits and ideals in a systematic, gradual and progressive way. Considered in this manner, the basic textbooks are the backbone of the curriculum content. Before the establishment of the Textbook Center, there was no one textbook series in any subject matter in Central America, and even now the only existing series is the one being written by the Center.

Expanding upon the general principle previously stated, the characteristics of the basic books are the following:

1. They take into consideration the interests, needs and capabilities of children at different stages of development.
2. They are based on a careful study of the sequence, graduation and scope of the subject matter to be taught through one book or through the whole series.
3. They are written in such a way that the vocabulary and sentence structure used are graduated in order of extension and difficulty.
4. They are accompanied by a teacher's manual.

More than anything else, this last characteristic has constituted an innovation in Central America. Before the appearance of the Center's textbooks the ones used in the classrooms did not have guides which would help the teachers properly use the books with their children. A few books had some recommendations for the teachers, but the idea of a teacher's manual, as a guide, did not exist. The teacher's manual is considered part of the basic textbook itself. It is indispensable, especially if new approaches in subject matter, sequence and methodology are included in the books. This is especially true of modern mathematics and science. Teachers' guides are necessary for any teacher, and particularly for teachers working in rural areas, where there are few, if any professional books.

Writing of Manuscripts

The writing of the manuscript of a certain book is preceded by the development of a plan by the whole team of author-teachers. To develop a plan, or to write a book by a team of writers has its advantages and its limitations. The actual writing of the manuscript by the group takes more time, because every main idea or methodological trend or device must be discussed, and should come out--in written form--as a consequence of group consensus. In this program the writing of manuscripts has been done in this way, in order to represent the needs, expectations, problems and limitations of six countries.

The plans must comprise the content of the whole book, usually sub-divided in units and sub-units or themes. Sometimes, ideas about the methodological approach are included, although this phase is taken care of at the time of the actual writing of the manuscript. As a point of departure, the content--including the possible sequence and graduation-- is taken from the "Modelo de Curriculum." Once the author-teachers know what and how much they are supposed to write, they distribute the work among themselves. From that point on, the work that is done within the group is an individual task which takes a great deal of imagination, initiative and research. General information and advice are given by the specific advisors and the consultants.

Even though the author-teachers write units as individuals, the final draft of the manuscript of a certain unit becomes the whole group's creation and responsibility, following the many changes adapted during frequent group discussions. In some instances, an author would not recognize his original work. The specific advisor works with the author-teachers continuously, with individuals and with the whole group, and he serves as the link between the group and the technical advisor and the editor.

Proof Edition, and Printing of the Book

The Regional Textbook Center prepares a proof edition for every book written. This is a must because the book has to be studied and approved by each one of the six Ministries of Education involved in the program. This step is the result of one of the recommendations made by the Ministries of Education. To send the proof edition for approval has its pros and cons. It is important to send it because once the written judgment ("dictamen") is received, the Center is sure that the book has been officially approved by a certain Ministry of Education enabling the teachers of that specific country to use the books without hesitancy. On the other hand, to send it has its difficulties, too. The Center must take into consideration the suggestions given by the Ministries, but they do not always agree on the nature and intentions of the modifications. Sometimes, the modifications suggested by two or more Ministries are conflicting and the Center must try to convince one of them to change their judgment.

Once a specific book has been approved by the Ministries of Education, and the proof editions corrected and/or modified, the Production Department of the Center prepares seven sets of negatives of the book. One set is sent to each one of the six countries to be printed. The seventh set is kept in storage by the Center. Once the book is printed, its distribution is the responsibility of the Ministry of Education, for early orientation of the teachers in the proper use of the text. Distribution has been a great problem for the Ministries. Never in the past has a particular Ministry had so many books in storage at once to be distributed. An accounting system for distribution and control had to be developed. As a result of this, the problem of distribution has been improved a great deal and the children, in general, have books which make them learn in a better and easier way.

Lessons Learned from the Project

Any new program or project is subject to both posi-

tive and negative criticism.   Usually, the fact that a program is new causes many people to seek out its errors,
failures or threats rather than to view its positive contributions.   Persons responsible for carrying out the objectives
and activities of a program should be aware of the criticisms
of the project emanating from the outside, and must consider their validity in order to improve the quality of the
program's accomplishments.

        This project has taught some valuable lessons.   Let
us first discuss the points in which the program has been
criticized.

    1.   The books have too many errors in concept, lan-
          guage and spelling.
    2.   The books do not develop a civic and national
          spirit in the children.   They deform their feel-
          ings and personality.
    3.   The reading and language books lack literary
          value.   They are dull and insipid.
    4.   The illustrations are poor.   Some of them are
          not artistic.   There should be more four-color
          illustrations.
    5.   Teachers and children do not like them.

        It is true that the books have had some errors.
Some errors have resulted from understaffing, especially
full-time proofreaders, and others from the pressures of
production.   The errors that some critics have found appeared to be numerous.   However, if we consider that the
program has produced 22 titles thus far, this assertion
seems exaggerated.

        The development of a civic and national spirit in
children is really a matter of philosophy.   Some critics do
not see the civic spirit the books try to develop.   It is
there.   It is true that a regional textbook has less opportunity to emphasize the study of all the phases of a specific
nation than a national textbook.   Each kind of book has different objectives.   The regional textbooks refer to the nations as parts of a whole.

        The criticism related to the lack of literary value in
the textbooks, in reading and language especially, has been
emphasized by the professional writers, literary experts,
linguists and printers, each with their own motives and interests.   According to the specific objectives of their intel-

lectual or commercial activity, they are right. Nevertheless, the textbooks, written by teachers, are not intended
as pieces of art, but instruments developed to teach reading
and language. Their criticism has had a great effect on the
attitude and solicitude of the author-teachers who are trying
to improve the literary quality of the textbooks. This criticism has done much good for the program, although it is
doubtful that the professional writers will ever be completely
satisfied.

Illustration of the books has been a big problem since
the beginning. It is very difficult to find good artists capable
of illustrating books for children because the children's book
market in the area has been restrained. The artists who
have illustrated the textbooks of the program have been
trained at the Center. Even so, the illustrations could and
would have been better, if the program had had more money
to pay for more four-color illustrations, or if the artists
could have had extra training.

Some have said that teachers and children do not like
the textbooks. This is the kind of criticism based on personal opinion and not backed by facts. According to observations made by the orientation specialists of the program
in the Central American countries, teachers and children do
like the textbooks. This is not, however, a conclusive appraisal.

Some Suggestions

There are some questions people usually ask in connection with the organization and development of programs in
which several regions or countries take part. The answers
to those questions may help solve some problems in advance,
or avoid some errors which have been made in the past.
Some of those questions and their respective comments are:

1. Is it possible to bring individuals from six countries together to work in harmony on a regional project of
integration?
There have been many intense discussions and expressions of differences between individuals from the six
countries during the life of this project. This was particularly true in the early years. Even so, the chief lesson
this seven-year experiment can pass on to other nations
which seek involvement in regional cooperative projects is

that integration can work.

If anybody wants to see, as close as possible, how integration and understanding work, in spite of national differences, he must watch any of the writers' groups of the Regional Textbook Center working as a unit.   Even though this might resemble viewing the complicated problems of integration through a microscope, it could provide some insight into understanding the forces, anxieties, prejudices, interests and inter-relations which take place in a group like this.

2.   Are there some areas which lend themselves more readily to integration projects than others?

The Center has found that there is relatively little dispute between countries in mathematics and science.   All seem to agree on basic issues, differing only on word interpretation and order.   In the language arts area too, there is little real conflict, although professional writers usually oppose the style in which the books for children are written.

In social studies the task has been more difficult. Nations still think of themselves as nations and want their own histories interpreted in their own way.   This is sometimes for political advantage but more often the only means of instilling strong national feelings.   It has been, therefore, impossible to write the third grade books regionally and the Center has served more as a coordinator for the Ministries.

3.   Is the team approach to writing textbooks the best way of doing it?

One of the concessions this project decided to make to secure six-country support for the textbook was that each country have a representative on each writing group.   Politically, this was a sound and necessary decision.   Operationally, it has slowed the writing process considerably and has been much more costly.

Perhaps the ideal procedure would be to have representatives of the Ministries and part-time writers by contract in the Center to write the books.

4.   Has the Textbook Project been helpful in the advancement of the movement towards Central American unity in education?

Perhaps more than the thousands of words which will have been produced in the 36 books of the Regional Textbook Center, the millions of daily interchanges between individuals --writers, principals, supervisors, teachers, parents and students--about education which were precipitated by the pro-

gram has done more to bring forth a feeling of Central American unity in education than anything else.

Curriculums have come closer together. Identical
material has been distributed and is in use; interchanges have
been made; new schools have been constructed; new teaching
methods have been adopted. The tempo of the times has
quickened in education and countries now look inward and
outward for ideas. Individuals from different countries know
each other better.

5. Can textbooks bring about curriculum changes?

Most of the elementary curriculum models in the six
Central American countries dated back 20 to 40 years when
the project originated.

Now, without exception, the six countries have instituted curriculum reforms. New subject matter content, a
new sequence, and a new methodology are being formulated.
While they are not exact copies of the regional textbooks,
and while none of the six reforms are exactly the same, they
do not conflict with the books or with each other. And so
the new curriculum and the new books can be used together.

It is hard to say if the curriculum changes would
have occurred if there were no books. All we can say is
that the first significant revisions of the curriculums of Central America took place within the first six years of the
Textbook Center operation.

6. Can textbooks change teaching methods?

The textbooks in this series are largely based upon a
practical, almost pragmatic philosophy of education. They
are full of ideas for experiments, group work, discussions
and field activity. These contrast sharply with the methods
used in the elementary schools of Central America.

There is some evidence, as yet inconclusive, that
teachers are changing their methods to fit those of the
books.[6] Certainly the advance work with the books at the
teacher training centers has helped. This process has been
assisted by extensive programs of in-service orientation
within each country and by use of the teacher's guides for
each book. However, one of the slowest things to change
in educational revolutions is teaching method.

7. What would be the first thing to do to start a
program like this?

The Regional Textbook Program was organized as the
answer to a felt urgent need: the lack of textbooks for children. The Program began its activities under a series of

assumptions. Several of those assumptions have proven to
be right, but if a program similar to the Textbook Program
were to be planned and organized, a survey related to needs,
priorities and attitudes which would have a definite implication on its achievements should be made.

The Regional Textbook Program has had its failures
and successes; optimistic and pesimistic supporters and non-
supporters but, for the first time, over two million children
have books which are helping them to understand the wonder-
ful things and the dangers of the age in which they are living and of the years ahead of their lives.

Notes

1. Manuel A. Arce, Proyecciones del Programa Regional
    de Libros de Texto. Asociación Nacional de Educa-
    dores, ANDE, Costa Rica, Nº17 y Nº18 (Abril-Mayo)
    1967, p. 16.

2. This organization aimed to improve education. Its ac-
    tivities were financed and carried out cooperatively
    by the governments of Guatemala and the United States.

3. Reunión de Presidentes de Centro América y Estados
    Unidos de América, Costa Rica: Talleres Tipográfi-
    cos de la Imprenta Vargas, 1963, p. 69.

4. Jerome S. Bruner, El Proceso de la Educación, México:
    Unión Tipográfica Editorial Hispano Americana,
    Traducción al español Lic. Carlos Palomar, 1963,
    p. 69.

5. Manuel A. Arce (ed.), Modelo de Curriculum, Guate-
    mala: ODECA-ROCAP, 1964.

6. Preliminary studies were made in El Salvador in the
    "Thirty Schools Study" of 1967 and in Costa Rica the
    same year by Donald A. Lemke. Copies of these
    studies are available from the USAID Education of-
    fices in each country.

9. SECONDARY EDUCATION REFORM IN HONDURAS
   Rafael Bardales B.

   The Ministry of Public Education, in its role as
director of Honduras's educational system, has developed a
Plan of Action designed to qualitatively and quantitatively
strengthen the educational system.   This will provide for
the increase of teaching services, school construction, establishment of libraries, revision of educational planning curricula, the incorporation of new teaching techniques, publications of textbooks and the upgrading of teacher skills
through in-service training.

   This plan of action in the past has been primarily
directed at the elementary school as constitutionally required
and has achieved positive results in increased matriculation,
decreased dropout figures, an increase in the number of six-
year schools, and the textbook program.   All of this has
combined to improve the physical conditions in order to
facilitate the teaching-learning process.   Outstanding in
these improvements is the construction of some 4,000 classrooms with furnishings.

   An analysis of the budget of the Ministry of Education
destined for primary education demonstrates that it receives 58 percent of the total with the remaining 42 percent
distributed among secondary education, higher education,
basic literacy programs and adult education.   This dispro-
portionate pattern had been maintained by past administrations but the current regime is modifying it while at the
same time confronting the problems which arise from the
school age population explosion.   Examination of precedent
demonstrates that secondary education has been systematically unattended and further, one observes a disarticulation between secondary education and the other levels.   The fact
that only 25 percent of the secondary schools are public has
not helped the control factor.

   Following the adoption of measures designed to increase primary school matriculations and decrease dropouts,

secondary education will soon be invaded by a rapid population explosion which must be met by expanding vocational education, offering new options and seeking the physical facilities and human resources that will assure a greater degree of support for secondary education on the part of the government.   The secondary level of education currently is confronted by numerous problems among which are the following:

A) Academic
    1) A limited number of curricular patterns.
    2) A lack of articulation between current educational programs and national plans for development.
    3) An insufficient supply of qualified teachers and technical personnel to meet current secondary school needs.
    4) An essentially theoretical curriculum divorced from individual needs.

B) Material Resources
    1) An insufficient number of public training institutes (there are currently nine, four in the capital).
    2) The educational and physical facilities of the majority of the secondary schools in use are inadequate.
    3) There are shortages of laboratories, shops and other teaching facilities.
    4) Low teacher salaries mandate teachers holding multiple positions which is detrimental to the teachers' efficiency and psychological well-being. This condition is particularly severe in private or semi-official institutions.

Fundamentals of the Reform

In November, 1966, an analysis of contemporary secondary education was completed.   This study documented the deficiencies in the developmental pattern of secondary education.   Noteworthy among the findings was the unsatisfactory condition of school buildings, most of which were originally constructed for other than instructional purposes.

There were 98 secondary schools in the nation, only nine fully supported by the government.   Total matriculations were 26,587 students representing 4.3 percent of the total secondary school age population.   Classrooms totaled

857, of which only 144 (16.8 percent) were public, being
attended by 6,176 (23.6 percent) students.   The total number
of teachers was 1,572, of whom only 218 had received academic preparations for secondary teaching.   The remainder
were primary school teachers, professionals prepared in
various disciplines or simply persons with some school relevant specialty.   There was also a shortage of research laboratory facilities, libraries, appropriate school furniture and
educational materials and supplies.

These problems mandated that the National Plan for
Educational Action direct its attention to the development of
secondary education through the formulation and application
of a Plan for Reform noted in the following basic assumptions:

1) It is no longer possible to continue ignoring that
   educational level which is called upon to prepare
   the secondary level para-technical personnel required to foster the socio-economic development
   of the nation.
2) It is an urgent necessity to modernize teaching
   methods and pursue a functional articulation
   among the levels which constitute the educational
   systems.
3) It is imperative to revise and restructure the
   curricular programs and plans, in order to provide the learners with the tools necessary to
   make them more effective producers and consum-
   ers and conscientiously responsible citizens.
4) There is an urgent need to extend educational opportunities in that current educational offerings
   are not responsive to demands of the present.
5) The democratization of secondary education in
   order to extend educational opportunity to the
   largest possible number of students is necessary
   in order to meet demographic, social and economic needs of the nation.

Goals

The implementation of the educational development
plan currently underway is devoted to the attainment of the
following goals:

First: To prepare citizens who possess a love of

country and the capacities necessary to make a positive contribution to the nation's economic development.

Second: To diversify the range of offerings at the
secondary level in order to propose a greater variety of
opportunities to the adolescent school age.

Third: To increase the capacity of secondary education to accept more students in order to facilitate a larger
proportion of secondary school age receiving an education.

Targets

As a function of the above cited goals, educational
reformers intend to attain the following:

a) Provide for a greater percentage of matriculation
   at this level in public schools.   Currently only
   25 percent of secondary enrollments are in public
   schools.   The target is to reverse the current
   pattern and provide public schools for 75 percent
   of the secondary school age population.
b) Provide in-service training in order to certify
   80 percent of the currently uncertified secondary
   teachers by 1975.   At present only 20 percent of
   the teachers have secondary certification certifi-
   cates or their equivalent.
c) Provide for areas of curricular specialization in
   order to reduce the pattern of extensive breadth
   of responsibility within general courses.
d) Initiate the system of full-time teachers as a
   means of raising the level of educational efficacy.
   Currently only 25 percent of the teachers are
   full-time employed.   By 1975 virtually all positions should be full-time.
e) Offer maximal opportunities for students to have
   an active input into the teaching-learning process.
f) Provide during the next 15 years for the necessary physical facilities to accommodate increases
   in enrollment caused by demographic growth and
   the backlog of population not provided for in past
   periods.
g) Improve the living standard of teachers through
   salary increases while demanding greater participation in school work.

Implementation of the Reform

     The detailed analyses presented in past research
point out the obvious necessity for initiating reform efforts
and the legitimacy of substantial increases in public resources
to be devoted to reform efforts. In principle it was necessary to finance these changes with resources from the federal budget but because of the magnitude of these needs and
their relatively low priority in national development plans
this was not possible.

     It was in this way that the Ministry of Public Educa-
tion, through the normal channels of the Central Government,
initiated the granting of loans by various international organizations to partially finance the cost of this reform.   Following a series of rejections on the part of some funding sources
that continue reasoning that educational costs should not be
considered as investments in that they do not demonstrate a
short term return, the granting in principle of a loan of 7
million dollars by the Agency for International Development
(AID) together with 3.5 million raised locally for a total of
10.5 million dollars was achieved.

     As has been indicated, the overall financial resources
required by this program is $10,500,000.   This will be
utilized as follows:

1)	Building Construction	$ 6,902,500
	First phase	5,850,000
	Second phase	1,052,500
2)	Acquisition of Equipment, Books,	
	Furniture	900,000
3)	Training of Personnel	460,000
	In-service training of 400 teachers	100,000
	150 annual scholarships in the Su-	
	perior Normal Teacher Training	
	Center.	360,000
4)	Technical Assistance	1,128,000
	Includes: Services of University	
	of Florida specialists; scholarships	
	and travel costs of Honduran	
	scholarship holders to Florida and	
	maintenance of Project Administra-	
	tive costs.	
5)	Architects and Building Design	1,108,500
	Total	$10,500,000

Development of the Program

Technical evaluations of the development of the project will be provided by the State of Florida Universities Consortium. Consideration of the proposals from various University Systems was made by a special committee consisting of representatives of the Ministry of Education; the Higher Commission for Economic Planning, and the Superior Normal Teacher Training School. The range of technical assistance contracted includes:

1. Assessment of the administrative reorganization of the Ministry of Education.
2. Assessment of the academic reorganization of the Superior Normal Teacher Training School.
3. Assessment of the educational reform of secondary education.
4. Training of nationals within the nations and abroad.
5. Organization of educational research services.
6. Assessment of the establishment of educational specifications for the architects that will have the responsibility of designing the new school buildings.
7. Assessment for equipping of libraries and laboratories.
8. Assessment of the restructuring of curricula and programs of secondary education based upon educational research.

In order to serve as a link between the Honduran Government and this team, the Ministry of Education has identified a Honduran Coordinator who has the responsibility to transmit all of the documentation attendant to the program's development and further serving as an intermediary in all the activities initiated by the Consortium. This functionary further coordinates the convening of meetings of nationals in order to make known reform projects presented by the Consortium.

The effort of this coordinator is further supported by the identification of permanent national counterparts that fulfill simultaneous responsibilities as technicians at the Ministry of Education, the National Autonomous University of Honduras, the Higher Commission of Economic Planning, the Alumni Association of the Higher Teacher Training School, the General Directorship of Primary Education, the General Directorship of Secondary Education, the Office of

Educational Planning and the Higher Teacher Training School.
As is evident, the integration of the task force consists of
Honduran educators of extensive teaching experience at all
levels of our education which guarantees that decisions will
be commensurate with Honduran educational realities.

When this group of Honduran technicians has studied
the various proposals in depth, they will make their recommendations and transmit them to the Ministry of Education
who, in turn, will tender the recommendations to the National Education Council, the final decision-making body.
This council will authorize or reject the adoption of the proposed program.   This Council is presided over by the Minister of Education and includes within it a representative of
the Autonomous National University of Honduras.

The training of personnel phase of the program will
be split into two stages: (1) the implementation of a special
degree program at the University of Florida for 58 individuals, the majority of whom are graduates of the Superior Normal Teacher Training College; the training of five key personnel from the Ministry of Education in administration,
program development, data processing and administrative
procedures; special training for 15 secondary school supervisors and 30 directors of schools and institutes; special
training for eight administrators and academic department
heads of the Superior Teachers College; and (2) in-service
training in Honduras.   It is proposed that two years of in-
service training be provided for all of the teachers and administrators of the Superior Normal Teachers College and
for teachers who will have the responsibility of directing
and administrating the new facilities to be constructed.

There were 21 teachers studying at the University of
Florida and 26 studying in Honduras.   Both groups finished
their training in 1971, when it was anticipated that the new
facilities would be opened.   This long-term training paralleled a short-term in-service training program initiated for
400 secondary school teachers.   This training in teaching
methods focused upon education, Spanish, social studies,
science and mathematics.   In the future this training will be
extended to include other areas, such as technical education,
art education, physical education, etc.

The physical facilities program includes the construction and equipping of 20 secondary schools, which will be
endowed with the best of educational facilities selected in ac-

cordance with the most modern pedagogical techniques designed to facilitate the preparation of professionals with theoretical and practical knowledge which will qualify them to
continue studying at the university level or be immediately
assimilated into the labor force. Within these facilities will
be research laboratories, well equipped work shops, gym-
nasiums, modern libraries, typing facilities, auditoriums,
business machine rooms, and specialized facilities for the
production of multi-media materials (photo developing labs,
projection equipment, etc.). The 20 buildings that will be
constructed will have a total of 358 rooms. It is important
to point out that the majority of these establishments are
semi-official, that is, they are partially maintained by the
government. Upon completion of the new buildings these
schools will become completely official.

The secondary reform project in Honduras will completely transform the educational system during the decade
of the 1970's. The extensive planning has resulted in a
balanced attack on all the old problems which traditionally
face the secondary systems in Latin America. The hope is
that this transformation will help supply trained individuals
to fill the gap of middle-level manpower positions which
Honduras so desperately needs to develop and to better prepare individuals to live in the world of the 20th century.

10. THE ADULT LITERACY PROCESS AS CULTURAL ACTION FOR FREEDOM*
Paulo Freire

Every educational practice implies a concept of man and the world.

Experience teaches us not to assume that the obvious is clearly understood. So it is with the truism with which we begin: all educational practice implies a theoretical stance on the educator's part. This stance in turn implies --sometimes more, sometimes less explicitly--an interpretation of man and the world. It could not be otherwise. The process of men's orientation in the world involves not just the association of sense images, as for animals. It involves, above all, thought-language; that is, the possibility of the act of knowing through his praxis, by which man transforms reality. For man, this process of orientation in the world can be understood neither as a purely subjective event, nor as an objective or mechanistic one, but only as an event in which subjectivity and objectivity are united. Orientation in the world, so understood, places the question of the purposes of action at the level of critical perception of reality.

If, for animals, orientation in the world means adaptation to the world, for man it means humanizing the world by transforming it. For animals there is no historical sense, no options or values in their orientation in the world; for man there is both an historical and a value dimension. Men have the sense of "project," in contrast to the instinctive routines of animals.

The action of men without objectives, whether the ob-

*Reprinted by permission from Harvard Educational Review, vol. 40, no. 2 (May 1970), 205-225. Copyright 1970 by the President and Fellows of Harvard College. The author gratefully acknowledges the contribution of Loretta Slover, who translated this essay.

jectives are right or wrong, mythical or demythologized,
naive or critical, is not praxis, though it may be orientation in the world. And not being praxis, it is action ignorant both of its own process and of its aim. The interrelation of the awareness of aim and of process is the basis for
planning action, which implies methods, objectives, and
value options.

Teaching adults to read and write must be seen, analyzed, and understood in this way. The critical analyst will
discover in the methods and texts used by educators and students practical value options which betray a philosophy of
man, well or poorly outlined, coherent or incoherent. Only
someone with a mechanistic mentality, which Marx would
call "grossly materialistic," could reduce adult literacy
learning to a purely technical action. Such a naive approach
would be incapable of perceiving that technique itself as an
instrument of men in their orientation in the world is not
neutral.

We shall try, however, to prove by analysis the self-
evidence of our statement. Let us consider the case of
primers used as the basic texts for teaching adults to read
and write. Let us further propose two distinct types: a
poorly done primer and a good one, according to the genre's
own criteria. Let us even suppose that the author of the
good primer based the selection of its generative words[1] on
a prior knowledge of which words have the greatest reso-
nance for the learner (a practice not commonly found, though
it does exist).

Doubtlessly, such an author is already far beyond the
colleague who composes his primer with words he himself
chooses in his own library. Both authors, however, are
identical in a fundamental way. In each case they themselves
decompose the given generative words and from the syllables
create new words. With these words, in turn, the authors
form simple sentences and, little by little, small stories,
the so-called reading lessons. Let us say that the author
of the second primer, going one step further, suggests that
the teachers who use it initiate discussions about one or
another word, sentence, or text with their students.

Considering either of these hypothetical cases we may
legitimately conclude that there is an implicit concept of man
in the primer's method and content, whether it is recognized
by the authors or not. This concept can be reconstructed

from various angles. We begin with the fact, inherent in
the idea and use of the primer, that it is the teacher who
chooses the words and proposes them to the learner. Insofar as the primer is the mediating object between the teacher and students, and the students are to be "filled" with
words the teachers have chosen, one can easily detect a
first important dimension of the image of man which here
begins to emerge. It is the profile of a man whose consciousness is "spatialized," and must be "filled" or "fed" in
order to know. This same conception led Sartre, criticizing
the notion that "to know is to eat," to exclaim: "O philo-
sophie alimentaire!"[2]

This "digestive" concept of knowledge, so common in
current educational practice, is found very clearly in the
primer.[3] Illiterates are considered "undernourished," not
in the literal sense in which many of them really are, but
because they lack the "bread of the spirit." Consistent with
the concept of knowledge as food, illiteracy is conceived of
as a "poison herb," intoxicating and debilitating persons who
cannot read or write. Thus, much is said about the "eradi-
cation" of illiteracy to cure the disease.[4] In this way, deprived of their character as linguistic signs constitutive of
man's thought-language, words are transformed into mere
"deposits of vocabulary"--the bread of the spirit which the
illiterates are to "eat" and "digest."

This "nutritionist" view of knowledge perhaps also
explains the humanitarian character of certain Latin American adult literacy campaigns. If millions of men are illiterate, "starving for letters," "thirsty for words," the word
must be brought to them to save them from "hunger" and
"thirst." The word, according to the naturalistic concept
of consciousness implicit in the primer, must be "deposited,"
not born of the creative effort of the learners. As understood in this concept, man is a passive being, the object of
the process of learning to read and write, and not its subject. As object his task is to "study" the so-called reading
lessons, which in fact are almost completely alienating and
alienated, having so little, if anything, to do with the student's socio-cultural reality.[5]

It would be a truly interesting study to analyze the
reading texts being used in private or official adult literacy
campaigns in rural and urban Latin America. It would not
be unusual to find among such texts sentences and readings
like the following random samples:[6]

A asa é da ave--"The wing is of the bird. "
Eva viu a uva--"Eva saw the grape. "
O galo canta--"The cock crows. "
O cachorro ladra--"The dog barks. "
Maria gosta dos animais--"Mary likes animals. "
João cuida das arvores--"John takes care of the
   trees. "

O pai de Carlinhos se chama Antonio. Carlinhos é
um bom menino, bem comportado e estudioso--"Charles's
father's name is Antonio. Charles is a good, well-behaved,
and studious boy. "

Ada deu o dedo ao urubu? Duvido, Ada deu o dedo
à arara.... 7

Se você trabalha com martelo e prego, tenha cuidado
para nao furar o dedo. --"If you hammer a nail, be careful
not to smash your finger. "8

****

Peter did not know how to read. Peter was a-
shamed. One day, Peter went to school and registered for a night course. Peter's teacher was
very good. Peter knows how to read now. Look
at Peter's face. [These lessons are generally illustrated.] Peter is smiling. He is a happy man.
He already has a good job. Everyone ought to
follow his example.

In saying that Peter is smiling because he knows how
to read, that he is happy because he now has a good job,
and that he is an example for all to follow, the authors establish a relationship between knowning how to read and getting good jobs which, in fact, cannot be borne out. This
naiveté reveals, at least, a failure to perceive the structure
not only of illiteracy, but of social phenomena in general.
Such an approach may admit that these phenomena exist, but
it cannot perceive their relationship to the structure of the
society in which they are found. It is as if these phenomena
were mythical, above and beyond concrete situations, or the
results of the intrinsic inferiority of a certain class of men.
Unable to grasp contemporary illiteracy as a typical mani-
festation of the "culture of silence, " directly related to underdeveloped structures, this approach cannot offer an objective, critical response to the challenge of illiteracy.

Merely teaching men to read and write does not work miracles; if there are not enough jobs for men able to work,
teaching more men to read and write will not create them.

One of these readers presents among its lessons the
following two texts on consecutive pages without relating
them.   The first is about May 1st, the Labor Day holiday,
on which workers commemorate their struggles.   It does not
say how or where these are commemorated, or what the
nature of the historical conflict was.   The main theme of
the second lesson is holidays.   It says that "on these days
people ought to go to the beach to swim and sunbathe...."
Therefore, if May 1st is a holiday, and if on holidays people
should go to the beach, the conclusion is that the workers
should go swimming on Labor Day, instead of meeting with
their unions in the public squares to discuss their problems.
Analysis of these texts reveals, then, a simplistic vision of
men, of their world, of the relationship between the two,
and of the literacy process which unfolds in that world.

"A asa é da ave, " "Eva viu a uva, " "o galo canta, "
and "o cachorro late, " are linguistic contexts which, when
mechanically memorized and repeated, are deprived of their
authentic dimension as thought-language in dynamic interplay
with reality.   Thus impoverished, they are not authentic
expressions of the world.   Their authors do not recognize in
the poor classes the ability to know and even create the
texts which would express their own thought-language at the
level of their perception of the world.   The authors repeat
with the texts what they do with the words, i.e., they introduce them into the learners' consciousness as if it were
empty space--once more, the "digestive" concept of knowledge.

Still more, the a-structural perception of illiteracy
revealed in these texts exposes the other false view of illiterates as marginal men. [9] Those who consider them marginal must, nevertheless, recognize the existence of a reality
to which they are marginal--not only physical space, but
historical, social, cultural, and economic realities--i.e.,
the structural dimension of reality.   In this way, illiterates
have to be recognized as beings "outside of, " "marginal to"
something, since it is impossible to be marginal to nothing.
But being "outside of" or "marginal to" necessarily implies
a movement of the one said to be marginal from the center,
where he was, to the periphery.   This movement, which is
an action, presupposes in turn not only an agent but also his

reasons. Admitting the existence of men "outside of" or "marginal to" structural reality, it seems legitimate to ask: Who is the author of this movement from the center of the structure to its margin? Do so-called marginal men, among them the illiterates, make the decision to move out to the periphery of society? If so, marginality is an option with all that it involves: hunger, sickness, rickets, pain, mental deficiencies, living death, crime, promiscuity, despair, the impossibility of being. In fact, however, it is difficult to accept that 40 percent of Brazil's population, almost 90 percent of Haiti's, 60 percent of Bolivia's, about 40 percent of Peru's, more than 30 percent of Mexico's and Venezuela's, and about 70 percent of Guatemala's would have made the tragic choice of their own marginality as illiterates. 10 If, then, marginality is not by choice, marginal man has been expelled from and kept outside of the social system and is therefore the object of violence.

In fact, however, the social structure as a whole does not "expel, " nor is marginal man a "being outside of. " He is, on the contrary, a "being inside of, " within the social structure, and in a dependent relationship to those whom we call falsely autonomous beings, inauthentic beings-for-themselves. A less rigorous approach, one more simplistic, less critical, more technicist, would say that it was unnecessary to reflect about what it would consider unimportant questions such as illiteracy and teaching adults to read and write. Such an approach might even add that the discussion of the concept of marginality is an unnecessary academic exercise. In fact, however, it is not so. In accepting the illiterate as a person who exists on the fringe of society, we are led to envision him as a sort of "sick man, " for whom literacy would be the "medicine" to cure him, enabling him to "return" to the "healthy" structure from which he has become separated. Educators would be benevolent counsellors, scouring the outskirts of the city for the stubborn illiterates, runaways from the good life, to restore them to the forsaken bosom of happiness by giving them the gift of the word.

In the light of such a concept--unfortunately, all too widespread--literacy programs can never be efforts toward freedom; they will never question the very reality which deprives men of the right to speak up--not only illiterates, but all those who are treated as objects in a dependent relationship. These men, illiterate or not, are, in fact, not marginal. What we said before bears repeating: They are

not "beings outside of"; they are "beings for another."
Therefore the solution to their problem is not to become
"beings inside of, " but men freeing themselves; for, in reality, they are not marginal to the structure, but oppressed
men within it. Alienated men, they cannot overcome their
dependency by "incorporation" into the very structure responsible for their dependency. There is no other road to
humanization--theirs as well as everyone else's--but authentic transformation of the dehumanizing structure.

From this last point of view, the illiterate is no
longer a person living on the fringe of society, a marginal
man, but rather a representative of the dominated strata of
society, in conscious or unconscious opposition to those who,
in the same structure, treat him as a thing. Thus, also,
teaching men to read and write is no longer an inconsequen-
tial matter of ba, be, bi, bo, bu, of memorizing an alienated
word, but a difficult apprenticeship in naming the world.

In the first hypothesis, interpreting illiterates as men
marginal to society, the literacy process reinforces the
mythification of reality by keeping it opaque and by dulling
the "empty consciousness" of the learner with innumerable
alienating words and phrases. By contrast, in the second
hypothesis--interpreting illiterates as men oppressed within
the system--the literacy process, as cultural action for
freedom, is an act of knowing in which the learner assumes
the role of knowing subject in dialogue with the educator.
For this very reason, it is a courageous endeavor to de-
mythologize reality, a process through which men who had
previously been submerged in reality begin to emerge in
order to re-insert themselves into it with critical awareness.
Therefore the educator must strive for an ever greater
clarity as to what, at times without his conscious knowledge,
illumines the path of his action. Only in this way will he
truly be able to assume the role of one of the subjects of
this action and remain consistent in the process.

The Adult Literacy Process as an Act of Knowing

To be an act of knowing the adult literacy process
demands among teachers and students a relationship of authentic dialogue. True dialogue unites subjects together in
the cognition of a knowable object which mediates between
them.

If learning to read and write is to constitute an act of knowing, the learners must assume from the beginning the role of creative subjects.   It is not a matter of memorizing and repeating given syllables, words, and phrases, but rather of reflecting critically on the process of reading and writing itself, and on the profound significance of language.

Insofar as language is impossible without thought, and language and thought are impossible without the world to which they refer, the human word is more than mere vocabulary-- it is word-and-action.   The cognitive dimensions of the literacy process must include the relationships of men with their world.   These relationships are the source of the dialectic between the products men achieve in transforming the world and the conditioning which these products in turn exercise on men.

Learning to read and write ought to be an opportunity for men to know what speaking the word really means: a human act implying reflection and action.   As such it is a primordial human right and not the privilege of a few. [11] Speaking the word is not a true act if it is not at the same time associated with the right of self-expression and world-expression, of creating and re-creating, of deciding and choosing and ultimately participating in society's historical process.

In the culture of silence the masses are "mute"; that is, they are prohibited from creatively taking part in the transformations of their society and therefore prohibited from being.   Even if they can occasionally read and write because they were "taught" in humanitarian--but not humanist --literacy campaigns, they are nevertheless alienated from the power responsible for their silence.

Illiterates know they are concrete men.   They know that they do things.   What they do not know in the culture of silence--in which they are ambiguous, dual beings--is that men's actions as such are transforming, creative, and re-creative.   Overcome by the myths of this culture, in-cluding the myth of their own "natural inferiority, " they do not know that their action upon the world is also transform-ing.   Prevented from having a "structural perception" of the facts involving them, they do not know that they cannot "have a voice"--i.e., that they cannot exercise the right to parti-cipate consciously in the socio-historical transformation of their society, because their work does not belong to them.

It could be said (and we would agree) that it is not possible to recognize all this apart from praxis, that is, apart from reflection and action, and that to attempt it would be pure idealism. But it is also true that action upon an object must be critically analyzed in order to understand both the object itself and the understanding one has of it. The act of knowing involves a dialectical movement which goes from action to reflection and from reflection upon action to a new action. For the learner to know what he did not know before, he must engage in an authentic process of abstraction by means of which he can reflect on the action-object whole, or, more generally, on forms of orientation in the world. In this process of abstraction, situations representative of how the learner orients himself in the world are proposed to him as the objects of his critique.

As an event calling forth the critical reflection of both the learners and educators, the literacy process must relate speaking the word to transforming reality, and to man's role in this transformation. Perceiving the significance of that relationship is indispensable for those learning to read and write if we are really committed to liberation. Such a perception will lead the learners to recognize a much greater right than that of being literate. They will ultimately recognize that, as men, they have the right to have a voice. On the other hand, as an act of knowing, learning to read and write presupposes not only a theory of knowing but a method which corresponds to the theory.

We recognize the indisputable unity between subjectivity and objectivity in the act of knowing. Reality is never just simply the objective datum, the concrete fact, but is also men's perception of it. Once again, this is not a subjectivistic or idealistic affirmation, as it might seem. On the contrary, subjectivism and idealism come into play when the subjective-objective unity is broken. [12]

The adult literacy process as an act of knowing implies the existence of two interrelated contexts. One is the context of authentic dialogue between learners and educators as equally knowing subjects. This is what schools should be--the theoretical context of dialogue. The second is the real, concrete context of facts, the social reality in which men exist. [13] In the theoretical context of dialogue, the facts presented by the real or concrete context are critically analyzed. This analysis involves the exercise of abstraction,

through which, by means of representations of concrete reality, we seek knowledge of that reality. The instrument for
this abstraction in our methodology is codification, [14] or representation of the existential situations of the learners.

Codification, on the one hand, mediates between the
concrete and theoretical contexts (of reality). On the other
hand, as knowable object, it mediates between the knowing
subjects, educators and learners, who seek in dialogue to
unveil the "action-object wholes." This type of linguistic
discourse must be "read" by anyone who tries to interpret
it, even when purely pictorial. As such, it presents what
Chomsky calls "surface structure" and "deep structure."

The "surface structure" of codification makes the
"action-object whole" explicit in a purely taxonomic form.
The first stage of decodification[15]--or reading--is descriptive. At this stage, the "readers"--or decodifiers--focus on
the relationship between the categories constituting the codification. This preliminary focus on the surface structure
is followed by analyzing the codified situation. This
leads the learner to the second and fundamental stage of decodification, the comprehension of the codification's "deep
structure." By understanding the codification's "deep structure" the learner can then understand the dialectic which
exists between the categories presented in the "surface" structure," as well as the unity between the "surface" and "deep"
structures.

In our method, the codification initially takes the
form of a photograph or sketch which represents a real existent, or an existent constructed by the learners. When
this representation is projected as a slide, the learners effect an operation basic to the act of knowing: they gain distance from the knowable object. This experience of distance
is undergone as well by the educators, so that educators and
learners together can reflect critically on the knowable object
which mediates between them. The aim of decodification is
to arrive at the critical level of knowing, beginning with the
learner's experience of the situation in the "real context."

Whereas the codified representation is the knowable
object mediating between knowing subjects, decodification--
dissolving the codification into its constituent elements--is
the operation by which the knowing subjects perceive relationships between the codification's elements and other facts presented by the real context--relationships which were formerly

unperceived. Codification represents a given dimension of reality as individuals live it, and this dimension is proposed for their analysis in a context other than that in which they live it. Codification thus transforms what was a way of life in the real context into "objectum" in the theoretical context. The learners, rather than receive information about this or that fact, analyze aspects of their own existential experience represented in the codification.

Existential experience is a whole. In illuminating one of its angles and perceiving the inter-relation of that angle with others, the learners tend to replace a fragmented vision of reality with a total vision. From the point of view of a theory of knowledge, this means that the dynamic between codification of existential situations and decodification involves the learners in a constant re-construction of their former "ad-miration" of reality.

We do not use the concept "ad-miration" here in the usual way, or in its ethical or esthetic sense, but with a special philosophical connotation. To "ad-mire" is to objectify the "not-I." It is a dialectical operation which characterizes man as man, differentiating him from the animal. It is directly associated with the creative dimension of his language. To "ad-mire" implies that man stands over against his "not-I" in order to understand it. For this reason, there is no act of knowing without "ad-miration" of the object to be known. If the act of knowing is a dynamic act-- and no knowledge is ever complete--then in order to know, man not only "ad-mires" the object, but must always be "re-ad-miring" his former "ad-miration." When we "re-ad-mire" our former "ad-miration" (always an "ad-miration" of) we are simultaneously "ad-miring" the act of "ad-miring" and the object "ad-mired," so that we can overcome the errors we made in our former "ad-miration." This "re-ad-miration" leads us to a perception of anterior perception.

In the process of decodifying representations of their existential situations and perceiving former perceptions, the learners gradually, hesitatingly, and timorously place in doubt the opinion they held of reality and replace it with a more and more critical knowledge thereof.

Let us suppose that we were to present to groups from among the dominated classes codifications which portray their imitation of the dominators' cultural models--a natural tendency of the oppressed consciousness at a given

moment.[16] The dominated persons would perhaps, in self-
defense, deny the truth of the codification. As they deepened
their analysis, however, they would begin to perceive that
their apparent imitation of the dominators' models is a result of their interiorization of these models and, above all,
of the myths of the "superiority" of the dominant classes
which cause the dominated to feel inferior. What in fact is
pure interiorization appears in a naive analysis to be imitation. At bottom, when the dominated classes reproduce the
dominators' style of life, it is because the dominators live
"within" the dominated. The dominated can eject the dominators only by getting distance from them and objectifying
them. Only then can they recognize them as their anti-
thesis.[17]

     To the extent, however, that interiorization of the
dominators' values is not only an individual phenomenon, but
a social and cultural one, ejection must be achieved by a
type of cultural action in which culture negates culture.
That is, culture, as an interiorized product which in turn
conditions men's subsequent acts, must become the object
of men's knowledge so that they can perceive its conditioning power. Cultural action occurs at the level of super-
structure. It can only be understood by what Althusser calls
"the dialectic of overdetermination."[18] This analytic tool
prevents us from falling into mechanistic explanations or,
what is worse, mechanistic action. An understanding of it
precludes surprise that cultural myths remain after the infrastructure is transformed, even by revolution.

     When the creation of a new culture is appropriate but
impeded by interiorized cultural "residue," this residue,
these myths, must be expelled by means of culture. Cultural action and cultural revolution, at different stages, constitute the modes of this expulsion. The learners must discover the reasons behind many of their attitudes toward
cultural reality and thus confront cultural reality in a new
way. "Re-ad-miration" of their former "ad-miration" is
necessary in order to bring this about. The learners' capacity for critical knowing--well beyond mere opinion--is established in the process of unveiling their relationships with
the historical-cultural world in and with which they exist.

     We do not mean to suggest that critical knowledge of
man-world relationships arises as a verbal knowledge outside of praxis. Praxis is involved in the concrete situations
which are codified for critical analysis. To analyze the

codification in its "deep structure" is, for this very reason,
to reconstruct the former praxis and to become capable of
a new and different praxis. The relationship between the
theoretical context, in which codified representations of objective facts are analyzed, and the concrete context, where
these facts occur, has to be made real.

Such education must have the character of commitment. It implies a movement from the concrete context
which provides objective facts, to the theoretical context
where these facts are analyzed in depth, and back to the concrete context where men experiment with new forms of prazis.

It might seem as if some of our statements defend
the principle that, whatever the level of the learners, they
ought to reconstruct the process of human knowing in absolute terms. In fact, when we consider adult literacy learning or education in general as an act of knowing, we are
advocating a synthesis between the educator's maximally systematized knowing and the learners' minimally systematized
knowing--a synthesis achieved in dialogue. The educator's
role is to propose problems about the codified existential
situations in order to help the learners arrive at a more
and more critical view of their reality. The educator's responsibility as conceived by this philosophy is thus greater
in every way than that of his colleague whose duty is to
transmit information which the learners memorize. Such
an educator can simply repeat what he has read, and often
misunderstood, since education for him does not mean an
act of knowing.

The first type of educator, on the contrary, is a
knowing subject, face to face with other knowing subjects.
He can never be a mere memorizer, but a person constantly
readjusting his knowledge, who calls forth knowledge from
his students. For him, education is a pedagogy of knowing.
The educator whose approach is mere memorization is anti-
dialogic; his act of transmitting knowledge is inalterable.
For the educator who experiences the act of knowing together with his students, in contrast, dialogue is the seal
of the act of knowing. He is aware, however, that not all
dialogue is in itself the mark of a relationship of true
knowledge.

Socratic intellectualism--which mistook the definition
of the concept for knowledge of the thing defined and this
knowledge as virtue--did not constitute a true pedagogy of

knowing, even though it was dialogic. Plato's theory of dialogue failed to go beyond the Socratic theory of the definition
as knowledge, even though for Plato one of the necessary
conditions for knowing was that man be capable of a "prise
de conscience, " and though the passage from doxa to logos
was indispensable for man to achieve truth. For Plato, the
"prise de conscience" did not refer to what man knew or
did not know or knew badly about his dialectical relationship
with the world; it was concerned rather with what man once
knew and forgot at birth. To know was to remember or
recollect forgotten knowledge. The apprehension of both doxa
and logos, and the overcoming of doxa by logos occurred not
in the man-world relationship, but in the effort to remember
or rediscover a forgotten logos.

    For dialogue to be a method of true knowledge, the
knowing subjects must approach reality scientifically in order
to seek the dialectical connections which explain the form of
reality. Thus, to know is not to remember something previously known and now forgotten. Nor can doxa be overcome
by logos apart from the dialectical relationship of man with
his world, apart from men's reflective action upon the world.

    To be an act of knowing, then, the adult literacy pro-
cess must engage the learners in the constant problematizing
of their existential situations. This problematizing employs
"generative words" chosen by specialized educators in a preliminary investigation of what we call the "minimal linguistic
universe" of the future learners. The words are chosen
(a) for their pragmatic value, i. e., as linguistic signs which
command a common understanding in a region or area of the
same city or country (in the United States, for instance, the
word "soul" has a special significance in black areas which
it does not have among whites), and (b) for their phonetic
difficulties which will gradually be presented to those learning to read and write. Finally, it is important that the first
generative word be tri-syllabic. When it is divided into its
syllables, each one constituting a syllabic family, the learners can experiment with various syllabic combinations even
at first sight of the word.

    Having chosen 17 generative words, [19] the next step
is to codify seventeen existential situations familiar to the
learners. The generative words are then worked into the
situations one by one in the order of their increasing phonetic difficulty. As we have already emphasized, these codifications are knowable objects which mediate between the

knowing subjects, educator-learners, learner-educators.
Their act of knowing is elaborated in the circulo de cultura
(cultural discussion group) which functions as the theoretical
context.

In Brazil, before analyzing the learners' existential
situations and the generative words contained in them, we
proposed the codified theme of man-world relationships in
general.[20] In Chile, at the suggestion of Chilean educators,
this important dimension was discussed concurrently with
learning to read and write. What is important is that the
person learning words be concomitantly engaged in a critical
analysis of the social framework in which men exist. For
example, the word "favela" in Rio de Janeiro, and the word
"callampa" in Chile, represent, each with its own nuances,
the same social, economic, and cultural reality of the vast
numbers of slum dwellers in those countries. If "favela" and
"callampa" are used as generative words for the people of
Brazilian and Chilean slums, the codifications will have to
represent slum situations.

There are many people who consider slum dwellers
marginal, intrinsically wicked and inferior. To such people
we recommend the profitable experience of discussing the
slum situation with slum dwellers themselves. As some of
these critics are often simply mistaken, it is possible that
they may rectify their mythical clichés and assume a more
scientific attitude. They may avoid saying that the illiteracy,
alcoholism, and crime of the slums, that its sickness, in-
fant mortality, learning deficiencies, and poor hygiene reveal the "inferior nature" of its inhabitants. They may even
end up realizing that if intrinsic evil exists it is part of the
structures, and that it is the structures which need to be
transformed.

It should be pointed out that the Third World as a
whole, and more in some parts than in others, suffers from
the same misunderstanding from certain sectors of the so-
called metropolitan societies. They see the Third World as
the incarnation of evil, the primitive, the devil, sin and
sloth--in sum, as historically unviable without the director
societies. Such a manichean attitude is at the source of
the impulse to "save" the "demon-possessed" Third World,
"educating it" and "correcting its thinking" according to the
director societies' own criteria.

The expansionist interests of the director societies

are implicit in such notions. These societies can never relate to the Third World as partners, since partnership presupposes equals, no matter how different the equal parties
may be, and can never be established between parties an-
tagonistic to each other. Thus, "salvation" of the Third
World by the director societies can only mean its domina-
tion, whereas in its legitimate aspiration to independence
lies its utopian vision: to save the director societies in the
very act of freeing itself.

In this sense the pedagogy which we defend, conceived
in a significant area of the Third World, is itself a utopian
pedagogy. By this very fact it is full of hope, for to be
utopian is not to be merely idealistic or impractical but
rather to engage in denunciation and annunciation. Our pedagogy cannot do without a vision of man and of the world.
It formulates a scientific humanist conception which finds its
expression in a dialogical praxis in which the teachers and
learners together, in the act of analyzing a dehumanizing
reality, denounce it while announcing its transformation in
the name of the liberation of man.

For this very reason, denunciation and annunciation
in this utopian pedagogy are not meant to be empty words,
but an historic commitment. Denunciation of a dehumanizing situation today increasingly demands precise scientific
understanding of that situation. Likewise, the annunciation
of its transformation increasingly requires a theory of transforming action. However, neither act by itself implies the
transformation of the denounced reality or the establishment
of that which is announced. Rather, as a moment in an
historical process, the announced reality is already present
in the act of denunciation and annunciation. [21]

That is why the utopian character of our educational
theory and practice is as permanent as education itself
which, for us, is cultural action. Its thrust toward denunciation and annunciation cannot be exhausted when the reality
denounced today cedes its place tomorrow to the reality previously announced in the denunciation. When education is no
longer utopian, i. e., when it no longer embodies the dramatic
unity of denunciation and annunciation, it is either because
the future has no more meaning for men, or because men
are afraid to risk living the future as creative overcoming
of the present, which has become old.

The more likely explanation is generally the latter.

That is why some people today study all the possibilities
which the future contains, in order to "domesticate" it and
keep it in line with the present, which is what they intend
to maintain. If there is any anguish in director societies
hidden beneath the cover of their cold technology, it springs
from their desperate determination that their metropolitan
status be preserved in the future. Among the things which
the Third World may learn from the metropolitan societies
there is this that is fundamental: not to replicate those
societies when its current utopia becomes actual fact.

When we defend such a conception of education--re-
alistic precisely to the extent that it is utopian--that is, to
the extent that it denounces what in fact is, and finds therefore between denunciation and its realization the time of its
praxis--we are attempting to formulate a type of education
which corresponds to the specifically human mode of being,
which is historical.

There is no annunciation without denunciation, just as
every denunciation generates annunciation. Without the latter, hope is impossible. In an authentic utopian vision,
however, hoping does not mean folding one's arms and waiting. Waiting is only possible when one, filled with hope,
seeks through reflective action to achieve that announced
future which is being born within the denunciation.

That is why there is no genuine hope in those who intend to make the future repeat their present, nor in those
who see the future as something predetermined. Both have
a "domesticated" notion of history: the former because they
want to stop time; the latter because they are certain about
a future they already "know. " Utopian hope, on the contrary,
is engagement full of risk. That is why the dominators,
who merely denounce those who denounce them, and who
have nothing to announce but the preservation of the status
quo, can never be utopian nor, for that matter, prophetic. [22]

A utopian pedagogy of denunciation and annunciation
such as ours will have to be an act of knowing the denounced
reality at the level of alphabetization and post-alphabetiza-
tion, which are in each case cultural action. That is why
there is such emphasis on the continual problematization of
the learners' existential situations as represented in the
codified images. The longer the problematization proceeds,
and the more the subjects enter into the "essence" of the
problematized object, the more they are able to unveil this

"essence. " The more they unveil it, the more their awakening consciousness deepens, thus leading to the "conscientization" of the situation by the poor classes.   Their critical
self-insertion into reality, i.e., their conscientization, makes
the transformation of their state of apathy into the utopian
state of denunciation and annunciation a viable project.

One must not think, however, that learning to read
and write precedes "conscientization, " or vice-versa.   Conscientization occurs simultaneously with the literacy or post-
literacy process.   It must be so.   In our educational
method, the word is not something static or disconnected
from men's existential experience, but a dimension of their
thought-language about the world.   That is why, when they
participate critically in analyzing the first generative words
linked with their existential experience; when they focus on
the syllabic families which result from that analysis; when
they perceive the mechanism of the syllabic combinations of
their language, the learners finally discover, in the various
possibilities of combination, their own words.   Little by
little, as these possibilities multiply, the learners, through
mastery of new generative words, expand both their vocabulary and their capacity for expression by the development of
their creative imagination. [23]

In some areas in Chile undergoing agrarian reform,
the peasants participating in the literacy programs wrote
with their tools on the dirt roads where they were working.
They composed the words from the syllabic combinations
they were learning.   "These men are sowers of the word, "
said Maria Edi Ferreira, a sociologist from the Santiago
team working in the Institute of Training and Research in
Agrarian Reform.   Indeed, they were not only sowing words,
but discussing ideas, and coming to understand their role in
the world better and better.

We asked one of these "sowers of words, " finishing
the first level of literacy classes, why he hadn't learned to
read and write before the agrarian reform.   "Before the
agrarian reform, my friend, " he said, "I didn't even think.
Neither did my friends. "

"Why?" we asked.   "Because it wasn't possible.   We
lived under orders.   We only had to carry out orders.   We
had nothing to say, " he replied emphatically.   The simple
answer of this peasant is a very clear analysis of "the culture of silence. "   In "the culture of silence, " to exist is

only to live.   The body carries out orders from above.
Thinking is difficult, speaking the word, forbidden.

"When all this land belonged to one latifundio, " said
another man in the same conversation, "there was no reason
to read and write.   We weren't responsible for anything.
The boss gave the orders and we obeyed.   Why read and
write? Now it's a different story.   Take me, for example.
In the asentiamiento, [24] I am responsible not only for my
work like all the other men, but also for tool repairs. When
I started I couldn't read, but I soon realized that I needed to
read and write.   You can't imagine what it was like to go to
Santiago to buy parts.   I couldn't get oriented.   I was afraid
of everything--afraid of the big city, of buying the wrong
thing, of being cheated.   Now it's all different. "

Observe how precisely this peasant described his former experience as an illiterate; his mistrust, his magical
(though logical) fear of the world; his timidity.   And observe
the sense of security with which he repeats, "Now it's all
different. "

"What did you feel, my friend, " we asked another
"sower of words" on a different occasion, "when you were
able to write and read your first word?" "I was happy because I discovered I could make words speak, " he replied.

Dario Salas reports, [25] "In our conversations with
peasants we were struck by the images they used to express
their interest and satisfaction about becoming literate.   For
example, 'Before we were blind, now the veil has fallen
from our eyes'; 'I came only to learn how to sign my name.
I never believed I would be able to read, too, at my age';
'Before, letters seemed like little puppets.   Today they say
something to me, and I can make them talk.' " "It is
touching, " continues Salas, "to observe the delight of the
peasants as the world of words opens to them.   Sometimes
they would say, 'We're so tired our heads ache, but we
don't want to leave here without learning to read and
write.' "[26]

The following words were taped during research on
"generative themes."[27]   They are an illiterate's decodification of a codified existential situation.

You see a house there, sad, as if it were aban-
doned.   When you see a house with a child in it,

it seems happier. It gives more joy and peace to
people passing by. The father of the family arrives
home from work exhausted, worried, bitter, and
his little boy comes to meet him with a big hug,
because a little boy is not stiff like a big person.
The father already begins to be happier just from
seeing his children. Then he really enjoys himself.
He is moved by his son's wanting to please him.
The father becomes more peaceful, and forgets his
problems.

Note once again the simplicity of expression, both profound and elegant, in the peasant's language. These are the
people considered absolutely ignorant by the proponents of
the "digestive" concept of literacy.

In 1968, an Uruguayan team[28] published a small book,
You Live as You Can (Se Vive como se Puede), whose contents are taken from the tape recordings of literacy classes
for urban dwellers. Its first edition of three thousand copies
was sold out in Montevideo in fifteen days, as was the second edition. The following is an excerpt from this book.

THE COLOR OF WATER

Water? Water? What is water used for?
   "Yes, yes, we saw it (in the picture). "
   "Oh, my native village, so far away.... "
   "Do you remember that village?"
   "The stream where I grew up, called Dead Friar ...
you know, I grew up there, a childhood moving from one
place to another ... the color of the water brings back
good memories, beautiful memories. "
   "What is the water used for?"
   "It is used for washing. We used it to wash clothes,
and the animals in the fields used to go there to drink,
and we washed ourselves there, too. "
   "Did you also use the water for drinking?"
   "Yes, when we were at the stream and had no other
water to drink, we drank from the stream. I remember
once in 1945 a plague of locusts came from somewhere,
and we had to fish them out of the water.... I was
small, but I remember taking out the locusts like this,
with my two hands--and I had no others. And I remember how hot the water was when there was a drought and
the stream was almost dry ... the water was dirty, mud-
dy, and hot, with all kinds of things in it. But we had

to drink it or die of thirst. "

The whole book is like this, pleasant in style, with great strength of expression of the world of its authors, those anonymous people, "sowers of words, " seeking to emerge from "the culture of silence. "

Yes, these ought to be the reading texts for people learning to read and write, and not "Eva saw the grape, " "The bird's wing, " "If you hammer a nail, be careful not to hit your fingers. " Intellectualist prejudices and above all class prejudices are responsible for the naive and unfounded notions that the people cannot write their own texts, or that a tape of their conversations is valueless since their conversations are impoverished of meaning. Comparing what the "sowers of words" said in the above references with what is generally written by specialist authors of reading lessons, we are convinced that only someone with very pronounced lack of taste or a lamentable scientific incompetency would choose the specialists' texts.

Imagine a book written entirely in this simple, poetic, free, language of the people, a book on which inter-disciplinary teams would collaborate in the spirit of true dialogue. The role of the teams would be to elaborate specialized sections of the book in problematic terms. For example, a section on linguistics would deal simply, though not simplistically, with questions fundamental to the learners' critical understanding of language. Let me emphasize again that since one of the important aspects of adult literacy work is the development of the capacity for expression, the section on linguistics would present themes for the learners to discuss, ranging from the increase of vocabulary to questions about communication--including the study of synonyms and antonyms, with its analysis of words in the linguistic context, and the use of metaphor, of which the people are such masters. Another section might provide the tools for a sociological analysis of the content of the texts.

These texts would not, of course, be used for mere mechanical reading, which leaves the readers without any understanding of what is real. Consistent with the nature of this pedagogy, they would become the object of analysis in reading seminars.

Add to all this the great stimulus it would be for those

learning to read and write, as well as for students on more
advanced levels, to know that they were reading and discussing the work of their own companions. . . .

    To undertake such a work, it is necessary to have
faith in the people, solidarity with them. It is necessary to
be utopian, in the sense in which we have used the word.

Notes

1. In languages like Portuguese or Spanish, words are
    composed syllabically. Thus, every non-monosyllabic
    word is, technically, <u>generative</u>, in the sense that
    other words can be constructed from its de-composed
    syllables. For a word to be authentically generative,
    however, certain conditions must be present which
    will be discussed in a later section of this essay.

2. Jean Paul Sartre, <u>Situations I</u>, Paris: Librairie Galli-
    mard, 1947, p. 31.

3. The digestive concept of knowledge is suggested by
    "controlled readings," by classes which consist only
    in lectures; by the use of memorized dialogues in
    language learning; by bibliographical notes which indi-
    cate not only which chapter, but which lines and
    words are to be read; by the methods of evaluating
    the students' progress in learning.

4. See Paulo Freire, "La alfebetizacion de adultos, critica
    de su vision ingenua; compreansion de su vision
    critica," in <u>Introducción a la Acción Cultural</u>, Santi-
    ago: ICIRA, 1969.

5. There are two noteworthy exceptions among these pri-
    mers: (1) in Brazil, <u>Viver e Lutar</u>, developed by a
    team of specialists of the Basic Education Movement,
    sponsored by the National Conference of Bishops.
    (This reader became the object of controversy after
    it was banned as subversive by the then governor of
    Guanabara, Mr. Carlos Lacerda, in 1963.) (2) In
    Chile, the ESPIGA collection, despite some small
    defects. The collection was organized by Jefatura
    de Planes Extraordinarios de Educación de Adultos,
    of the Public Education Ministry.

6. Since at the time this essay was written the writer did
    not have access to the primers, and was, therefore,
    vulnerable to recording phrases imprecisely or to
    confusing the author of one or another primer, it was
    thought best not to identify the authors or the titles
    of the books.

7. The English here would be nonsensical, as is the Portu-
    guese, the point being the emphasis on the consonant
    "d"--Editor.

8. The author of this reading text may even have added
    here, "If, however, this should happen, apply a
    little mercurochrome. "

9. [The Portuguese word here translated as marginal man
    is "marginado. " This has a passive sense: he who
    has been made marginal, or sent outside society; as
    well as the sense of a state of existence on the
    fringe of society. --Translator.]

10. UNESCO: "La situación educativa en América Latina, "
    Cuadro no. 20, page 263 (Paris, 1960).

11. Paulo Freire, op. cit.

12. There are two ways to fall into idealism: The "one
    consists of dissolving the real in subjectivity; the
    other in denying all real subjectivity in the interests
    of objectivity. " Jean Paul Sartre, Search for a
    Method, trans. Hazel E. Barnes, New York: Vintage
    Books, 1968, p. 33.

13. See Karel Kosik, Dialectica de lo Concreto, Mexico:
    Grijalbo, 1967.

14. [Codification refers alternatively to the imaging, or
    the image itself, of some significant aspect of the
    learner's concrete reality (of a slum dwelling, for
    example). As such, it becomes both the object of
    the teacher-learner dialogue and the context for the
    introduction of the generative word. --Editor.]

15. [Decodification refers to a process of description and
    interpretation, whether of printed words, pictures,
    or other "codifications. " As such, decodification and
    decodifying are distinct from the process of decoding,

or word-recognition. --Editor.]

16. Re the oppressed consciousness, see: Frantz Fanon,
    The Wretched of the Earth, New York: Grove Press,
    1968; Albert Memmi, Colonizer and the Colonized,
    New York: Orion Press, 1965; and Paulo Freire,
    Pedagogy of the Oppressed, New York: Herder &
    Herder, 1970.

17. See Fanon, The Wretched; Freire, Pedagogy.

18. See Louis Althusser, Pour Marx, Paris: Librairie
    François Maspero, 1965; and Paulo Freire, Annual
    Report: Activities for 1968, Agrarian Reform, Train-
    ing and Research Institute ICIRA, Chile, trans. John
    Dewitt, Center for the Study of Development and So-
    cial Change, Cambridge, Mass., 1969 (Mimeo).

19. We observed in Brazil and Spanish America, especially
    Chile, that no more than 17 words were necessary
    for teaching adults to read and write syllabic languages
    like Portuguese and Spanish.

20. See Paulo Freire, Educação como Pratica da Liberdade,
    Rio de Janeiro: Paz e Terra, 1967; Chilean edition,
    Santiago: ICIRA, 1969.

21. Re the utopian dimension of denunciation and proclama-
    tion, see Leszek Kolakowski, Toward a Marxist Hu-
    manism, New York: Grove Press, 1969.

22. "The right, as a conservative force, needs no utopia;
    its essence is the affirmation of existing conditions--
    a fact and not a utopia--or else the desire to revert
    to a state which was once an accomplished fact.   The
    Right strives to idealize actual conditions, not to
    change them.   What it needs is fraud not utopia. "
    Kolakowski, op. cit., pp. 71-72.

23. "We have observed that the study of the creative aspect
    of language use develops the assumption that linguistic
    and mental process are virtually identical, language
    providing the primary means for free expansion of
    thought and feeling, as well as for the functioning of
    creative imagination, " Noam Chomsky, Cartesian Lin-
    guistics, New York: Harper and Row, 1966, p. 31.

24. After the disappropriation of lands in the agrarian re-
      form in Chile, the peasants who were salaried work-
      ers on the large latifundia become "settlers" (asen-
      tados) during a three-year period in which they re-
      ceive varied assistance from the government through
      the Agrarian Reform Corporation. This period of
      "settlement" (asentamiento) precedes that of assign-
      ing lands to the peasants. This policy is now chang-
      ing. The phase of "settlement" of the lands is being
      abolished, in favor of an immediate distribution of
      lands to the peasants. The Agrarian Reform Corpor-
      ation will continue, nevertheless, to aid the peasants.

25. Dario Salas, "Algumas experiencias vividas na Super-
      visão de Educação basica, " in A alfabetização fun-
      cional no Chile. Report to UNESCO, November,
      1968. Introduction: Paulo Freire.

26. Dario Salas refers here to one of the best adult educa-
      tion programs organized by the Agrarian Reform Cor-
      poration in Chile, in strict collaboration with the
      Ministry of Education and ICIRA. Fifty peasants re-
      ceive boarding and instruction scholarships for a
      month. The courses center on discussions of the
      local, regional, and national situations.

27. An analysis of the objectives and methodology of the in-
      vestigation of generative themes lies outside the scope
      of this essay, but is dealt with in the author's work,
      Pedagogy of the Oppressed (op. cit.).

11. STUDY, WORK AND MILITARY SERVICE IN CUBA
Concepción E. Castañeda

"Give me a six-year-old child and I
will make of him a good communist. "
--V. I. Lenin

When Fidel Castro took over the Cuban government in
1959 he knew, as it later happened, that the majority of the
people who seemed to support him, would desert the government as soon as he put into effect many of his revolutionary
laws, such as the Agrarian Reform and the Urban Reform
laws. And, indeed, people did desert as soon as Castro declared Cuba as a socialist country with Russian hands. This
created a strong force of people against Castro, enough to
endanger the new government. Not only were the adults
against Castro, but also many of the youngsters.

It is impossible for any government to change a whole
political system if this government does not have the youth's
help. The youth of a country are its main political force
and hope for the future. Castro knew this fact, just as he
knew that it was almost impossible to change most adults'
minds. He needed to politically indoctrinate the new generation of Cuban students and workers according to Leninist
doctrine.

Thus, Castro's primary task was to change the educational system from the elementary school to the universities. The effort to create a new Cuban man, one who was
able to accomplish the tasks set for him by the Cuban revolution was Castro's goal. As he himself said, "All revolution is an extraordinary process of education.... Revolution
and education are the same thing. " And the best place to
start that educational revolution was the high schools, where
the student's age ranged from 12 to 17 years.

But the not yet well defined communist regime needed
an avant-garde to initiate the educational changes. For that

145

purpose the Jóvenes Rebeldes (Young Rebels), later called
Jóvenes Comunistas or (Young Communists), were created.
And their motto "Estudio, Trabajo, Fusil" (Study, Work,
Military Service) became the rules to follow in every school
in Cuba. Hence, to understand Castro's educational system
we have to explore the Young Rebels' motto and see what the
present Cuban regime is accomplishing in the educational
system, still in its experimental stage and continuously
changing.

Study

On May 11, 1961 Castro's government took over the
private schools in Cuba. There were 1,300 of these schools.
At the same time all textbooks in Social Science, or any
other matter, which were not in accord with the communist
line, were forbidden. Other books were revised to conform
to the official line of communism. Teachers were fired and
only partisan teachers were allowed to remain in their
schools under direct supervision of the Young Rebels, who
were the Revolution's watch-dogs in this field.

After the regime was nearly consolidated among the
students, the teacher's staff was given special political indoctrination. Teachers were told what to teach and how to
teach the new generation. Destruction of old beliefs, values
and institutions was sought. Old established historic facts
had to be changed to fit the new political system. Even the
thoughts and teachings of José Marté, the Cuban patriot and
Independence Mentor were to be interpreted and taught by
the communistic pattern; such as, "every one of Martés'
words was a word said against the United States...." So
prepared teachers were taken again to the schools ready to
re-train the youth.

It was not a hard task to give the students a new political outlook. The Cuban educational system was characterized by its lack of political indoctrination at the school
level, so the Cuban youth were not very interested in any
particular political system at that point. The students enthusiastically accepted the new role they had in revolutionary
activities. Nothing could be said against Castro's government. Even parents could not stand between the Young Rebel
and "the counter-revolutionary student." Many of those
counter-revolutionary students and teachers were incarcerated
for opposing the pro-communistic teaching in the schools.

The students who distinguished themselves the most by their
political achievement and work (not academic), were hired
as teachers and political instructors in other schools.   After
the Campaign against Illiteracy in 1961, a campaign by students, some as young as 13, to teach 985,000 illiterates
how to read and write, [1] the students who participated were
taken to special internship (political) schools, to prepare
them as "teachers."[2]   They became political instructors,
not teachers of general knowledge.

     Thus it was that the Cuban school system became di-
rected toward the sociopolitical aspect rather than science
and letters.   These new teachers were placed in the primary
school to shape the six-year-old child's mind to be what
Lenin called "a good communist," the type of citizen necessary for the regime's survival and growth.   Those youths
are the called "Pioneers of the Revolution" and are taught,
from kindergarten to the 9th grade, communist slogans,
thoughts and the meaning of sacrifice, cooperation, discipline and hard work.   In these elementary schools, from
the age of 12 onward, there is encouragement toward technical studies, farming and sports.   Sports and farming are
extra studies beyond the regular curriculum, but they receive special care.

     Teaching training programs receive very special care
also and students are urged to follow teaching careers.   As
soon as they finish the 6th grade, those students with special
skills and aptitudes for teaching are placed as teachers of
the lower grades.   A student who wishes to join the teaching profession is very welcome and is taken to a special
internship in the mountains to study teaching methodology as
well as politics.   The teacher doesn't need a college degree
to be a high school teacher.   The student teacher is promoted from lower grades to higher grades merely by taking
the weekly seminars that are offered by more experienced
teachers.   Many of these self-made teachers reach university rank, for political reasons and needs.   The same method is followed in every branch of teaching.   Either in general studies or in technical studies, the teacher has to show
a clear communist ideology.   If not, he is not promoted and
is finally fired.   So, the Castro government has created,
little by little, its own elite of teachers, qualified to indoctrinate politically the Cuban youth.

Work

     The new Cuban curriculum plan encourages work.
From the very beginning at the primary school through university and technical school years, a student has to spend
part of the year working in cooperative farms.   A little
teaching is given during the 45-day period that the student
spends working and living in poor conditions.   This, according to Castro, is to enable the young to learn to love work
under any circumstance, and to give their help to increase
national wealth, "now that the land belongs to the people and
not to the United States capitalists." Work is an integral
part of the educational system.

Military Service

     When the young are 14 years old, they can join the
armed militia, and (or) at 16 they should serve two years
of compulsory military training.   Either way, he is taught
to love "all communist" countries and to hate whatever op-
poses the communistic ideal.   He is prepared to help the
Vietcong, the Angolans and to teach guerrilla warfare in
South America.   He has learned through his political indoctrination at school to obey and to serve International Communism.

     But Cuba has been in dire need of skilled workers
and technicians.   Modern science and technology are needed
in the creation of wealth.   So every productive process on
any sector of the Cuban economy has to be modernized by
bringing technology to bear on production.   That is why
much attention has been given to the creation of a scientific
attitude in every Cuban.   This is seen as a kind of vocational training, the teaching of skills to the young student,
and the proliferation of technical schools.   To accomplish
this goal, the Cuban revolution has to rely on the Cuban
young people, because from them can be formed the true
communists.   And only through political indoctrination and
hard work can this be done.

     The gloomy reality of this plan of studies is that the
new generation in Cuba is being indoctrinated against the
United States and any form of democratic government, to
the point of no return.   A Cuban lawyer, Mario Lazo says,

     Education in Cuba has been misused by Castro to

diseminate lies and to instill hatred of the United
States; to condition his followers, especially the
young, to the task of overthrowing U.S. democracy
along with the societies of Latin American countries. [3]

Notes

1. 710, 000 persons were taught how to read and to write
   in a period of nine months.

2. Those schools were named "Makarenko" after the
   Russian educator Anton Makarenko.

3. Mario Lazo, Dagger in the Heart, Santa Monica, Cal.:
   Fidelis Publishers, Inc., 1969, p. 414.

12.   CHANGES IN CUBAN EDUCATION*
Rolland G. Paulston

The objective of this article is to examine the antecedents, ends and process of the change produced in Cuban
education during the last decade. With the purpose of pre-
senting a perspective analysis, I will also sketch the development of the educational structures and services during the
pre-revolutionary era. This approach has the advantage of
facilitating the comparison of Cuba's educational systems before and after the revolution and, by means of contrast,
demonstrating the authentic revolutionary character resulting
from the change in education since 1959.

The study is divided in three sections: the first
deals with the change in the social organization and in the
functions of education during the periods of Spanish or North
American influence; the second describes the revolutionary
innovations and changes produced in education since 1959; the
third examines some of the characteristics, problems and
tendencies of the present educational system. I have used
an ample variety of Cuban material from original sources
in the preparation of this study, mainly information from
the Cuban delegation in UNESCO, [1] as well as data collected
during field work in Cuba during December 1970.

Obstacles to Change in Education

My experiences as technical counselor in Latin American Ministries of Education, most recently in Venezuela
and Peru, have presented vivid lessons about the obstacles
that have hindered qualitative change--or educational reform,
if one chooses--in traditional Latin American societies.
These structural and socio-cultural obstacles have been well

*A revised version, reprinted (and translated) by permission
of "Cambíos en la Educación Cubana, " Aportes: Una Revista
de Estudios Latinoamericanos 5 (July 1971), p. 60-82.

documented by Ivan Illich, Seymour Lipset and Aldo Solari,
John Gillin, Richard Adams and others.[2] All of these
authors have emphasized the fact that social values that
stand out in terms of function of power are those of the
upper class. A large segment of the middle sectors tend
to identify themselves--although as soon as they are alone
this is more like a social aspiration--with the upper class
and to accept and defend the values of said class. According to the Brazilian sociologist Florestan Fernandes, the
democratization of teaching--that is to say, the creation of
a mass system of education--has resulted in the extension
of the aristocratic school of the past through a great part
of Latin American society.[3]

        This process has created in different levels, in all
of Latin America, systems of public schools that inculcate
traditional, neocolonial values that may be highly functional
to legitimize elite status and power, but are not very functional for individual and economic development. Theoretical
and humanistic studies that are considered adequate and
desirable contradict in great part the practical and technical
activities related to productive work. Thus, Latin America,
as Burns observes, faces a paradox: in order to improve
education it must first change its social order, but in order
to change its social order it must develop and more equit-
ably distribute its economic recourses. Given existing re-
ward structures, however, educational systems are not able
to furnish enough qualified technical personnel in order to
carry out this task. Moreover as the Alliance for Progress
has pointed out, the Latin American elites have rarely
shown more than a superficial interest in the reform of
their social, economic or educational institutions. These
rather effectively serve to maintain elitist privilege but do
little to foster national development. Nevertheless, the
United States remains loyal to the model of the Alliance
which advocated evolutionary change or gradual reform.
But because of the existing elites' reticence or incapacity to
surrender a part of their power or privilege, the structural
and economic changes produced vis-à-vis this effort have
been few. As Ortega y Gasset has stated, "the tiger does
not de-Tigerize himself." In notable contrast, we have the
incontestable success of Cuba in "de-Tigerizing the tiger,"
in creating new social institutions and a basic social and
cultural realignment that completely repudiated the "personalismo" egocentric model in favor of another more "sociocen-
tric" model which morally rewards socially conscious behavior strengthening group solidarity and well-being.

The Pre-Revolutionary Educational Situation

As the last Spanish colony in America along with
Puerto Rico, Cuba shared little in the widespread development of public schools that occurred in many of the Latin
American republics during the second half of the 19th century. In contrast to this pattern, Cuban education continued
the colonial model within which a relatively small elite of
large landowners, administrators and professionals educated
their children in private schools or abroad. There were a
few public and religion schools which served the small urban middle sectors, while children of the vast rural lower
class were largely unschooled. Public primary education in
colonial Cuba began in 1857 with the "Spanish Law of Public
Instruction. " In 1880, public secondary education was
created by the "Colonial Plan for Public Instruction, " which
founded 80 urban secondary schools (bachillerato) exclusively
dedicated to pre-university studies. In 1898, the total number of students matriculated in these schools did not exceed
30, 000. Less than one-third of the total populations could
be classed as literate. [4]

After independence in 1898 and two periods of United
States military occupation from 1898 to 1902 and from 1906
to 1909, Cuba entered into a period of forced modernization
and Americanization. In 1898, the United States nearly over
night became a major colonial power. In that fateful year
the United States annexed Hawaii and after a brief and victorious war with Spain, annexed Puerto Rico and the Philip-
pine Islands, and occupied Cuba. President William McKinley ambiguously instructed the commander of the American
military forces occupying Cuba to "prepare the people for
independence" and more specifically to conduct the occupation "in the interest and benefit of the Cuban people and
those who have property and interests in the island. "[5] General Leonard Wood, who commanded the first occupation,
indicated that he considered his job to be to create a Republic "based strictly upon the model of our great Republic ...
in a Latin country where more than 70 percent of the population is illiterate. "[6]

With development priorities on public education together with the construction of sewers and roads, public
health measures and commercial activities, U. S. developmental efforts turned Cuba into an area of intensive capital
investment. Free public primary education became the
principal educational activity of the period of occupation in

that the North American policy makers considered literacy
as a necessary prerequisite to the establishment of stable
government.

A new school law patterned after that of the State of
Ohio created local school boards, requiring compulsory attendance, normal school to prepare teachers, textbooks and
lesson plans. As Cuba is not Ohio, the law survived only
so long as there were North American troops on the island.
During their period of intense Yankee tutelage, however, the
Cubans learned many new educational ideas and practices;
manual training, kindergartens, the construction of modern
schools, citizenship education and many other practices that
reflected U.S. values inherent in the model of the North
American public schools. [7] The contrast of the U.S. educational model to the Spanish colonial model could not have
been more extreme.

In quantitative terms the North American contribution
was massive. Thousands of public schools were built and
enrollments, principally urban, tripled relative to the figures
of the pre-independence period. But less than half of the
school-age children were attending classes and the majority
dropped out of school before becoming literate. In the United
States, the North American policy of trying to establish a
democratic government through a literacy education in a
plantation economy was criticized as ineffective and unrealistic. Rather, it was suggested that what the Cubans really
needed was a practical education designed to aid them in
adopting themselves to their rural, agricultural setting. [8]

Following military occupation, Cuban educators adapted
series of North American practices and attempted to extend
the new and vulnerable system of public education. Most
notably, Enrique José Varona, Minister of Education and
proponent of neopositivism, worked diligently but in vain to
redirect the curriculum from a classical, humanistic orientation to one with greater emphasis on the sciences. The
1909 teacher certification law sought to provide for a more
professional training, placement, and supervision of teachers.
In 1915, normal schools were created and in 1927, schools
were founded for the training of accounting and administrative personnel. [9]

After the rise in the price of sugar during the first
World War, public education was raised both qualitatively
and quantitatively. Table 1 points out that the number of

Table I. Number of Schools, Teachers and Students in Private and Public Education in Cuba, 1902-1968.

PRIMARY SCHOOLS

Year[a]	Public			Private		
	Schools	Teachers	Students	Schools	Teachers	Students
1902	3,474	3,583	163,348	---	---	---
1912	3,916	4,055	234,625	---	---	---
1925	3,627	6,896	388,349	575	1,956	38,064
1931	3,816	7,567	452,016	568	1,608	32,450
1939	4,386	9,386	424,091	360	1,906	31,023
1950	7,614	21,148	593,361	---	---	79,645
1955	7,905	20,119	728,087	---	6,619	107,000
1958	7,567	17,355	717,417	665	7,000	120,000
1962	13,780	36,613	1,207,286	0	0	0
1968	14,807	48,994	1,490,754	0	0	0

SECONDARY SCHOOLS

Year[a]	Public			Private[c]		
	Schools	Teachers	Students	Schools	Teachers	Students
1902-39	no entry in any category					
1952	119	1,952	26,413	---b	---	---
1955	116	1,963	46,914	165b	850	13,459b
1958	184	2,580	63,526	165	---	14,850
1962	335	7,380	123,118	0	0	0
1968	434	10,703	186,358	0	0	0

UNIVERSITIES (Public and Private[a])

Year[a]	Schools	Teachers	Students
1902	1	---	---
1912	1	---	---
1925	1	---	---
1931	1	---	---
1939	1	---	---
1952	4	711	20,971
1955	7	975	24,273
1958	6	1,053	25,514
1962	3	1,987	20,537
1968	3	4,151	27,523

[a]Beginning in September and ending in June.
[b]1956.
[c]Only schools with bachelor's degree.
[d]Until 1962 all were public.

Sources: "Cuban Economic Research Project," Study in Cuba (Coral Gables, 1965); UNESCO, Statistical Yearbook 1963-68 (Louvain, Belgium, 1963-68); and Carmelo Mesa-Lago. "Availability and Reliability of Statistics in Socialist Cuba," Latin American Research Review 4 (summer 1969), p. 72-74.

primary school teachers and students doubled between 1902
and 1925.   Further, between 1921 and 1927 state expenditures
for education tripled, and expenditures per capita increased
from 2.01 pesos to 4.9 pesos (see Table II).   Matriculation
of school-age children (five to 14 years) increased from 46
percent in 1901-1902 to 63 percent in 1925-26; a greater
percentage than in any other Spanish-speaking Republic at
that time.   Thus, in 1926, Cuba led all of the Latin American nations in the percentage of children attending school.
During the last years of the 20's, Cuban educators, with the
aid of North American colleagues had progressed to the point
where they were able to offer technical assistance to up-
grade teacher skills in a number of South American nations,
especially in Venezuala.   Also during the 1920's, public
school graduates increased over 70 percent while its organization and content until the 1930's more closely resembled
the North American system of education than that of any
other Latin American nation. [10]

    The educational system, nevertheless, suffered from
numerous serious defects.   Nelson observed that corruption
and abuse plagued school administration; that required school
attendance rapidly lost its value; that local school boards,
in principle locally elected, ended up being appointed from
Havana, and that because the public education system could
never afford its own buildings, the majority of the classes
were taught in inadequate rented or borrowed facilities. [11]
Perhaps, the most serious problem of all was that the Cuban
educational system clearly failed to meet the educational
needs of the large rural population. [12]   This great majority
of Cubans lived in a poor, underdeveloped world, trailing
centuries behind the rapidly modernizing sector.

    Following the world depression and the social and po-
litical agitation of the 1930's and thereafter, the percentage
of school age children matriculated in public schools fell
from the 1925-1926 level of 63 percent to 35 percent in
1942-1943.   During World War II and the postwar period of
economic recovery, the number of public primary schools
and their graduates increased 80 and 70 percent respectively.
There occurred, also, an emphasis upon the rural schools
under a type of military organization.   But the increase in
overall population and the inattention paid the rural area
during the 30's were counterproductive factors.   Thus, although the proportion of illiterates fell to about 23 percent
in 1953, the matriculation of school-age children in primary
schools was only 36 percent, that is, approximately 10 per-

Table II.   State Cost[a] of Public Education in Cuba, 1902-1966
(in millions of pesos of the current price)

Year[b]	State Budget	Cost of Education	Percentage of State Budget in Education	Cost per capita (in pesos)
1902	17. 5	3. 7	21. 2	2. 01
1906	24. 2	4. 2	17. 4	2. 09
1921	62. 7	10. 4	16. 6	3. 37
1927	81. 0	15. 1	18. 6	4. 90
1940	79. 0	11. 4	14. 4	2. 66
1952	299. 8	58. 2	19. 4	10. 07
1958	382. 0	75. 5	19. 8	11. 53
1962	1, 853. 9	221. 2	11. 9	31. 30
1966	2, 717. 9	272. 3	10. 0	34. 91

[a]The comparisons between prerevolutionary and revolutionary figures can provoke confusion.   In 1902-1958, the dates refer to the cost of the Ministry of Education, excluding the cost of the provinces, cities and special funds, such as those of the universities and private schools.   The dates from 1962 to 1966 include all of the costs of Education.
[b]This refers to the economic year: from the first of July to the following 30th of June.

Sources: Mercedes García Tudurí, "La enseñanza en Cuba en los primeros cincuenta años de independencia, " Historia de la Nación Cubana 10 (La Habana, 1952), "Cuban Economic Research Project, " Study in Cuba (Coral Gables, 1965), and JUCEPLAN, Boletín Estadístico 1966 (Havana, s.f.), p. 20.

cent less than the proportion of the population enrolled when the republic was founded.   Further, the proportion of the secondary school-age population enrolled in 1953 was only 12 percent of the adolescents from 15 to 17 years of age.   Thus, in marked contrast to the leadership position Cuba enjoyed in the 1930's, all but three of the other Latin American countries reported primary school enrollment figures higher than Cuba's during the first years of the 1950's.

The report Informe sobre Cuba, prepared by the World Bank, described public education in the first years of the 50's as being in a state of deterioration.   The report indicated that, although there had been some progress in the development of the secondary school system and some specialized types of schools during the 1940's, the general tendency during the period after the 20's had been one of retrogression. A smaller number of school-age children attended school and the numbers of hours of instruction offered daily had fallen to four and in many districts to only two hours. Only one-half or fewer of the school-age children attended school and of some 180, 000 children who began the first grade, fewer than 5, 000 reached the eighth grade. While apathy and absentism were common among the teachers, administration of the public schools has been described as afflicted by an excessive centralization in the ministry of education in Havana, the absence of continuity due to frequent political changes, lack of professionalism and of any type of civil service system, and a demoralizing tradition of patronage and abuse. [13]

The problem of abuses in school administration reached an all time high during the term of President Grau San Martín (1944-1948), when Minister of Education Aleman, during the period in which he occupied that position, literally robbed millions of dollars of appropriations from the education budget, enabling him very quickly to become one of the richest men in Cuba. [14] His blatant theft of the public funds allocated for education denied the public schools of sorely needed resources. In 1952 and 1958, nearly one-fifth of the state budget was devoted to public education and theoretically, the per capita expenditure was in excess of ten dollars, that is to say, more than double the figure of the golden 20's. At the same time that Cuba was last in line in Latin America in terms of the percentage of school age children enrolled, only two or three Latin American nations "spent" more public funds on education than Cuba.

Cuban teachers benefited from life-time appointment in their roles as public servants and received a full salary, irrespective of their meeting classes or not. Understandably, the appointment of teachers became a major focus of patronage. Appointments were bought at prices ranging from 500 to 2, 000 pesos. The higher prices were paid for appointments as "specialists, " those who received the same salaries as the teachers who taught all subjects but who taught only such subjects as music, art, or English for only two or three hours a week-end, and often this without an adequate knowledge of their specialties. The World Bank report caustically observed, "some specialists were too incompetent to do work such as this and were appointed as inspectors, generally in Havana, where the majority preferred to live. "[15]

It would be difficult to exaggerate the pernicious effect the thefts and patronage practices had on the educational system and the morale of many dedicated teachers. Absenteeism, apathy and social antagonisms, especially in the case of those teachers assigned to rural primary schools (secondary schools were nearly non-existent in rural areas), intensified the already marked differences between urban and rural education. Many Cuban educators have testified most openly on this topic:[16]

> the majority of the teachers and inspectors live in the capital or in an important provincial city. They are late for work every day, and from the moment that they do arrive at their respective schools, they have only one thought: to leave in time to catch the last bus that would take them home. The actual work done by these teachers is worthless and their schools are good for nothing.

Another Cuban writer has said:

> If you catch a train early in the morning from Havana to Matanzas some sixty miles away, you will see getting off at every station along the way, a few well-dressed people. They are teachers who live in Havana and who take the train to work every day. They hate their work, they hate the towns where they teach, they hate their students and they hate their students' families. Whenever they can they say they are sick and don't go. They do everything they can in order to be transferred to Havana.

A distinguished Cuban with an intimate knowledge of Cuban schools dating back to the first day of the republic, has spoken of the qualitative decline of public schools as compared to private schools in the 1940's and 1950's:

> All of my children attended public schools. I knew the schools and the teachers, and I knew that the public schools were better than the private ones. But none of my grandchildren goes to a public school, even though some of their mothers are teachers in those schools. The reason for this is that they know and I know that the public schools today are worthless.

The quantitative and qualitative decline of Cuban education
during the pre-revolutionary decades can be attributed not
only to the sharp fluctuations in earning from sugar, the influence of dictators, abuse, patronage, and political unrest,
but also to the social class differentiation which followed independence. With the increase in urbanization and commercial activity, Cuban society had gradually changed, until by
the 1950's the transformation from the essentially dualistic
social structure of the colonial period had arrived at a tri-
partite hierarchy: an elite, composed of plantation owners,
businessmen, some prosperous professionals, politicians,
and tradesmen; a middle stratum, composed of nearly all of
the professionals, skilled workers, administrative personnel,
small landowners, and military officers; and the lowest stratum, consisting of unskilled urban workers, the rural proletariat, peasants, and the unemployed.

Paralleling the rise of new social groups, the educational system became differentiated also and established an
educational hierarchy with schools serving each level. The
elite group, for example, continued educating their children
in private elitist schools, or abroad, generally in the United
States. The growing middle sector, from which were re-
cruited the major portion of the teachers and administrators
for the public rural and urban schools, in most cases transferred their children to private schools after the period of
the 1930's and the entry of larger and larger numbers of
working class children into the public educational system.
In 1939, private secondary schools were "incorporated" into
the public system and in 1950 the establishment of private
universities was approved.

Table I demonstrates that the number of private primary schools nearly doubled between 1939 and 1958, nearly
tripling their enrollments in the same period. Before the
1950's there had been only a single university and it was
public. In 1955, there were seven, four of which were private. Political agitation and violence in public primary and
secondary schools and in the university were also important
causes for the expansion of private schools. On the eve of
the Cuban revolution, approximately 15 percent of total primary level enrollments, 25 percent of secondary enrollments
and 20 percent of university enrollments were in private institutions. The rapid growth of private schools, many of
which were neither authorized nor registered by the Ministry
of Education, reflected a much increased demand on the part
of the middle sector for an education that was oriented toward

the preparation of elites and was therefore more prestigious.
All over the island, many middle-sector families with modest
incomes saved diligently in order to send their children to
private schools. [17] In the lowest stratum, the majority of
the urban proletariat sent their children to urban public
schools, while the children of the rural proletariat and similar groups attended the very inferior rural public schools
or received no schooling at all.

In other words, the pre-revolutionary Cuban educational system provided educational opportunities which were
tremendously unequal for its clientel according to their socio-
economic level and place of residence.   The system intensified rural-urban differences, inculcated the values of the upper class and engendered patently unrealistic aspirations for
the great majority of Cuban children and prepared very little
by way of human resources for national development.   In
reference to this problem the report of the World Bank
noted, "unless Cuba significantly improves its educational
system in the near future it is impossible to be optimistic
regarding the probability of successful economic development. "[18]

One needs to add further that considering the upper-
class values dominant in Cuban public schools in 1958 the
possibilities of social and political development from the educational system were disheartening.   In fact, the primary
function of education was to maintain the status quo in a
grotesquely maldeveloped society economically dependent on
the United States.   Education was divorced from day-to-day
needs and rooted in transcendental values that reinforced the
tradition of the speculative philosopher and man of letters.
It reinforced the belief in personalism, the strength of family
ties, and the importance of hierarchy.   The system of education in Cuba during the last years of the 1950's, to para-
phrase Rudolph Atcon, had become in fragmented microcosm
an accurate reflection of the fragmented macrocosm of the
overall society.

Innovations During the Revolution

Even before the revolutionary forces had come to
power, the central role that formal education would play in
the creation of a new and more just society had been
stressed by Castro.   He strongly criticized the existence of
private schools which, he said, discriminated according to

social class and represented commercial exploitation. He
strongly criticized education--and with reason--as being ver-
balistic, intellectually false, nonscientific, disassociated from
real life, and perpetuating an open divorce between theory
and practice. He underlined, also, the limited capacity of
education alone to contribute to economic development and,
especially, how links with North American interests gave the
school system a neocolonial appearance. [19] In his famous
"History Will Absolve Me" speech six years prior to coming
to power, Castro declared that a revolutionary government
would undertake the integral reform of the Cuban educational
system for the purpose of eliminating these deficiencies and
accelerating the creation of a new society. [20]

In keeping with this policy, when the revolutionary
forces were victorious in January of 1959, high priority was
given to intensive educational programs, in order to carry
the socio-political and educational revolution to the traditionally ignored rural areas and to the urban lower-class neigh-
borhoods and slums. During the first year the government
built more than 3, 000 new public schools and 7, 000 new
teachers entered the classroom to teach more than 300, 000
children who attended school for the first time. Such educational expansion was only possible thanks to the raised level
of efficiency of the existing school system and the recruitment of young volunteer teachers, such as the "Frank Pais"
Brigade, that taught in the most remote mountainous regions,
regions which in 1957-1958 had supported the revolutionary
forces.

No matter what opinion one may have of Castro and
his revolution, the quantitative achievements of Cuban education during the last decade are impressive. Between 1957
and 1968 the number of public primary and secondary schools
nearly doubled, greatly improving the accessability of schooling in rural areas. The number of teachers tripled and the
number of hours of annual instructions doubled. Primary
school enrollments doubled and secondary school enrollments
tripled. In the 1958-1966 period state expenditures for education nearly quadrupled and expenditures per capita more
than tripled. Even taking into account the influence of such
factors as the incorporation of private schools into the public
system (which resulted in an impressive statistical increase
in 1962 without a de facto increase in educational services
available) and rising inflation, there is no doubt but that the
increases have been substantial. The Ministry of Education
states with pride that "no Cuban child lacks education today,"

and that "attendance is reflected in the following figures:
93 percent (of the school-age children) attend primary school
and 95 percent attend secondary school."[21] In 1968 some
240,000 complete scholarships were granted which have
greatly facilitated this expansion. Also, pre-school education,
special education for handicapped children and school health
programs have been expanded in an impressive manner.

Differences in access to educational services according to earning power have been largely eliminated. Many
military facilities and homes of upper- and middle-class
families that fled from the revolution have been utilized for
educational purposes. All the government private schools
were nationalized on 6 July 1961 soon after the unsuccessful
mercenary invasion of Playa Girón (Bay of Pigs). In re-
viewing these educational changes produced during the first
years of the revolution, Jolly has observed (a) that great
value has been vested in a series of formal and non-formal
educational programs as both a basic item of current expense and as a basic investment for economic development;
(b) that the large-scale exodus of technically qualified refu-
gees, along with the imperative to rapidly industrialize by
1964, created a high priority for technical education programs; (c) that the inequities, privileges and distinctions engendered by the pre-revolutionary society were attacked and
insofar as possible eliminated by the new system of education, especially by the means of nationalizing the private
schools; and (d) that the introduction of a new political culture brought with it a heavy ideological content to education,
the need to teach Cuba's variation of Marxism-Leninism.[22]

During the first revolutionary decade--especially after
1964--the educational objectives adopted by the government
gradually became more concrete, creating specific programs
in schools designed to achieve certain operational objectives.
The dual objectives of adult literacy and participation of
youth in the voluntary task of rural development were both
served by the "National Literacy Campaign" of 1961. More
than 100,000 students and volunteer workers lived with rural
families for six months teaching the value of literacy and of
the revolution, and apparently illiteracy (of the population
over ten years of age) was reduced from 23.6 percent in
1953 to 3.9 percent in 1961.[23]

Continuing this massive adult education enterprise,
the government launched the "Battle of the Sixth Grade, "
designed to raise the level of education of more than

700,000 adults, made literate during the "Year of Education" in 1961. This worker-peasant program has enrolled since that time more than half a million adults annually. More than one-third of a million have already received their sixth-grade certificate. [24]

Involving students in productive work while they continue their formal studies has been achieved via the establishment of various programs. The most important is the "Schools to the Countryside" program which enables youth to gain "revolutionary experience" and contribute to rural development. When initiated in the 1965-1966 school year, over 20,000 students volunteered for productive activities in agriculture such as harvesting coffee, planting fruit trees and occupying themselves in other socially and economically useful tasks. In 1966-1967 some 140,000 students participated; in 1967-1968 some 160,000, and in 1970 the major portion of the secondary school population of all the provinces participated part-time in some agricultural activity. [25] The recent "Countryside School" program seeks to place all junior high schools in rural areas and directly involve all youth in agricultural production. To date only seven or eight of these expensive boarding schools have been constructed.

The need to prepare more technically qualified students to work in areas of agricultural and industrial development has led to the creation of numerous special programs for technical and professional education. For example, during the past decade the Cuban government has founded 13 industrial-technological institutes for the preparation of paraprofessionals in 33 areas of engineering specialization. Forty-five technical institutes have been created for the preparation of skilled workers and agricultural technicians, and various fishing schools have been developed to prepare skilled workers for the new and rapidly growing fishing fleet.

In the interest of integrating school and labor experience, the so-called "Six by Six" program strives to increase, via the application of technical-educative concepts, the specialization of middle-level technicians and skilled workers in productive industries and service sector enterprises. After a brief period of technical training, students alternate six months of work in industry with six months studying in school. The program began with more than 8,000 students in 1966-1967, but, without explanation, the number of participants fell to only some 300 the following year. [26]

The "Minimum Technician" program, begun in 1962, intends to provide industrial, agricultural and commercial workers some minimum technical knowledge of their work and of the machinery being used. Classes are held at the work cite and they strive to increase worker productivity and responsibility by explaining to the workers how their contribution affects the entire process of production. During the first years of the revolution special instructional programs were created to serve large numbers of prostitutes and maids (many of whose employers had fled the nation) by providing them with new skills which would permit them to dedicate themselves to new more ideologically acceptable occupations. [27] The Ministry of Armed Forces established a section of technical education in the latter part of 1963. Enrollment in this program increased from 4,115 in 1964 to 32,966 in 1968. [28]

The highest priority has been given to a new campaign to raise the educational level of school teachers, as a means of increasing effectiveness or expertise in various sectors of the system. On 16 February 1970 there appeared in _Granma_ a long and detailed official announcement of the "Teacher Certification Plan." It presents the objective and the means to certify 26,031 primary and secondary school teachers, this being nearly 40 percent of the current teaching population. The objectives of the plan, which seems to reflect a kind of the-return-of-John-Dewey, are to prepare:

> (a) teachers who understand the essence of the educational process and are capable of controlling the process, (b) teachers who master the subject matter which they teach, and (c) teachers who are capable of teaching children how to understand and not [just] memorize encyclopedic facts. [29]

Cuban universities have also been seen to have undergone marked alterations via significant university reform. Coming with the nationalization of private schools, the earlier established seven universities were concentrated into three: one for the Western part of the Island (University of Havana), one for the central part (University of the Villas), and the third for the Eastern part (University of Oriente). New departments, schools and chairs have been created and others have been eliminated or reorganized. Lifetime appointments have been terminated. The university

Table III.   Percentages of University Registration by Discipline in Cuba, 1959-1967[a]

Year[b]	Humanities[c]	Law	Education	Social Sciences[d]	Natural Sciences[e]	Engineering Architecture	Medical Sciences	Agricultural Sciences[f]
1959	4.3	11.2	19.7	25.3	6.3	13.0	15.5	4.7
1961	3.1	3.9	18.5	21.8	3.7	25.4	19.2	4.3
1963	3.0	1.7	15.4	25.3	6.2	21.0	23.1	4.3
1965	2.5	1.4	24.4	13.1	6.6	24.0	22.8	5.2
1967	2.1	0.8	26.0	7.1	9.5	23.7	20.8	10.0

[a] Does not include registration in the Preparatory Faculty Field-Work.
[b] The school year begins in September and ends in the following June.
[c] Philosophy and literature.
[d] Principally economics (commerce in 1959), political science, history and sociology.
[e] Mathematics, physics, chemistry, biology, geology, pharmacy, psychology and geography.
[f] Agronomy, veterinary and animal care.

Source: Computations based on approximate data from JUCEPLAN, Compendio Estadístico de Cuba, 1968 (Havana, 1968), p. 34-35.

has been made more open than before, by means of a notable
broadening of the admissions policy. University enrollment
decreased in the first years of the revolution, but by 1968 it
had passed the 1958 level by 2, 000 students. The number of
professors, in contrast, quadrupled (see Table I).

Further, the basic philosophy of higher education has
undergone a genuine revolution. While the traditional, pre-
revolutionary university was essentially divorced from national development and placed emphasis upon humanistic, legal
and social science careers, the current university is linked
to national human resources needs. (According to the 1953
census, the number of lawyers was greater than the combined
total of engineers, agronomists, veterinarians and teachers
with university diplomas.) A comparison of the shift in enrollments to key areas of study between 1959 and 1967, as
presented in Table III, offers proof of this reorientation.
The proportion of enrollees matriculated in humanities and
law, for example, has decreased from 15. 5 to 2. 9 percent,
while that of engineering, natural sciences and agriculture
has increased from 24 to 43. 2 percent. There has also
been recorded a notable increase in matriculation in medical
science and education. Table III reflects the overall strategy
of change for Cuban development. While the emphasis was
on industrialization (1959-1963), the most noticeable increase
in matriculations was in engineering, while in agricultural
sciences there was a relative decline. When the shift in
emphasis moved to agriculture, the decline in engineering
enrollments was overtaken by an increase in agricultural
sciences. In social sciences we see that, in 1959, the
school of business (which would later become economics) received a goodly number of students, in fact 95 percent of the
total, while in 1967 the proportion had fallen to 70 percent
(with only one-fifth of the magnitude of the 1959 enrollment
total). The separation on the part of the Cuban structure
from the private enterprise system has resulted in considerable pressure to eliminate the professional careers of public
accountancy and business, which explains the decline in enrollments in economics. [30] At the same time, there have
been modest increases in enrollments in history, sociology
and political science.

An important innovation at the university level is the
Worker-Peasant Preparatory School, which is designed to
link agriculture, industry and higher education. The purpose
of the program is to prepare industrial workers and peasants
between the ages 18 and 40 for university study. After a

number of years of preparatory courses in the universities,
candidates begin regular courses of study. Matriculation in
this particularly innovative program increased from 85 students in 1959-1960 to 8,156 in 1967-1968. [31]

Current Trends

During the last decade, the intent of putting into practice and consolidating the revolution in and through educational
activities has created what Cuban leaders call an "authentic educational state." Educational leaders point out that the revolution has been the principal source of motivation for innovation and change in education and also has constituted the
ideologically major instructional message. The constant
strengthening of the ideological code via educational effort--
be it in the school, the factories, or the fields--as the nucleus for the creation of material abundance and the social
consciousness required by the societal striving toward the
communist ideal, is perhaps the most outstanding characteristic of the Cuban educational revolution.

The bedrock of ideological emphasis on education un-
derlies priorities on modern science and technology as key
elements in the raising of agricultural and industrial productivity. This emphasis permeates not only the directives affecting vocational education, but also formal educational programs in which a raised level of appreciation of the role of
science and technology in the process of development is
taught. The entire educational system is guided by a basic
interest in producing students that know how to think, that
understand the use of the scientific method as a means of
solving problems, and that comprehend "how" things function.
Castro has raised the question, "What role can the scientifically literate man, the technologically literate man play in
the community of the future?"[32] For anyone familiar with
the general Latin American preference for more traditional,
fatalistic, and mystical ways of knowing, this emphasis on
empiricism and science represents a genuine epistemological
revolution.

Another theme which is constantly repeated is the
great importance which leaders of the revolution ascribe to
the work ethic. Work, according to Che Guevara, brings
out the best in a man. Castro says that work is youth's
best teacher. Cuban education reflects a belief in moral
and ideological growth for youth arising from their partici-

pation in socially useful work.   They say that young people
grow and develop, as well as the nation, when they are involved in work; manual tasks are especially emphasized in
this respect.   Further, the objectives of the educational system to change traditional Latin American values regarding
the dignity of physical labor and the individual's range of
responsibility to the society at large, are extremely revolutionary.

The importance given to equality in the educational
system is increasingly evident.   Every year the government
enthusiastically supports increasing numbers of students.
Opportunities to continue studying are now almost entirely
based upon ideological attainment and scholastic achievement,
while socio-economic criteria used to be preëminent in the
process of educational selection.   The symbols of special
privileges in school and in the society at large are being
submerged by an omnipresent emphasis on the social equality
of the common man.   The socialization of the means of production and of property, as well as the elimination of enormous inequities in the distribution of wealth, are concrete
evidence of the decision of the government to radically modify the relations between those who own property and those
who are without it.   Unfortunately we lack data on efforts
directed toward social responsibility and their efficacy in
replacing individual and familial orientations or on the effectiveness of educational activities in achieving this basic
value reorientation.

Another constant theme in revolutionary Cuban education is its instrumental emphasis on mobilization of the population.   The literacy campaign, especially with its brigades,
literacy army, battalions, marches and such, has the aura
and rhetoric of a classical military offensive.   Other mo-
bilizing efforts such as the "Peasant Schools" campaign have
similar military overtones.   The campaigns are generally
considered to be powerful motivating and socializing experiences that serve to reinforce personal understanding of and
identification with the revolutionary effort.

There is no doubt as to the very considerable progress
achieved by the revolution in the area of Cuban education.
Nevertheless, this does not mean that there are not serious
problems that continue to limit the achievement of educational objectives and, in various ways, circumscribe the impact
of education in the overall process of change.   Apparently
the system contains a number of inherent contradictions that

may engender antagonisms and create problems.

Possibly the most serious educational quandaries are
the problems of quality and motivation.   The emphasis on
the right of all children to receive an education and of all
adults to read and write at a sixth-grade level was established during the first years of the revolution.   These programs were developed much more rapidly than the growth of
the teacher supply and other facilities.   The exodus of thousands of teachers made the teacher shortage all the more
severe.   The nationalization of the private educational sector,
the confiscation of the homes of exiles, and above all the intensive teacher certification program, as well as the use of
volunteer teachers, served to fill the need.   But in many
cases educational standards declined, particularly in terms
of the knowledge and economic potential of school graduates.
Educational attainment vis-à-vis formal schooling also probably suffered because of the extensive participation of students in mobilization programs which took them out of school
to engage in agricultural work for long periods.

It is not yet known in what way higher education can
structure its programs to incorporate the philosophic intent
of the Worker-Peasant Preparatory School, which introduces
industrial workers and peasants to the university.   Neither
does it appear that educational planners have the capacity to
resolve the more general quandary arising out of the goal of
developing a high level of scientific and technological compe-
tency without creating a new privileged scientific and technological elite, as has occurred in the U.S.S.R. and Eastern
Europe.   In this respect, the People's Republic of China requires that education be both "red" and "expert," that is to
say, education must teach ideological orthodoxy as well as
technological sophistication.   But both the Chinese and the
Cubans are finding that it is very difficult to pursue both
these objectives simultaneously in a balanced and rational
way.

The importance placed on ideological orthodoxy has
possibly had negative effects upon scientific research, diversity of thought and ideas, and open access to higher education.   Elizabeth Sutherland says, "The Revolution seemed to
expect that new men with creative, nonconformist mentalities
would arise from an educational experience which was not
nonconformist."[33]   The mobilizing-military model offered to
Cuban youth seems to have provided excellent results in
terms of discipline, community solidarity and commitment

to national objectives, but it is very possibly an obstacle to the development of initiative and originality in the search for alternative solutions to complex problems.

Ideological orthodoxy has also been a disuasive factor for the politically noncommitted students who wished to pursue advanced studies. As Sutherland points out, there is a shortage of production experts,

> but some promising students have not been considered sufficiently prorevolutionary to receive instruction. They have been denied admission as students to the university for this reason. Is it that Cuban development does not need their knowledge more than their political loyalty?[34]

All of the scholarships granted by the Ministry of Education to study abroad (with the exception of those to Mexico prior to 1965) are to study in socialist nations, principally the U.S.S.R. and East Germany. Scholarships to Yugoslavia were completely terminated in 1967 and those to Czechoslovakia were reduced from 296 in 1963-1964 to 72 in 1968-1969.[35] Thus, the Cuban student educated abroad has nearly no possibility to encounter divergent points of view, not even within the socialist camp.

Another constant obstacle to the revolutionary educational programs resides in the widespread resistance to cultural change. In spite of the slogans, the activities, and many revolutionary changes, Cubans have not been wont in a single decade to completely overcome, either individually or collectively, the weight of precedent. As Richard Fagen has noted, one of the lessons of development which the Cubans have had most to learn is that cultural systems have a great deal of inertia and tenaciously resist change.[36] And when the changes desired represent nearly a complete break with the traditional modes of learning--modes established within the context of the traditional value system, world view and cultural organization--as has occurred in Cuba--the persistance of older values and behavior patterns, even among the most revolutionary Cubans, becomes a serious problem not yet fully understood. For example, more than 500,000 Cubans, the majority from the upper and middle classes, have preferred to flee their country rather than accept the new system of values. Although many Cubans who were raised in the pre-revolutionary society have become loyal citizens of the new state, the children raised within the revolutionary

ambience which only now is beginning to take shape are the
only ones considered sufficiently pure and uncorrupted by
egotism, capitalism and elitism to become the new "whole
man," the true communist.

The Cuban educational strategy for the 1970's, as it
was described in the 1968 UNESCO national report on education, calls for a continuing dual emphasis on ideology and
technology in which education will be at once red and expert.
Castro explains this strategy in the following way:

> No social revolution can achieve socialism without
> a technological revolution ... nor can it achieve
> communism solely through the achievement of
> abundance. Communism can only be reached through
> the achievement of education and abundance. Abun-
> dance can not be achieved without technology and
> technology can not be achieved without widespread
> popular education. [37]

Another theme which constantly arises is the necessity
for greater unity between the school and society and between
theory and practice. As Castro has observed, Cuba today
is "a great school." According to the UNESCO Cuba report,
Castro states that the sphere of activity of the schools will
be extended in the future and they will be more closely
linked to everyday life, in order that all of the environment
will be studied and will become educative. The UNESCO
Cuba report predicts also that the time will soon come when
today's extracurricular activities will constitute a part of
scholastic activities and the boundaries between the two will
disappear. Further, it states that by combining physical and
intellectual labor every citizen will be capable, with the aid
of technology, of performing both manual and intellectual
tasks.

The government also declares that in 1975 all children
and youth will receive not only free education and books, but
also food and clothing. Compulsory attendance at general and
polytechnical schools shall be extended to include the basic
secondary level of education. Enrollments in higher education will increase rapidly and universities will be decentralized with branches in rural, industrial, research and productive enterprizes of the nation. Adult education will continue
to be emphasized via the "Battle of the Sixth Grade" until
all of the educational deficits of the preceding regime have
been eliminated and all of the citizens possess the minimum

level of knowledge necessary to participate successfully in
the technical advance of industry and agriculture.

It is extremely difficult to assess the degree to which
the Cuban educational revolution has attained its partly utopian goals.   It is clear that education has played a central
role in the replacing of the old elitist and hierarchical society with a new social order committed to egalitarianism
and development.   Nevertheless, what the effectiveness of the
schools has been in the change of attitudes, especially of
basic values, and in promoting appropriate behavior, we do
not know and will have to wait to know until extensive research into this area has been conducted and published.

We do know however that while Cuba strives to lay
the foundations for the communist millenium through nation-
wide mobilization, popular education, and other tactics rooted
in the revolutionary model, the educational system daily becomes more functional as an instrument of national development.   If we compare it to the objectives of the Alliance for
Progress' strategy for educational reform in Latin America--
that is, the elimination of illiteracy, the reduction of the
drop-out rate, and the increase of technical education, administrative efficiency, and improved scientific and rural ed-
ucation--it is evident that Cuba is among the vanguard of
Latin American nations vis-à-vis the successful implementa-
tions of these necessary reform measures.   Cuba is in addition the only Latin American nation in which the privileged
elites and the system of values which maintained them have
been eliminated as an essential requisite to economic development, socio-cultural integration and educational reform.

In conclusion, we might note Lambros Comitas' observation that in any social system, educational institutions
have two principal functions: to maintain and strengthen the
existing social order and, more rarely, to promote and insure the rebuilding of culture and society by means of the
deliberate introduction of a type of education substantially
different from the one made available to the preceding generation. [38] Cuban education before 1959 was clearly conse-
crated to the first function, that is, the maintenance of the
status quo.   Since 1959, the educational system, in its efforts to reform and change the values of society, has presented an example of the second revolutionary function.   Evi-
dently an authentic social revolution requires the development of a new educational system which will aid in building
the new society and act as a safeguard against the possible

collapse of the new system and the rejection of the revolutionary values.

As Cuba ends its 13th year of revolutionary change and Cuban education begins to move from its revolutionary function to that of maintaining the new social order, other nations of the "Third World," and especially those of Latin America, continue watching Cuba and its promise of rapid and complete socio-cultural and economic reform. Although "Fidelismo" and the Cuban model are possibly unique; there is no doubt but that Cuba has undergone a profound transformation, and that both formal and non-formal educational activities have become increasingly crucial in attempts to forge a radically new status quo. [39]

Notes

1. National Mission of UNESCO, Cuba, Educación y Cultura, Havana, 1963; Ministry of Education, Informe a la XXIX Conferencia Internacional de Instrucción Pública (called by the OIE and UNESCO, Ginebra, 1966), Havana, 1966; and Ministry of Education, Informe a la XXXI Conferencia Internacional de Instrucción Pública (called by the OIE and UNESCO), Havana, 1968.

2. This work is commented upon in "Estratificación social, poder y organización educacional," Rolland G. Paulston, Aportes No. 16 (April 1970), p. 91-111.

3. Cited in Elites in Latin America, Seymour Lipset and Aldo Solari, eds., New York, 1967, p. 19.

4. See a description of the educational development during the pre-revolutionary period in "La enseñanza en Cuba en los primeros cincuenta años de independencia," Mercedes García Tudurí, Historia de la Nación Cubana, Pérez Cabrera Remos y Santovenia, eds., vol. 10, Havana, 1952.

5. Cited in Life of William McKinley, Charles S. Olcott, New York, 1916, p. 196.

6. Cited in Prelude to Point Four: American Technical Missions Overseas, 1838-1938, Merle Curti and Kendall Birr, Madison, Wis., 1954, p. 83.

7. Ibid., p. 90-92.

8. Foreign Policy Association, Commission on Cuban Affairs, Problems of the New Cuba, New York, 1935, p. 138.

9. García Tudurí, Mercedes, "Resumen de la historia de la educación en Cuba: su evaluación, problemas y soluciones del futuro," Temática cubana: Primera Reunión de Estudios Cubanos, New York, 1970, p. 108-142.

10. See Our Cuban Colony: A Study in Sugar, Leland H. Jenks, New York, 1928; Rural Cuba, Lowry Nelson, Minneapolis, 1950, p. 61, 186, 235, and 239-244; and The Crime of Cuba, Carleton Beals, New York 1933, p. 281, 294 and 297. See also the chapter by Richard Jolly, "Education: Pre-Revolutionary Background," in Cuba: The Economic and Social Revolution, Dudley Seers, ed., Chapel Hill, N.C., 1964.

11. Nelson: Rural Cuba, p. 61, 186.

12. Foreign Policy Association, Problems of Cuba, p. 130-131, 134.

13. International Bank for Reconstruction and Development, Economic and Technical Mission in Cuba, Informe sobre Cuba, Baltimore, 1952, p. 404.

14. Personal information received from Carmelo Mesa-Lago, May 1970.

15. Informe sobre Cuba, p. 426.

16. Ibid., p. 414-429.

17. Ibid., p. 414.

18. Ibid., p. 434-35.

19. Revolución, September 7, 1961, p. 6.

20. Castro, Fidel, La historia me absolverá, Havana, 1961, p. 60-71.

21. Ministry of Education, Informe a la XXXI Conferencia,
     p. 157.

22. Jolly, "Education" [see note 10].

23. See the objective evaluations of the impact of the cam-
     paign in the information of the experts of UNESCO
     Anna Lorenzetto and Karl Neys in Report on the
     Method and Means Utilized in Cuba to Eliminate Il-
     literacy, Ministry of Education, Havana, 1965,
     p. 17-18, and in the Spanish version of UNESCO,
     p. 53-128. The multiple role of the literacy cam-
     paign, the massive mobilization, the internalization
     of new values, etc., is broadly covered by Richard
     R. Fagen in The Transformation of Political Culture
     in Cuba, Stanford, Cal., 1969, chapter 3.

24. Ministry of Education, Informe a la XXXI Conferencia,
     p. 165.

25. See Report on the Method and Means, Ministry of Edu-
     cation; The Youngest Revolution, Elizabeth Suther-
     land, New York, 1969; "Student Power in Action, "
     Arlie Hochschild, Trans-action No. 6 (April 1969),
     p. 16-21; "Cuba Report, " José Yglesias, The New
     York Times Magazine, January 12, 1968, and
     " 'Column' of 40, 000 Aids Cuban Farms; An Army
     of Young People is Deployed in Camagüey, " The
     New York Times, April 26, 1970.

26. Ministry of Education, Informe a la XXXI Conferencia,
     p. 167.

27. Jolly, "Education, " p. 209-19 [see note 10].

28. JUCEPLAN, Compendio Estadístico de Cuba, 1968, Ha-
     vana, 1968, p. 40.

29. "Directivas del MINDED sobre el plan de titulación de
     maestros, " Granma, February 16, 1970.

30. Lataste, Albán, Cuba: ¿hacia una neuva economía po-
     litica del socialismo? Santiago, Chile, 1968, p. 20.

31. JUCEPLAN, Compendio Estadistico de Cuba, 1968,
     p. 34-35.

32. Castro, Fidel, Discurso a la sesión final de los sindi-
    catos obreros cubanos, August 30, 1966, Havana,
    1966.

33. Sutherland, Youngest Revolution, p. 129.

34. Ibid., p. 136. See also University Students and Revo-
    lution in Cuba, Jaime Suchlicki, Coral Gables, Fla.,
    1969.

35. JUCEPLAN, Compendio Estadístico de Cuba, 1968,
    p. 39.

36. Fagen, Transformation of Culture, p. 147-52.

37. Ministry of Education, Informe a la XXXI Conferencia,
    p. 165.

38. Comitas, Lambros, "Education and Social Stratification
    in Contemporary Bolivia," Transactions of the New
    York Academy of Sciences, 2nd ser. 29, No. 7
    (May 1967), p. 935-948.

39. See "Revolution: For Internal Consumption Only,"
    Richard R. Fagen, Transaction No. 6 (April 1969),
    p. 10-15.

13. RURAL PRIMARY SCHOOLS IN PARAGUAY
Paraguayan Ministry of Education and Culture

One of the main targets of most Latin American educational systems is the extension of primary schools to all
grade levels in order to make available a complete elementary education for all youth.   Presently most countries have
this universal primary education as a law, but few education
ministries in Latin America have yet been able to attain this
goal.   In the larger cities and urban centers the transportation problem is less acute.   But in the rural areas--where
only footpaths connect large areas and where swollen rainy-
season rivers often divide sections--children must walk miles
to reach a school.   And the pressure of family farm work
is so strong that parents discourage more than a few years
of schooling.

The result is that rural schools frequently end after
first, second or third grade.   Thus, even the students who
may want to continue have no opportunity.   This eliminates
the practical application of universal primary education.
Recognizing this problem, the Ministry of Education and Culture in Paraguay has been working to meet its responsibility
of extending complete primary schooling in the rural areas
since 1965 with a unique plan for the gradual changeover.

This task implies the elimination of the numerous
rural schools staffed by only one or two teachers and, as a
consequence, the restructuring of the system along the lines
of two fundamental types of school organizations: the complete unit of a single teacher, and the multi-teacher primary
school of six teachers.   The complete primary school will
eventually include no more than 40 children.   In the initial
phases, complete primary schools will consist of: (1) two
teachers for 40 to 70 children; (2) three teachers for 70 to
100 children; (3) four teachers for 100 to 130 children;
(4) five teachers for 130 to 160 children; and (5) complete
graded schools of six teachers and 160 or more children.

The educational system itself should be considered as a criterion of development and the unitary school is the initial stage, the point of departure for a process of constant change. In this way the intention is to develop not only a dynamic and flexible system but a practical and functional one. The objectives identified require planning and continuity. Their importance and their implication for the strengthening of the educational level of the citizenry are such that they constitute a central role in the plans for the socio-economic development of Paraguay. The success realized in the implementation of these objectives will facilitate not only the implementation of the Constitutional guarantee to all of the inhabitants of the Republic of the right to receive an education but also the more efficacious and productive investment of the funds authorized for this purpose. Efforts are now being concentrated upon the technical improvement of the one-room schools and the functioning of more and better multi-classroom schools. This effort focuses upon in-service training of currently working teachers, and the preparation of future teachers and school administrators.

Basic Principles of the Unitary School

The unitary rural school "is a one-teacher school that serves a student group and seeks the extension and the perfection of this effort, thus fostering the development of the entire community."[1] Therefore, the unitary school, through its goals, its socio-economic conditions and the distinctive characteristics of its operational and organizational structure, permits and demands the application of certain basic modern educational principles:

(1) Educational realism is a process that begins in reality, in life, but does not remain there. Through the process of abstraction and generalization, the student arrives at the concept and applies it for the betterment of the quality of life in the community.

(2) Teaching to the nature of the child in a unitary school permits the teacher to structure learning groups on the basis of individual student abilities, and to develop their progress in accordance with their achievement and capacities. This educational continuity permits the child continuous advancement while neither repeating subject areas nor failing.

(3) The activity principle recognizes the essentially active character of learning and the educational value of pur-

poseful work.   The teacher directs and orients the student
only as necessary.

(4) The principle of intuition reaffirms the value of
intuition as the basis for all our knowledge.   Teach things
for their own sake; it is better to learn that which one sees
than that which one hears, and better also than that which
one does.   It is recognized that intuition motivates knowledge
as the first step and that this knowledge needs to be extended
thereafter by our cognitive capacities.   The process runs
from the concrete to the semi-concrete to the abstract: first
the event, later its representation and, finally, the verbal
expression of the ideas.
(5) The consolidation of educational output is a social
responsibility and obligation.   The evaluation of educational
output of the child is constant; the teacher maintains a daily
individualized check of his pupils' learning.   In this way, the
teacher helps maximize student potential and insures continuous progress.
(6) The prediction and planning principle refers to the
necessity for forward-looking educational policies, "capable
of accelerating educational development, of articulating it
with the general need for the development of nations and of
imprinting the actions of educational administrators with direction, coherence and continuity."[2]   The work of the unitary
school is not conceived without detailed planning of all its
activities.   Given the circumstances of having to work with
children of differing ages and levels of instruction, it is indispensable for the teacher to elaborate an annual plan,
weekly plans and an overall guide.

On the other hand, the unitary school is the vital
component, the cultural center of the community, and the
reason for providing integral and realistically relevant school
activities that should be linked with the community's objectives for socio-economic development.   These objectives
might best be described as the following: (1) acquisition of
knowledge; (2) development of reflective thought through the
teaching of problem solving and the nurturing of the child's
reflective powers; (3) cultivation of useful activities: social
graces, cooperative work habits and, ultimately, the acquisition of habits and abilities; and (4) understanding of the
phenomena of culture and its importance in human, economic
and social development.

Characteristics of The Unitary School Program

The success of the task of creating complete primary
schools in rural areas includes, among its multiple implications, problems concerning the revision of school plans and
programs and the reform of the evaluative and promotion
systems as they affect students.   The transcendental enor-
mity that these two problem areas have for extension of primary teaching is evident.

In light of the above, the task force of specialists in
the textbook production section of the Department of Psychopedagogical Research in Paraguay was charged with developing a curriculum project for the unitary schools appropriate
to the spirit, organizational characteristics and operating
style of this type of school.   The proposed project was presented and subjected to analysis at the seminar on "Complete
Schools in Rural Areas" held in Asunción in 1968.

The unitary schools are organized along the same
lines as the graduated schools, that is, on a year-by-year
basis.   This multi-group is directed by a single teacher,
who should have a basic psychological understanding of Paraguayan school children and cultural understanding of her region of this developing nation, in order to interpret social
and economic changes and progress.

The selection of the content of the curriculum is
rooted in the proposition that there exists a minimum of
knowledge necessary in a given society without which life in
that society can not operate.   This minimum is incorporated
in the basic activities developed and knowledge transmitted
which shall aid the child in acquiring habits and developing
understanding, skills, attitudes and values within the limits
of individual capacities.

The program was further elaborated with well defined
short-range objectives.   However, these were based on the
following requirements and characteristics of the total school
program: (1) to be subordinated to educational objectives;
(2) to be open-ended in order to provide the capacity for
modifications, additions and substitutions appropriate to exigencies of time and place; (3) to be flexible, in order to accommodate the range of individual capacities to be found in
the local and school communities; (4) to be continuous in
order to provide an unbroken continuity based upon the recognition of education as a gradual process of growth; (6) to be

integrative in order to avoid an artificial fragmentation of knowledge; and (7) to be functional in order to provide for the actual necessities of the children and the community.

The unitary school teachers will direct a single academic program and three instrumental disciplines (idiomatic language, arithmetic and geometry) with special attention to the basic objectives that have been cited above. The second responsibility shall be to group the students by sections and levels on the basis of their school achievement and accommodation to the various subject matters. The sections shall be basic, intermediate, and advanced.

The basic section shall consist of children who have not yet learned to read and write. This section shall work with the teacher during the majority of the time and shall be integrated to the intermediate section during certain activities and time periods, in order to familiarize them with the children in the other ability groups and thereby facilitate their socialization. The intermediate section will consist of children of average achievement levels and the advanced section will consist of the most advanced achievers. Direct observation, past educational experience and a detailed exploration of the mental maturity and level of instruction of each child, shall be the means for grouping students.

The collaboration of the most advanced students with leadership characteristics is always necessary and useful in working with different groups and is most important in the unitary school. The contribution of the leader shall not exactly consist of teaching the younger and lesser advanced, but to help them to understand instructions and directions for self-instruction be it oral or written, while the teacher is otherwise occupied with some other group in the class.

Self-Instruction

Self-instruction is that work that each section, level or student will pursue independent of the teacher's presence, guided by oral or written instructions. The objectives of this work may be short and/or long range. The first are designed to advance the students' constructive use of leisure time, and the second to the acquisition of work attitudes and habits.

The self-instruction may take the following forms:

(1) Participation in individual activity by everyone in a group
on the basis of oral or written instructions; for example, re-
write a letter, paint a poster or build something; (2) individually complete a commonly assigned task such as copying,
arithmetic drills, penmanship; and (3) free work, that each
student shall do after completing tasks assigned by the teacher: in order to facilitate this effort a list of activities will
be available from which each student may select an activity
which he likes to do during his free time.

Teacher and Materials

Unitary school teachers will have the same preparation as graduated school teachers, and shall subsequently
receive special training in small group work and community
development in order to prepare themselves to face the
multi-faceted responsibilities presented by children at various age, academic and social levels.

Their direct contact with families will place them in
an advantageous position and will, at the same time, demand
a knowledge of the fundamental principles of rural sociology
in order to view the child as a member of a community
whose goals and modes of behavior should be compatible
with the educational offerings and should be enhanced via
the educational program. The teacher needs to be a scholar
who dedicates a portion of her time to the concerns of the
nation's educational policy, the systems of education, of
texts and other teaching resources, and who shall maintain
contact with the supervisor in her zone in order to apprise
herself of the recommendations emanating from the Central
Office.

The unitary school, more than any other, requires a
wealth of educational material in order to function and achieve
its objectives. In that a single teacher must simultaneously
teach a number of groups, at least the following basic and
auxillary materials will be needed:

* basic reading texts
* work books
* dictionaries
* lecture display posters
* illustrated anatomy and hygiene posters
* three-dimensional and two-dimensional materials
  for use in arithmetic and geometry

   * measuring devices and tools for work in geometry
   * chemicals and scales in order to perform scientific
    and agricultural experiments
   * plans, maps, globes

The auxilliary materials should include:

   * magazines, periodicals, bulletins
   * reference books
   * story books
   * laminated illustrations for geography, history,
    science and others.

   The effort to provide a complete primary school education for all youngsters, especially in the rural areas, in Paraguay is by no means limited to the physical shifting of students. To be successful, it must also include a complete revision of the elementary school curriculum to meet the new demands which the structure will provide. This revision is now underway. The successful completion of this program in Paraguay, or in any other Latin American country, is dependent upon the availability of resources in the educational budget. However, the long-range projection for the termination of the project has now been established and accepted. With this comes a commitment to the rural youth of Paraguay which cannot be revoked.

Notes

1. Prado, Abner M., <u>The Unitary Rural School</u>, Secretary of Public Education, Mexico.

2. Romero Luzano Simon, "The Systematic Planning of Education," UNESCO, Boletin No. 30, 1966.

14. GUATEMALA'S APPROACH TO RURAL EDUCATION
Peter C. Wright and Luis Arturo Lemus

In January 1970 Guatemala began a pilot program in practical problem-centered education for the rural area. The program was designed to transform a traditional curriculum--teaching methods and training--and give education a meaning and importance it has never held for the rural population. The pilot schools are pivotal to a five-year, $15,000,000 loan financed program of qualitative improvement of rural education formulated after two years of intensive study.

Emphasis in Guatemalan primary education has been in urban rather than rural education. The rural population, comprising 66 percent of the nation's total, in 1967 was provided one classroom for every 140 children aged seven to 14, whereas in urban areas one classroom was provided for every 49 pupils. Moreover, only 8 percent of the rural schools offered six grades, while all urban areas provided six grades. The primary curriculum for rural schools is urban centered, but 24 percent of the rural teachers have received training for rural posts.

At first glance the major primary education problem is the upgrading and more efficient use of existing rural facilities, rather than the construction of more rural schools. Of a rural school-age population of 699,000, 21 percent enrolled, but only 17 percent attended school in 1967. However, it is estimated that 60 percent of rural grade-one population did attend school, while less than 1 percent of the rural sixth-grade population attended school. Of the country's 3,423 rural schools, 73 percent offer no more than three grades and about 92 percent of the rural children in school in 1967 were in the first three grades. Rural sixth-grade attendance comprised only 5 percent of the nation's total attendance in grade six. One fourth of the rural schools are private schools on large fincas and few of these offer more than two grades of education. See Tables I and II.

Table I.   Rural Attendance by Grade as Percent of
Total Rural Primary Attendance 1967

	Public	Private
1st grade	56. 6%	59. 0%
2nd grade	23. 5%	24. 2%
3rd grade	12. 9%	11. 9%
4th grade	4. 3%	3. 0%
5th grade	1. 9%	1. 3%
6th grade	. 9%	. 04%

Table II.   Rural Schools (Public) Offering 1, 1-2, 1-3, etc.,
Grades as Percent of Total Public Rural Schools

One-grade schools	8%
Two-grade schools	19%
Three-grade schools	45%
Four-grade schools	16%
Five-grade schools	6%
Six-grade schools	6%

Where rural primary school facilities do exist, a
fourth of those who enroll do not attend, and the majority
of those who do attend any one grade do not continue to the
next higher grade even where a higher grade is offered.
For example, where two grades of school are offered, less
than 45 percent go on to the second grade.   Where three
grades are offered, only 28 percent reach third grade;
where four grades are offered, 19 percent; and where there
are six grades, 16 percent attend the final grade.   However,
attendance is greater in any given grade where the next
higher grade is offered.   Second-grade attendance as a percentage of first-grade attendance ranges from a national
average of 44 percent where two grades are offered to 52
percent where six grades of school are offered.   Third-
grade attendance ranges from 28 percent in three grade
schools to 38 percent in six grade schools; and fourth-grade
attendance from 19 to 27 percent.   An analysis of the nation by municipio and department clearly shows that the
highest rate of drop-out occurs in schools offering one to
three grades (73 percent of all rural schools) and the lowest
rate of drop-out in schools offering four to six grades (27
percent of all rural schools).   Drop-out and socio-economic
conditions are closely related.   The highest drop-out rates

occur in subsistence agricultural communities. Attendance
increases with the degree of urbanization; from aldea to
cabecera municipal, cabecera departamental to the capital
of Guatemala.

In addition to this "halo" effect of upper grades on increased attendance, noted above, low attendance and high
rural drop-out are ascribed to the following six factors:

1. Unqualified Teachers. Of existing rural teachers,
32 percent have received special training for rural teaching,
20 percent are without titles or diplomas, and the balance
have been trained for urban posts. The GOG National Council on Economic Planning sums up the teaching profession
as follows:

> Teachers have isolated themselves from the social
> and economic problems of the country. The teach-
> ing profession of the Republic lacks preparation to
> assume the responsibility that belongs to them....
> Teachers have not been capable of transmitting to
> children motivation to change.... The school has
> not served as an instrument to enable the child to
> live his own life.

While there is a surplus of graduates of urban normal
schools, rural normal schools currently only produce about
77 rural teachers a year. The immediate need for over
1,000 rural teachers is being met with urban graduates
whom experience shows rarely live in or become members
of the rural communities in which they teach, do not identify with the problems of the community and are ill prepared
to handle a curriculum which should be directed to the improvement of rural economics and living conditions.

2. Curriculum and Teaching Materials. The typical
rural school curriculum is urban-oriented, passive, theoretical and given to rote learning. It has very little relation to
the social, economic or political needs of the country, nor
to the interests of the children themselves. Until the advent
of the ROCAP-ODECA textbooks, now available for the first
three grades, no general textbooks were used, and few are
yet available for fourth through sixth grades.

The Guatemalan rural school, as well as "urban"
schools in rural cabeceras and municipales, largely serves

a subsistence economy and traditional peasant social organization. AID-sponsored research conducted in the eastern departments of Guatemala between 1961 and 1965 clearly shows that formal education holds little meaning for the campesino; that its principal value is conferred status; and the campesino does not see education as relevant to his life or improvement of his life.

Diminishing per capita land resources and diminishing land productivity pose an increasing and recognized threat. The response of the young illiterate campesino has been to attend evening literacy classes that might provide "light." Research also indicates that young adults who have achieved literacy in night classes, employing a curriculum directed to agriculture, health and nutrition, are more sophisticated about matters of health and nutrition than illiterates or those who have attended public school for a year or two. However, without textbooks or reading materials, those who have attended primary school from one to three years, as well as those who have been to literacy classes rapidly lose their marginal abilities to read and write. In one study conducted in the Department of Jutiapa, literacy loss after three years of primary school ran as high as 40 percent.

3.   Unqualified and Inadequate Supervision. Guatemala has not developed a corps of supervisors trained to assist rural teachers in problems of curriculum, instruction and teaching materials. Lack of supervision is also responsible for inequitable teaching loads, lack of distribution of available teaching materials and maintenance of buildings and equipment. Within departments pupil-teacher ratios in aldeas ranged in 1967 from 10 pupils per teacher to 146 pupils per teacher. Departmental averages for schools at different grade levels ranged from four pupils per teacher to 54 per teacher. Directors or "principals" of schools are without preparation for handling administrative tasks of personnel, curriculum, school-community relations, discipline.

4.   Communication. Rural communities in Guatemala are dispersed and largely inaccessible. Many campesinos live on their milpa, rather than in a local community where a school may be located. In the Department of Jutiapa, which is typical of areas throughout Guatemala, less than one fourth of the communities are accessible by vehicle. School attendance, supervision and materials supply are affected.

5. <u>Language</u>. Language presents another communication barrier to the educational and economic development
of Guatemala. In addition to Spanish, spoken in urban areas
and throughout the eastern and coastal regions, seven Indian
dialects (among 20 used in the country) are used predominantly in rural communities of 10 departments. With the illiteracy rate among Indian mothers as high as 95 percent in
these areas, children from rural Indian homes enter school
unable to speak Spanish, the language in which the primary
school curriculum is taught.

6. <u>Planning, Harvesting, Migration</u>. These have
been traditionally cited as causes for low attendance and high
drop-out. Coffee harvesting beginning in November reduces
school attendance in these areas. Seasonal migration of
families to coastal areas beginning in October and planting
and harvesting in local communities from May through September also affects attendance.

The (In)Efficient Use of Facilities

Analysis of pupil-teacher ratios in rural schools reveals that schools offering four to six grades make substantially better use of teachers and school rooms than those offering one to three grades. In 20 of 22 departments,
schools offering four grades have higher pupil-teacher ratios
than those with two grades or three grades. Five- and six-
grade schools generally have higher pupil-teacher ratios than
those with fewer grades. Classroom use follows the same
pattern. In short, four- to six-grade schools not only insure a higher rate of retention in all grades, but are more
economical.

Poor supervision has aggravated the inequities of
pupil-teacher ratios. Schools have been identified with four
teachers and less than 25 pupils, while as noted earlier
there are other schools with one teacher and over 100 pupils. In rural areas 398 classrooms are not in use, and
123 teachers can be moved to schools needing more teachers.
However, there are other rural communities which need 866
teachers and over 1,000 classrooms to bring the pupil-teacher and pupil-classroom ratios into a balance of 40 pupils
per teacher and classroom.

The above summarizes the findings of an intensive
analysis of Guatemala's rural primary system conducted by

the Office of Planning of the Ministry of Education (OPIE)
with technical assistance provided by AID.   OPIE's conclusions and recommendations were consistent with those made
earlier by Guatemala's National Planning Council and studies
by the Ministry of Education and UNESCO: rural education
could best be served by qualitative up-grading of the existing system rather than an extension of the system through
continued construction of one- and two-room schools.   This
meant a program of up-grading present one- to three-grade
schools, a hard look at the purposes of education and hence
the curriculum, and improved preparation and in-service
training of teachers.   In a sector loan approach to improving national education, Guatemala turned to USAID for assistance in primary education, to the IRBD in secondary and the
IDB in University education.   The loan proposal to AID was
based upon the study and recommendations of OPIE and focused upon the qualitative improvement of rural education.
AID in 1968 approved a loan of $8.6 million with a provision
for a follow-on loan if the program proceeded as planned.
The Guatemalan Government agreed to provide counterpart
funds of $6.6 million for the program.   At the same time
AID agreed to provide grant funding needed to establish and
equip four rural pilot schools designed to print the direction
of rural education and teacher training to be carried out
under the loan.

Briefly stated, the loan funded program calls for the
construction of two rural normal schools each with a capacity of 500 students, the construction of 50 regional rural
education and in-service teacher training centers, the construction of approximately 2,500 classrooms to up-grade
existing schools and alleviate congestion and provision of
textbooks and teaching materials and equipment in the
amount of $1.6 million.   To undertake the detailed plan-
ning and implement the program, including the four pilot
schools, the Ministry of Education created in August 1969
a special project office (PEMEP--Proyecto de Extensión y
Mejoramiento de la Educación Primaria).   Staffed by full-
time specialists in curriculum development, education administrators, architects and engineers, PEMEP was constituted as an independent office of the Ministry of Education
responsible to the Ministers of Education and Finance.   The
staff is aided by an architectural and engineering consulting
firm.   The first construction is expected in 1971, two years
after the signing of the loan.

Planning of the pilot schools was begun late in 1968.

The first two schools opened at the start of the school year
in January 1970.   The stated purpose of the pilot schools is
to improve the existing Programa de Estudios, a three-
volume guide for primary teachers, by making these programs (1) more applicable to the life of the rural community, (2) useful in improving social and economic life, (3)
successful in orienting the child toward education, and (4) effective in techniques for developing the child's potential in
problem-solving and academics.

     The traditional Programa de Estudios sets forth the
philosophy and objectives of the subject matter to be covered
in each of the six primary grades and suggests to the teacher a very wide range of exercises and activities, which,
however, few teachers can implement for lack of motivation,
training, and facilities.   The average rural teacher, bur-
dened with several grades, selects those items which are
within his competence and repeats them year after year.
Children dutifully copy the instruction in their notebooks.
Few teachers, moreover, understand or identify with rural
life or its problems, or are able to help the student understand the value of mathematics, language arts, natural and
social sciences in their lives.   The result is that education
for the rural student is theoretical and most often has little
application or meaning to the life he is destined to live.   In
the average rural school, educational emphasis is on teaching what the teacher knows.   What the rural student must
know if he is to improve the future of rural Guatemala has
not been taught.   The dilemma for the child is the lack of
an intersection between real, immediate problems and the
academic education which is necessary for on-going solutions.
The rural child cannot accept the doctrine of "learning as
preparation, " because he has not experienced that academic
education does in fact prepare for anything.

     The pilot schools were visualized as laboratories for
the development of a meaningful rural curriculum, as models
for 50 regional schools to be built with loan funds, and as
experimental schools to be operated in conjunction with two
new rural normal schools.   Two schools were located in
Eastern rural Ladino section of Guatemala and two in the
Indian Highlands, all within an hour's drive of the planned
Normal Schools.

     To accelerate the project, existing six-grade schools
in rural areas were selected as pilot schools.   Each local
community was provided a minimum of five acres of land.

USAID provided agricultural, shop, and industrial arts facilities, a model home for instruction in home-making and nutrition, and a multi-purpose building for combined classes,
library, teacher training and adult education.   Simple, low-
cost prefabricated construction was used.   Equipment includes
wells, pumps, irrigation system for year-round gardening,
sewing machines, shops and agricultural tools, generators
where needed, 16mm and overhead projectors.   USAID established a budget for local purchase of materials to build
chicken houses and pig-pens, seeds, fertilizers, teaching
supplies and miscellaneous costs.   All buildings and equipment were planned jointly by Guatemalan and USAID personnel.

Responsibility for the pilot school program rests with
a supervisor of pilot schools who reports to the Director of
PEMEP.   He is assisted by two teams of three Guatemalan
technicians in the areas of agriculture, industrial arts and
home economics.   Each team has developed a schedule for
working with teachers in either the two Ladino or two Indian
pilot schools.   AID supplies vehicles for the supervisor and
technicians.   AID has also placed at the disposal of PEMEP
four U.S. contract technicians in problem centered curriculum development.   Each of these technicians is scheduled to
make two or three visits a year averaging two to three
weeks each.   They work directly with the Guatemalan technicians and pilot school teachers as determined by the Supervisor.   While the U.S. technicians provide ideas and reinforcement, the responsibility for the program and day-to-day
activities are firmly in the hands of the Guatemalan staff.

The critical factor in introducing what might be called
a 180 degree change in the direction of education is the staff.
A decision was made not to change the teaching staff of the
schools selected as pilots.   These teachers were considered
typical products of and wedded to a traditional curriculum
and education by rote.   Those who saw the need for a more
"practical" rural curriculum thought of it in terms of an
hour or two a week devoted to a school garden, shop, home-
making, and health as additives to be squeezed into the on-
going instruction in language, arithmetic, and natural and
social studies that had long since been packaged in the
teachers' minds.   The pilot schools, designed to experiment
broadly with curriculum, teaching methods, and pupil-
teacher relationships, posed an obvious threat to the well-
known and trusted paths of traditional pedagogy.   Between
the close of the school year in early October 1969 and the

scheduled opening of the pilot schools in January 1970,
teachers and technicians were exposed to a series of programs designed to open their eyes to a new educational environment, to stimulate self-assurance and acceptance of a
more flexible approach to teaching, and to introduce a new
philosophy of education engaging them directly in the planning of new approaches to their January classes.   The technicians, supervisor and school directors were sent to Mexico for two weeks to participate in a training seminar for
rural teachers conducted by the Mexican Ministry of Education.   Upon their return they and the pilot school teachers
attended a two-week sensitivity training course conducted by
Rafael Landivar University in Guatemala City.   This was
followed by a one-month seminar which covered the purpose
and philosophy of the pilot schools, demonstrations of a
problem-centered approach to learning, and the participation
of the teachers in developing learning situations of interest
to campesino children.   Dr. Robert Dwyer and Mrs. Jane
Elligett, consultants to the program and authors of Teaching
Children through Natural Mathematics, participated in the
seminar and returned to Guatemala to work with the teachers
and technicians during the early weeks of January 1970.

    The pilot schools in practice are creating the inter-
section between the interests and practical problems of rural
life and academic education.   The intersection is created at
the very beginning of the child's school education.   In the
pilot schools, the child is not introduced to reading, writing
and arithmetic.   He is introduced to solving problems that
are real to him, and that he is able to solve at his age
level: problems of getting and sharing things he likes to
eat and play with, problems of taking care of things he likes
to keep, problems of doing things he likes to do.   He meets
reading, writing and arithmetic (academics) as tools to solve
these problems today.   If he finds that he can solve these
problems through today's academics, he will not have to be
coerced or coaxed to use tomorrow's academics to solve
his more advanced problems tomorrow.   The gradual expansion of problems and the growth of academic skills to
solve them will occur together.   The child's natural motivation and natural learning process remains at the center of
his school life.   This "educational intersection" and the
philosophy underlying it has been given the name "técnica
educativa integradora."   Enthusiastically endorsed by both
Guatemalan and U.S. technicians, the philosophy has engendered coordination of the activities of the several technicians working on the project.   In addition to Dr. Dwyer

and Mrs. Elligett of the University of South Florida, consultants to the program are Dr. Donald Wyckoff of the American Crafts Council and Dr. Thomas Rich, chairman of the
Behavioral Sciences Department at the University of South
Florida.

Teacher training is begun with a brief discussion of
the difference between environmental academics and traditional approaches, followed by a demonstration of the technique
in practice.   This demonstration takes the form of a regular lesson.   The consultants and technicians role-play the
teacher, and the teachers role-play the pupils in whatever
manner they wish.   The teachers are encouraged to role-play
pupils with learning or behavior problems.   By so doing,
the teachers help the demonstration to reveal the effect of
the technique on these pupils.   The demonstration is followed
by a period of questions, suggestions for improvements, and
ways of adapting the lesson to a particular environment.   In
environmental academics, the lessons are based on the environment, and the instructional materials are items from
the environment.   Thus the curriculum of each school has
its individual content.

The fundamental process of training, however, is the
study and review of whatever educational program is in present use.   This review is conducted mainly by the teachers
themselves.   The consultants and technicians serve only to
keep the discussion focussed on one point: in this lesson,
what is the real problem for the child?   If in fact no problem for the child can be found (other than to learn whatever
was presented), the discussion is refocussed: can we design
a real problem for the child, in which this material is involved?   If it is possible, it is done.   If it is not possible,
it is discussed whether the teaching of this academic material can be deferred until a real problem is feasible.   Teacher training and curriculum design thus proceed together.   In
the process of their training, the teachers create a relevant
curriculum.   In the process of creating a relevant curriculum, they acquire the training they need to become their
own architects of learning situations.

The training has been conducted in two stages.   In
the first stage, the technicians and supervisors received
training during a workshop with the consultants.   In the
second stage, these technicians and supervisors are taking
over much of the responsibility of training the pilot school
teachers themselves.   The consultants are participating in

regular and extended stays at the schools.   The pilot schools
will thus be laboratories where Guatemalan educators can experiment with and develop an education for rural children
that will be so important to them and to their parents that
children will complete their primary education and education
will make it possible for them to improve their lives, their
community and their nation.   In the pilot schools the land,
buildings, equipment, special facilities and activities make it
possible to associate each learning activity with an activity
important to the community, the parent, and the child, and
which the child can do himself.

    The job of the pilot school staff is to enrich the exist-
ing curriculum by using the pilot school facilities and the
special knowledge of the technicians as the basis for learning
mathematics, language arts, social studies, science, health
and safety.   The basic activities of the schools are agriculture, industrial arts, home economics, nutrition, and esthe-
tics.   Through these activities the students learn mathematics,
language arts, social studies, science, health, and safety by
basing them on real situations which are important to them, their
parents and the community.   For example, instead of being
taught entirely in the classroom, mathematics is learned more
quickly and with greater promise for future application if measurement, sums, averages, productivity and costs become a part
of agricultural instruction, "educación para el hogar, " and
nutrition and other subjects.   Natural sciences have more
meaning if they are a part of a study of plant growth, animal and human diseases, human nutrition, soil analysis, and
farm production.

    This does not mean abandonment of all traditional
classroom work.   It does invite experimentation with education outside the classroom and putting more time and emphasis on learning outside the classroom.   Time previously
spent wholly in the classroom is now divided between problem-solving in the shop, field or model home, and in the
classroom where discussion and practice will still take place.
It is the job of the technicians and supervisor to work with
and train the pilot school teachers to make use of the pilot
school facilities and develop lesson plans.   The lesson plans
and the technicians' evaluation of them will become the basis
for a program of studies to be used in 50 regional schools
which will have similar equipment and facilities.   The pilot
schools will also provide background and experience for rural
teacher education in the two new loan funded rural normal
schools and for the in-service training of teachers now hold-

ing positions in rural schools.

In a country where over 70 percent of the rural population cannot read the instruction on a package of seed or
the formula on a bag of fertilizer, much less comprehend
their significance to their deteriorating subsistence economy,
the role of the pilot schools and the planned 50 regional
schools goes far beyond primary education.   The schools
are seen as centers of rural development, offering the services of the technical staff, and agricultural, shop, health
and nutrition facilities to adults and schools in the satellite
communities which lie within a radius of three miles of the
pilot school.   Each school has a minimum of four satellite
communities.   "Promotores sociales, " individuals selected
from each satellite community for their qualities of leadership and demonstrated interest in community development,
are being given a six weeks' rural development course, including two weeks of sensitivity training at Landivar University.   These "promotores" will stimulate and organize community participation in development projects, adult education
and demonstration projects which require the services and
facilities of the schools.   One promotor social has already
brought 50 campesinos together in a communal corn fertili-
zation project with the help of a pilot school agricultural
technician.

At the writing of the article the first two pilot schools
at Santa Rosa de Lima in the Department of Santa Rosa and
Quezada in the Department of Jutiapa have been in operation
four months.   How are they doing?   A level of excitement
never before seen in Guatemalan education pervades the students, teachers and technicians.   The school day begins
earlier and closes later than a year ago.   Drop-outs in 1968
and 1969 have asked to be re-admitted.   Children too young
to attend school came to watch their older brothers and sis-
ters.   In Santa Rosa de Lima the children have planted
flower and vegetable gardens, made flower pots of clay and
bamboo, built cobblestone walks, tables and benches.   All
of these activities served as vehicles for learning "academics"
involving measurement and the use of tools, as well as
learning new names and working together.   One visitor ex-
claimed that he had never seen third-grade children learning
geometry without being conscious of what they were doing.
Another gave the following report:

> How exciting to observe students out of the class-
> room planting and cultivating their own gardens--

utilizing the best approaches so that they can, in
turn, instruct their parents. In talking with the
students they respond without hesitation, telling the
size of their gardens, how vegetables grow, how
they will be used, how to spell their names. The
teacher is part of the group: she does not prompt
the students, and furthermore the teacher is learning along with the students. In another class the
teacher was introducing leadership training by having a student direct the entire class in group sing-
ing. Poise before the group, ability to speak up
and ability to include the entire group were all
part of education. And then the class evaluated
the student's leadership ability. New words and
key phrases were placed on the blackboard, referred to, spelled out all in an integrated way. The
students had a good time learning how to handle an
important leadership and social problem. There
is a climate for learning that is in sharp contrast
to the average school where students are chanting
their lessons or teachers lecturing the student.

In the first two pilot schools the students and teachers
appear to be generating their own problem-centered activities,
calling upon the technicians only for advice on how to carry
out projects. Sometimes the children decide how to go about
a project. The attitude of the teacher and technician is that
the child will learn by his mistakes. To date, the pilot
schools have operated with a minimum of the equipment and
teaching materials ordered for them. Initial reliance has
been in the resources of the environment. Such teaching
aids as simple microscopes, overhead and 16mm projectors,
sewing machines, arts and crafts materials, maps, etc.
will be gradually introduced during the school year. Rabbits
will be introduced before chickens and pigs, and each carefully prepared for in advance, utilizing each steps of preparation as a learning experience.

Evaluation of the program will be longitudinal and in
depth. In the first year a process evaluation will be conducted, with detailed descriptions of steps in implementation.
This will include a narrative of activities, methods, problems and reactions from students, teachers, technicians,
consultants and the community. In addition, baseline data
on school attendance, drop-outs, proportions of school-age
children in school and other related statistics will be provided. Parallel to the initial steps, in-depth evaluations are

being planned. Special achievement tests and attitude studies
will be basic in this phase. Methods of selecting teachers
and development of teacher training must also be considered.
This evaluation, over a five-year period, should clearly document the progress and effectiveness of this program. The
beginning is auspicious. Students, teachers and community
are enthusiastic. However, there is a long road ahead.
There is always the danger that a new method will too quickly
become traditional through being done by the students in a
lock step; there is also the danger of the teacher's feeling
overworked when the novelty wears off. There will be problems of keeping alive the experimental approach. Much will
depend upon the selection and training of new teachers. Imagination, flexibility and dedication are in short supply
among teachers paid as little as $70 a month. However,
interested, motivated students have a way of stimulating and
bringing out the best in a teacher. The process works both
ways.

Section III

PLANNING FOR CHANGE

The evolution of national and educational planning offices in underdeveloped countries has been triggered by the
necessity to spread thin resources over broad areas. This
has led to the growth of power centers in planning offices,
sometimes as an integral unit designed to develop new programs, sometimes as entities unto themselves with strength
and talent to make studies but without the power to enforce
them. Often these planning offices have been the main focus
of international agencies with the hope that they would serve
as the quick spark for educational change and impact. As a
result they are highly publicized.

Their development has led to a new type of academic
discipline, one not previously organized even in the developed
countries. Much time and money has been put into this organizational effort and the development of models which could
be successfully applied to any country in a similar development stage. These organizations and these models, often
with the international push, have become much more sophisticated than the rest of the educational system. To some
extent this has made them leaders in the movement to change
education. But the very real danger exists that sophisticated
models in the process of becoming organized lose their contact with the schools and their problems, especially in rural
Latin America. This foreseeable danger has caused a split
in planning office directions, between the theoretical and the
practical.

But, as statistical figures became more available,
close critical looks at the over-all educational system came
to be common. These were first done by economists who
related education to the process of economic growth. Later,
other social scientists have compared education with political
and social problems, with historical antecedents and with
anthropological roots. Personnel who look honestly at the
Latin American educational statistics are inevitably over-

199

whelmed by the immensity of the task which faces public education in the 1970's. Some propose changes within the structure, some a complete re-ordering of the structure itself.

These nine essays move from a description of a large public education planning office to the advocation of a complete re-ordering of the structure. In between, one will find proposals for rather unique planning and curriculum models, an education minister's own planning projection, an analysis of political and social influence on public schooling in Latin America, a summary of the statistical position of education and a broad description of potential growth in the region "if" education and the other areas can catch up to the problems. All are written by Latin Americans and Latin American specialists.

Some kind of long-range or general plan for the future of education in Latin America is perhaps the only hope remaining for changes significant enough to make a difference, or which will be in time. The idyllic hope that what now exists is good enough and that change can come about in a slow, easy way is negated by the statistics. This is a time for dreamers or philosopher-kings to assume positions of influence in Latin America and to institute immediate change. The real question is not what kind of formal and/or informal educational structure can be created for the 1970's, but what will be needed in the 1980's and beyond.

15. A SIX-NATION EDUCATIONAL PLANNING OFFICE
Ovidio Soto Blanco

Educational planning units around the world have been, historically, one-country ventures. In Central America a unique experiment is underway in which six countries have banded together to form a single planning office. This does not eliminate the individual planning offices within each country, but tends to coordinate their efforts, to distribute the results of their studies and programs and to be the instigator of new experiments. Some of these concepts of integration existed for a long time and, as a consequence, the organization of Central American States, ODECA, formulated a document, the Basic Unification of Education which has now been ratified by all of the Central American governments. Article 5 of this document "recognizes the necessity of education being rooted in overall planning. In this way, integral educational planning should be articulated with and strengthen national level economic and social planning."

Fundamental factors that necessitate Central American regional educational planning may be synthesized in the following points:

a) Agreement among educators, economists, and planners in economic and social sectors regarding the necessity to eliminate isolated educational development efforts so that educational development constitutes an integral part of Central American development;

b) There is evidence that the separate Central American nations are devoting much money and energy to the task of strengthening their educational systems. Nevertheless, economic integration and especially the Central American Common Market have served to foster an urgent sense of necessity for seeking a coordinated set of new solutions to the quantitative and qualitative problems of teaching that will provide significant and rapid answers for improved education in Central America;

c) If this conviction really exists, education should

truly be an agent of economic and social growth, to the extent that educational systems are capable of meeting the demands for changes in the economic and social structure. Educational efforts of the past should be carefully reviewed but the focus should be on current technological necessities. The need is to prepare the quantity and quality of labor force personnel required by Central American development, thereby to create attitudes favorable to development and social change;

d) It is indispensable that Central American educational development have a policy of focused effort; a rational utilization of human resources and the best possible use of the Central American finances devoted to this purpose;

e) It is necessary to take advantage of the experiences of the individual nations in order to accelerate educational development, producing structural changes and teacher reforms that facilitate the implementation and maximum utilization of educational services;

f) Certainly, the outstanding utility of Central American educational planning as an efficacious instrument for orienting the process of study, of structural and institutional reforms, has been implicitly recognized in the act of implementing the Central American Basic Unification of Education Document.

Based upon earlier completed studies, the Cultural and Educational Council of ODECA decided to create the Central American Educational Planning Office (OCEPLAN), beginning in August 1968, as a regional entity of educational planning for Central America and Panama and as a permanent technical organ of the Cultural and Educational Council. OCEPLAN has the following specific responsibilities:

a) Undertake the permanent task of diagnosis, identification of trends and prediction of educational needs as these are linked with the objectives, goals and requirements of Central American economic and social development.

b) Implement the Central American Basic Unification of Education Document, mediate the processes of integration, research and devise work plans oriented to these ends.

c) Conceive and formulate multinational projects, directed to the resolution of common educational problems and meet the needs of individual nations' onerous and isolated problems.

d) Direct the application and evaluate the results of the adoption of educational materials within the region.

e) Identify the educational aspects of the region that are amenable to unification and integrated development.

f) Prepare the studies necessary for the obtaining of foreign financing and technical assistance for regional educational activities.

g) Coordinate and evaluate the National Educational Planning Offices of the region, with those International and Central American organs of integration that conduct economic and social development programs in the area.

h) Contribute to the strengthening of the mechanisms and the technical upgrading of the process of planning implemented by the individual nations.

OCEPLAN has initiated its work with the following organizational pattern:

--Consultive and Coordinating Group

--Administration

--Instrumental Services: a statistical analysis and projections unit and a documents unit

--An interdisciplinary team of technicians and specialists.

The Consultive and Coordinating Group is the organ of OCEPLAN that provides the coordination and evaluation of OCEPLAN's activities in its conception, content and implementation of plans and work programs and in the regional coordination of national educational plans. The function of the group is to be the permanent vehicle of OCEPLAN within the National Educational Planning Offices and with those organs represented in Central American integration to the end of maintaining permanent, institutionalized relationships. Thus, the directors of the National Educational Planning Offices of the six nations of the Central American Isthmus, one representative of the permanent secretariat of the University Higher Education Council of Central America (CSUCA), and a representative of the Permanent Secretariat of the General Economic Integration Agreement (SIECA) are members of the Consultive and Coordinating Group. The Administration of OCEPLAN is currently provided by one of the functionaries of the central coordinating office.

The OCEPLAN budget consists of annual quotas from each Central American country. These funds are administered by the Secretary General of ODECA in accordance with its rules and regulations. Further, the Secretary General's office has provided equipment, office space, duplication and publication services and secretarial support. It is obvious,

however, that the growth of OCEPLAN and the development
of its programs will require increased financial support.

As stated earlier, the work of OCEPLAN was initiated
in August, 1968. Activities that have been completed since
that date are arranged in the following pattern:

a) Preparation of the documentation for Meetings of
the Educational and Cultural Council;
b) Preparation of the documentation for the first
meeting of the Consultive and Coordinating Group;
c) Secretarial support for the first meeting of the
Consultive and Coordinating Group;
d) Work session concerning the Project to Reform
the Honduran Secondary Education [see article number 9];
e) Preparation, organization and completion of a
large curriculum study for the secondary level.
f) Organization of individual studies in the areas of
special education, audio-visual aids, fund-raising and educational administration with the goal of implementing these on
an experimental basis.

An in-depth look at goals and objectives of one of the
major current studies presents a view of operational techniques.   That study, "Trends and Necessities of Central
American Education, " has three basic objectives:

1) To present a diagnosis of Central America's educational situation.   Nevertheless, it is not solely a descriptive document but a study which identifies necessary changes
and activities.   It deals, then, with the identification of
some projects of a regional level which facilitate the implementation of the document of the Central American Basic
Unification of Education.
2) To contribute to the evaluation that the Ministries
of Education are conducting in order to determine the efficacy of their educational systems vis-à-vis the extension of
of educational opportunities.   This assessment is basic to
the ability to advance education in Central America in accordance with individual national and global regional needs.
3) To generate useful conclusions pointing the way
for educational policy for the region.   The information
gathered together is of importance to the organs of integration and especially, to the Cultural and Educational Council
of ODECA.   The alternatives identified indicate that a study
such as the one being carried out should, at least, be directed toward identifying action programs for the region that

will stamp educational integration with its particular dynamism.

The study will consist of four parts: the first will
be descriptive, containing basic data to serve as points of
reference while defining the current efficacy of educational
services; the second will be characteristically diagnostic;
the third is intended to present an objective portrait of future exigencies to arise in Central American education; and
the fourth part will indicate the bases for judging an educational policy for the nations.   The flavor that OCEPLAN had
desired to give a study of this type is one that does not
smack of an ODECA technician's effort, but rather one which
incorporates the authentic participation of each one and all
of the personnel who contribute to the conduct of educational
efforts of the region.   Only in this way can a working document constitute a point of departure for cooperatively and
conscientiously seeking solutions to Central America's educational problems.

We have provided sufficient information regarding that
which OCEPLAN has accomplished in its time of existence
to provide a general view of its work and, more specifically,
its potential contribution to Central American education.
There are many signs which advocate a dynamic modification in aspects of education during the coming decades;
among others; those which emanate from the categorical importance of making the integral development of our nations
a practical alternative.

Educators must ever remain aware of the fact that
within the concept of a balanced Central American development, education has a very important role to play.   Robert
McNamara, president of the World Bank, has said: "Our
purpose in this instance shall be to give assistance which
will contribute most to economic development.   This means
placing more emphasis upon educational planning as a point
of departure for the integral process of strengthening education. " Further, educators must be capable of identifying
those forms that produce the highest quality and greatest
quantity of educational opportunities so that future generations of Central Americans shall benefit by the effective integration of the respective nations.   It is essential to underline the significance of an even more widespread form of
coordinated regional educational effort.   But as all the individual nations have their own educational problems, their
offices of educational planning should obviously be strength-

ened.   OCEPLAN was created not as a substitute for national planning units, but rather to coordinate international
efforts and to evaluate with technical and policy planning
groups.   This purpose should be made most clear in order
to avoid counter-productive misunderstandings.

16. EDUCATIONAL DEVELOPMENT IN BOLIVIA
Thomas N. Chirikos and John R. Shea*

Recent years have witnessed a burgeoning interest throughout Latin America in planning educational development. Almost all nations of the region have established educational planning units on a formal basis, and several have recently published long-range plans.[1] This development is not without relevance to students of educational reform, because planning activities are carried out in large measure to help decision-makers establish explicit criteria for assessing the performance of educational systems and for guiding their future development. Since educational reform frequently stems from a shift in the criteria used to evaluate the program of the school system, anticipation of probable changes in the thrust of Latin American education requires an understanding of how planning criteria are applied in specific cases.

Although Latin America is certainly not a homogeneous region, Bolivia is reasonably representative of several Latin countries and of a number of less-developed economies elsewhere in the world. For this reason, it is hoped that a discussion of planning criteria and their application within the context of this country's problems will have relevance for other countries with similar characteristics. The people of this landlocked, predominantly rural nation of approximately 4.5 million inhabitants manage to live on a per capita national income of less than $125 per year. Consequently, there is a need for the people of Bolivia to use their scarce resources as judiciously as possible. With respect to education, illiteracy is endemic, the educational structure is traditional, and expectations for expanded educational opportunities are growing rapidly, particularly in rural areas of the country. If rhetoric can be believed, the national authorities are committed to improving the school system at

*The writers wish to thank Herbert S. Parnes and Frederick A. Zeller for helpful comments on a draft of this paper. The views herein expressed are those of the authors alone, and not necessarily those of U.S.A.I.D. or the Government of Bolivia.

all levels. Recently, comprehensive educational planning
has been enlisted as a means of identifying major problem
areas and strategic decision requirements.

The purpose of this essay is to describe the use of
planning criteria in delineating a long-term strategy for educational development in Bolivia.   We begin with a brief
description of school enrollment and student flows as of
1966.   The essential educational policy issue of whether to
concentrate on rapid expansion in matriculation or on accel-
eration of economic growth is then posed.   This is followed
by a brief overview of the manpower requirements approach
to educational planning, one of several techniques that may
be employed in linking educational policy to economic development targets.   While this approach played an important
role in the Bolivian case, matters of efficiency were often
critical in policy deliberations.   The relevance of these two
criteria--manpower requirements and the efficiency of the
school system--are illustrated through examination of ways
to meet the country's future demand for high-level and middle-
level manpower.

In 1966, the various levels and branches of the formal education system in Bolivia enrolled approximately
711,000 students. Of this number, over four-fifths were in
primary and pre-primary classes.   Nearly 15 percent
studied in the nation's public and private secondary schools,
while universities and related institutions of higher education
enrolled the remaining 3 percent of all students.   The size
of the school system had grown substantially since the Revolution of 1952.   Estimates show that over this period enrollments at the primary and secondary levels increased at an
average annual rate of about 7 percent.   There has been a
corresponding increase in the volume of resources allocated
to education.   This remarkable growth notwithstanding, the
proportion of Bolivian children actually enrolled in school
remains quite low.   The scholarity rate for all children
between the ages of six and 12, for instance, is estimated
to have been roughly 60 percent in 1966; and for ages 13 to
19, less than 28 percent.   These rates are substantially
lower in rural areas, where the majority of the population
resides, and as expected, significantly lower for girls than
for boys.

Of considerable significance is that while the structure
of the school system reflects, in part, a fairly rapid rate of

growth in new students at the first level, very high dropout
and failure rates account for the shape of the educational
pyramid.   On the basis of both cross-sectional and time
series data, it is estimated that only one in five students
completes at least six years of primary school; indeed,
fewer than one in three enters the fourth grade.   Furthermore, only 16 of every 100 students enrolling in secondary
schools complete such programs.   The probability of a first
grader completing university studies is on the order of one
in 250.   Since not all school-age children enroll in school,
even this number overstates the educational attainment probabilities for the typical child born in Bolivia.

Even if desirable, Bolivia is not in a position simply
to expand enrollments by creating additional classrooms
throughout the countryside.   At the present time, some 80
percent of all youngsters enter first grade.   Although many
children live in very small communities in areas not accessible to schools, there is nevertheless, considerable senti-
ment within the country in favor of a policy to expand scholarity rates.   At the same time, a number of leaders would
like to pursue a strategy to maximize the contribution of the
educational system to the economic growth and development
of the country.   Regardless of how the problem is perceived,
there is a need to choose an appropriate growth path for the
system.   The need to make such a choice, in turn, places
great weight on the criteria used in evaluating alternative
courses of action.   In this context, the utilization of criteria
means including an explicit test of preferredness for one
rather than other possible courses of action.

While the need to accelerate economic development
is increasingly accepted in the Third World as an appropriate
goal of educational policy, there is extensive debate on the
relationship between policy and development goals:

Manpower Requirements.   In Bolivia, the planning
method used to relate the two involved the determination of
manpower requirements.   That is, quantitative estimates
were made of the future numbers and types of human resources needed to achieve economic development targets.
The use of such a criterion for educational policy involves
(1) projection of an optimal and feasible growth path and
structure of economic activity over the planning period; (2)
translation of such economic output targets into a set of occupational needs; (3) determination of the number of persons
to be trained in each occupational group by determining nor-

mal attrition from each occupation and probable growth in
the labor force; and (4) specification of some level of education, training, and experience for entrants into each occupation.   This procedure yields a set of target output figures
for the educational system which is consistent with demographic realities and the requirements of an over-all program for accelerating economic development.

Of course, little can be said within a manpower requirements framework about how an educational system ought
to be expanded or modified until certain judgements are
made concerning the relationship between occupational performance and job-related skills. [2]   Linking occupations to an
optimal (or even desirable) pattern of education and training
is an even more troublesome element in the manpower requirements approach to educational planning. [3]   Decisions
reached with respect to the "required" pattern of education
for each occupation, along with projected (policy determined)
dropout, repetition, and transition rates, will determine the
future size of the educational system necessary if economic
and social development goals are to be reached. [4]   Obviously,
other things the same, the lower the educational attainment
targets established for each occupation, the lower the resource commitment necessary to meet projected manpower
requirements.

Except for certain occupations, such as licensed
physicians and a few other groups, occupational categories
used in employment projections cover a variety of specific
jobs which are far from homogeneous in terms of the knowledge and skill required for acceptable performance.   In addition, most jobs are not rigidly structured by existing technology and, as a consequence, may be performed in some
fashion by individuals possessing somewhat different capabilities.   Certainly this is the case for teachers, hospital
administrators, and many other important occupational
groups.   The worker whose tasks are so circumscribed
that, for example, he must turn dials in a precise way at
a set speed is certainly the exception rather than the rule.
In using projections of future manpower requirements by occupation and educational attainment for the determination of
educational policy, a further complication arises.   Various
ways exist for acquiring occupational competencies.   Formal
schooling, on-the-job training, and learning through experience in lower level or related occupations are three important activities which generate job-related knowledge and skills.
Moreover, as a general rule it is not clear in the absence of

careful study which alternative is more efficient.

Efficiency. The shape of the educational pyramid in
Bolivia required using a second criterion--efficiency--in
evaluating the direction of future educational change. The
notion of efficiency refers to the relationship between "inputs" and "outputs." With respect to school systems, efficiency may be measured usefully in terms of (1) the ratio
of non-student educational resources (e. g., teachers, classrooms, etc.) to student outputs (e. g., graduates) and (2) of
student inputs (e. g., entering students) to student outputs.
The former measure emphasizes physical facility requirements, teachers, and budgets. The second focuses on con-
straints on student flows through the system, both within
and among specific educational tracks. In both cases, the
internal operation of the educational system is evaluated by
how well it utilizes scarce resources and by how much lee-
way is left to the policymaker in varying the number of
"outputs" (i. e., graduates) over the planning period.

Implicit in viewing the educational system within an
input-output framework is that resources are used more effectively when pupils complete any given educational program
rather than drop out prior to that time. This assumption
does not deny that benefits often accrue to students regardless of whether a program is completed, but it does imply
that a pupil may fail to gain in either of two ways. First,
he will not be awarded a title or certificate of completion,
which may bar him from entry to some occupations for
which he might otherwise be qualified. Second, he may not
learn all that a program is designed to teach and, as a
result, his productivity may remain low. Another, and
perhaps even more important, reason for concern with efficiency is that a static set of failure, dropout, and transition
rates within and between levels of a school system and between schools and the labor force provides very little flexibility in meeting short-term and intermediate-term graduation targets and places enormous (and in some cases, in-
feasible) demands on available resources for education to
achieve higher student output targets even in the very long
run.

An example may help to clarify these points. If all
student flow coefficients (failure, dropout, and repetition
rates, along with transition probabilities) were fixed, it
would be impossible to change the projected number of university graduates in Bolivia for approximately 17 years, and

even then such a change would depend upon altering the number of first graders during the first year of the planning
period. [5] The number of graduates in any year during the
interim is already implicit in existing enrollments and flow
coefficients.   It follows that, if additional engineers were
needed over a short-run planning period, for example, they
could be developed, but only at the expense of fewer graduates in other fields.   In the long-run, of course, more
graduates could be obtained, but only if expansion in the
number of first-year pupils were feasible and, then, only
by tolerating additional dropouts and an overall expansion in
the educational system and its resource base.   In the case
of Bolivia, the existence of such rigidity would mean that to
increase university graduations over and above trend by a
single person within 17 years would require approximately
250 additional pupil spaces in the first grade of primary
schools during the first year of the plan.

It should be clear that if student flow coefficients
were inflexible and if projected manpower requirements were
to call for more graduates than are already implicit in
existing enrollments, such graduates would be forthcoming
only after many years.   Even this statement assumes some
possibility of expanding first year enrollments immediately.
It follows, in principle, that to the extent that repetition and
dropout rates can be reduced to less than what they otherwise would be, it would be possible to produce more graduates, reduce beginning enrollments to obtain the same number of graduates, or pursue some intermediate strategy in
developing the school system.   While leaders in a country
will rarely entertain the possibility of reducing (in an absolute sense) first year enrollments in primary schools, it
would be possible with declining dropout and repetition rates
or with increased transition or labor force participation
rates to meet projected manpower requirements with fewer
students in the system and, therefore, fewer dropouts and
resources.

It is important to observe that as in most countries
the determinants of existing student flow coefficients are
complex and often not subject to easy manipulation.   Evidence suggests that much of the dropout problem in Bolivia
stems from conditions exogenous to the school system: the
nation's poverty and the related need for children to work,
particularly in rural areas, and malnutrition, chronic ill
health, and epidemics.   Various conditions internal to the
school system, however, are partly responsible for the low

levels of measured efficiency. Among the important in-
school variables undoubtedly linked to dropout and repetition
rates are (1) existing fail-pass standards; (2) limited student
places and transportation barriers in many sparsely populated
rural areas; (3) the often poor quality of the teaching force;
(4) the nonexistence of school lunch programs in many areas;
and (5) obsolescence of the curriculum.

The question of curricular relevancy exists, of
course, in both advanced and developing nations. Since
problems of curriculum are important to the selected educational issue about to be considered, a few additional observations are appropriate. A major curriculum problem is to
fulfill the perceived needs of many students who in the normal course of events will not proceed through the various
levels of the school system, but will terminate their studies
sometime before. The content of education in most parts of
the Bolivian system is designed for those who anticipate attendance at one of the universities. This curriculum was
instituted during a period when education was for an elite
minority. Despite the fact that enrollments have expanded
rapidly since the 1952 Revolution, there has been very little
corresponding adaptation of the curriculum.

The utilization of the planning criteria described
above in an assessment of the national educational system
in Bolivia pinpointed a wide variety of problem areas where
policy changes were required. Many problems corresponded
to initial expectations; others, however, did not. While it
is impossible in the space remaining to discuss even a frac-
tion of these findings, one important set of problems may
be used to illustrate how the planning criteria were applied.
The problem relates to the size, structure, and efficiency
of university education in Bolivia and resultant policy implications for other parts of the school system. To begin with,
the projection of a set of long-term manpower requirements
demonstrated the need to upgrade a very large percentage
of new entrants to the labor force over the planning period,
particularly at the professional and technical levels of the
occupational structure. Of significance in this regard is
that the "output" of the university system not only would
have to grow at a fairly rapid rate if these occupational targets were to be met, but that the structure of the system in
terms of areas of specialization would have to change substantially. In particular, the analysis demonstrated the need
to prepare a substantial number of graduates in the fields of
public and business administration. The need stemmed from

the economic requirement for substantially more managers and public officials and the necessity of preparing persons specifically for these functions rather than in the general areas of law and economics as has been the case. This appeared to be so even in light of the fact that the relationship between managerial performance and educational preparation is not an unambiguous one.

Because the school system in Bolivia is terribly inefficient, the planning exercise demonstrated that even marginal increases in university graduates would require an intake of new students in the first grade of primary school exceeding the number of children in the relevant age cohort! Stated in slightly different terms, unless educational policy could influence the efficiency of the school system, it would not be possible to satisfy rather modest educational output targets predicated upon manpower needs. Indeed, even within the range of feasible improvements in the efficiency of the system, it proved possible to meet output targets only by tolerating a significantly large number of dropouts, for which both appropriate training and an adequate labor market would have to be found. Analyses showed, for example, that it would be necessary to tolerate some 70,000 university and 338,000 secondary school drop-outs between 1969 and 1980.

One important implication of the figures is that educational programs had to be designed to provide useful training to persons dropping out of school. Rather than rely on the formal school system to perform this task, however, it was recommended that a National Manpower Training Institute--financed by a payroll tax and operated outside the formal school system--be established. Indeed, it was recommended that such an organization train more than 75,000 workers over the planning period. This general approach was chosen for a variety of reasons: the limited size and quality of the nation's existing secondary school vocational-technical programs; the largely dysfunctional nature of the nation's single post-secondary industrial school;[6] and the anticipated responsiveness to actual needs that a new institution would have. The alternatives were to ignore the massive problem of academic dropouts without specialized skills or radically to restructure the secondary level of the formal school system. Because of severely limited training capacity in the private sector, the absence of incentives to train workers on-the-job, and the moribund nature of the formal school system, the semi-autonomous agency approach

was proposed.   Time and hindsight may tell how rational
such an overall strategy has been.

Notes

1.   Both writers were engaged in the research and planning
     efforts sponsored by the Government of Bolivia and
     U. S. Agency for International Development summarized
     in: Chirikos, T. N., Kelley, S. C., Sanders, D. P.,
     Shea, J. R., et al., Human Resources in Bolivia:
     Problems, Planning, and Policy, Columbus: Center
     for Human Resource Research, Ohio State University,
     1971, 382 p.

2.   For an excellent discussion of the complexity of this re-
     lationship see P. J. Foster, "The Vocational School
     Fallacy in Development Planning, " Education and Eco-
     nomic Development, C. A. Anderson and M. S. Bow-
     man (eds.), Chicago: Aldine, 1966, p. 142-163.

3.   Herbert S. Parnes, "Relation of Occupation to Education-
     al Qualifications, " in: Planning Education for Eco-
     nomic and Social Development, Paris: OECD, 1963,
     p. 147-157.

4.   The basic task in Bolivia was to determine minimum
     feasible conditions and resource commitments.   It
     was recognized, of course, that the Bolivian people
     might wish to do even more than necessary in order
     to achieve other education-related goals requiring
     somewhat different resource patterns.

5.   The Bolivian system consists of six years of primary
     school, six of secondary, and five years in most uni-
     versity faculties; a total of 17 years.

6.   This school, with curricula running from five to seven
     years in length, was designed to produce high-level
     technicians and skilled craftsmen.   Partly because of
     limited breadth in labor markets for such skills, how-
     ever, there is reason to believe that over 50 percent
     of its graduates migrate each year to neighboring
     countries for work.

17. A PEDAGOGICAL MODEL FOR CURRICULUM PLANNING
Ralph Tyler and Mario Leyton Soto

Let us assume that the curriculum planner has selected a small list of important objectives which are possible
to achieve. Because these objectives have their origin in
several sources, they probably are stated in diverse ways.
In order to prepare a single list, therefore, it is imperative
to state them in such a way that they are useful in the selection of learning activities and in orienting the learning
process. While these objectives are sometimes stated as
tasks the teacher must do (such as introduce the theory of
evolution, demonstrate the nature of inductive experimentation, or introduce the romantic poets), these postulates are
not really educational objectives. The objective of education
is not that the teacher carry out specific pre-determined activities, but that significant changes be brought about in student behavior. It is essential to keep in mind when stating
educational objectives, therefore, that these refer to desired
changes to take place in the students. Once the statement
of behavioral objectives is made, it is possible to infer the
specific activities which the teacher ought to plan in order
to achieve the objectives. The difficulty that arises by er-
roneously stating objectives as teacher tasks is that there
is no way to evaluate whether or not they should be carried
out. Thus, whenever objectives are mistakenly formulated
in this way, a type of circular reasoning is involved which
does not satisfactorily guide the succeeding steps of material selection and the development of methodological processes.

Another method frequently used to state objectives is
to make a list of topics, concepts, generalizations and other
content elements which should be covered in one or more
classroom periods. Thus, in a Chilean history course, the
objectives might be stated as: "the Colonial Period, " "the
Autocratic Republic, " "the War of the Pacific, " etc. In
science courses, the generalizations might be: "nothing is
created or lost in nature"; or "green plants transform the
sun's energy into glucose by a process called photosynthesis."
To express educational objectives as topics or generaliza-

tions or in other forms is unsatisfactory (even when the content areas in which the students should work is indicated)
since what the students are to do with those elements is not
specified.   What do we expect the student to do with generalizations?   Do we hope that he will memorize them?   Or
that he will consider them as coherent unifying theories
which will help him to understand the scientific method?
Or that he will apply them to concrete situations in his
everyday life?   When the objectives are stated as topics,
the changes to be brought about in the students remain un-
certain.   What do we expect students to gain in their study
of "the Colonial Period" of Chilean history?   Should he remember certain facts about the period?   Should he be able
to identify the developmental tendencies and apply them to
other historical periods?   The problems which arise as a
result of stating educational objectives as themes, topics or
generalizations are obvious; they do not constitute a convenient base for orienting the progressive development of the
curriculum.

A third method often used to state objectives is to
present them in the form of general behavior models which
do not specifically indicate the area of life or content.   According to this method, objectives are stated as follows:
"develop critical thinking, " "develop appreciation, " "develop
social attitudes, " "develop wide interests. "   When objectives
are expressed in this form, it is expected that education
will bring about some changes in student behavior.   This
kind of statement provides a general indication of the types
of changes which the educational program should expect.
Nevertheless, from what is known about transfer of learning,
it is unlikely that such general objectives can be realized.
It is indispensable to specify in more detail the context
within which the behavior is functional or the area of life
in which it is to be applied.   It is not enough to simply
speak about "the development of critical thinking"; reference
must be made to the context or to the types of problems to
which this thinking will be applied.   It is not sufficient to
formulate an objective saying that its purpose is to "develop
wide interests. "   It is necessary to specify the areas in
which these interests should be awakened and stimulated.   It
is unsatisfactory to state that the objective is "to develop
social attitudes" without specifying clearly and precisely
which are the context areas in which these attitudes should
be developed.   Thus, it is also inadequate to formulate objectives only in terms of general behaviors if they are not
expressed as specific guides for curriculum development

and high level instruction.

A New Model

The most useful way in which to express educational objectives is to indicate both the type of student behavior desired as well as the context or area of life in which this behavior ought to operate.

Thus, the objective "to write clear and well-organized reports of social science projects" indicates both the type of behavior--"write clear and well-organized reports"--as well as the areas of life to which these reports refer--"social science projects." In the same way, the objectives "to be familiar with reliable sources of information related to nutritional problems, " states the kind of behavior--"to be familiar with reliable sources"--as well as the content--"sources related to nutritional problems. "

Since a clearly stated objective consists of two dimensions, behavior and context, it is useful to employ a bidimensional chart which facilitates a clear, precise expression of the objectives. The double-entry chart, example given below, demonstrates its use in expressing objectives for a secondary school biology course. It is not intended that the objectives contained in the chart are ideal, they are provided here merely to demonstrate how each objective pursued can be expressed more completely and be more clearly defined in both its behavioral and content dimensions.

A glance at the chart shows that there are seven kinds of behaviors pursued in this biology course: "an understanding of principles and important facts"; "familiarity with reliable sources of information"; etc. Even a superficial analysis of the behavioral aspects sketched in the chart indicates that the goal of this natural science course goes far beyond the mere acquisition of information. The way in which the seven kinds of behaviors are presented immediately suggests the need to establish learning activities which increase the student's familiarity with sources of information, increase his ability to interpret facts and apply principles, deepen his experience through proper study methods and ways of reporting research results, stimulate interests, develop favorable attitudes towards the social applications of science, etc. The mere formulation of these behavioral categories makes possible the deduction of various

Chart I. Example of a Bi-Dimensional Plan for the Formulation of Objectives For a Secondary School Class in Natural Sciences

Content Aspects of Objectives	Behavioral Aspects of the Objectives						
	1. Understanding of Principles and Important Facts	2. Familiarity with Reliable Information Sources	3. Ability to Interpret Data	4. Ability to Apply Principles	5. Ability to Study and Report Results	6. Well-defined, Broad Interests	7. Social Attitudes
A. Functions of the human organism							
1. Nutrition	X	X	X	X	X	X	X
2. Digestion	X		X	X	X	X	
3. Circulation	X		X	X	X	X	
4. Respiration	X		X	X	X	X	
5. Reproduction	X	X	X	X	X	X	X
B. Use of Vegetable and Animal Resources							
1. Relations With Energy	X		X	X	X	X	X
2. Environmental factors affecting Animal, Vegetable Growth	X			X	X	X	X
3. Heredity; Genetics	X		X	X	X	X	X
4. Use of Soil				X	X	X	X
C. Evolution; Development	X		X	X	X	X	X

ideas concerning the manner in which the required curriculum should be planned.

Nevertheless, a simple enumeration of behaviors is not sufficient for adequately expressing objectives. Thus, the chart also includes the content elements which the objectives ought to include. The bi-dimensional scheme given shows that the course has been planned to develop different kinds of behavior in relation to nutrition, digestion, circulation, respiration and human reproduction as well as the use of vegetable and animal resources and thus gives superficial consideration to energy relations, environmental factors which influence vegetable and animal development, heredity and genetics, soil utilization, etc. It should also be pointed out that the behavioral objectives are also evolutionary and developmental. Without doubt, the statement of the content aspects helps to define more clearly the task to be carried out in the biology course.

Finally, the chart demonstrates the way in which the bi-dimensional aspects of educational objectives are related. The intersections of the behavioral columns with those corresponding to content categories are marked with an "X" where the behavioral aspect is applied to a determined context area. For example, the first intersection which occurs between the first behavior stated and contents 1, 2, 3, 4 and 5 of category A (Functions of the Human Organism), 1, 2, 3, and 4 of category B (Use of Human and Vegetable Resources), and category C (Evolution and Development), indicates clearly that a student ought to develop familiarity with reliable sources of information--in this case, nutrition and reproduction, environmental factors which condition vegetable and animal growth, etc. The fact that no intersection is produced between behavior 2 and contents 2, 3, and 4 of the same category A and aspect 1 of category B, indicates that-- in this instance--the acquisition of familiarity with reliable sources concerning digestion, circulation, etc. is not a specific objective.

The foregoing examples are valid, of course, for the diverse intersections that occur in the scheme between the behavioral and content aspects determined for this course.

By the same token, the ability to interpret data is specified as something to be developed in relation to each content area. The ability to apply principles, however, does not include the area of evolution and development. The

ability to study and to write research results as well as to
develop wide, well-defined interests is also common to the
several content areas in this specific course. It should be
noted in the chart that social attitudes should be developed
in specific relation to nutrition, reproduction, energy relations, environmental factors which condition animal and vegetable growth, heredity and genetics, soil utilization, evolution and development. Thus, it should be clear that each
"X" indicates precisely the kinds of behavior that ought to
be developed in this course as well as the content areas or
activities to which they are related.

    When objectives are expressed in a bi-dimensional
scheme, they assume the nature of concise specifications
which permit an evaluation of the subsequent development of
the course. The teacher may observe the different columns
of this chart in order to determine with relative ease the
kinds of learning activities he should present in the classroom. The activities chosen should permit the students to
develop an understanding of facts and significant principles
not only on the memory level but should also encompass
analysis, interpretation and application of data. In other
words, the activities ought to contain the necessary mental
operations which direct the student to interpret and understand on a more sophisticated level. In a similar way, the
second column, "familiarity with reliable sources of information, " adds a second specification. It is not enough that
the student understand and remember important facts and
principles; he should also know where to go for additional
needed information. Thus, it is indispensible to select activities which will permit students to consult various sources
of information and acquire practice in evaluating sources.
Thus, in order to develop the behavioral aspect specified,
it is imperative to take into account the need to propose many
different kinds of learning activities in order to carry out the
objective stated in the first column. In the same way, objectives originating in the third column permit the establishment of specifications vis-à-vis the learning activities to be
planned. Thus, in order to develop the ability to interpret
facts, the student ought to carry out activities which give
him the opportunity not only to come into contact with them
but also to deal concretely with their interpretation. Further,
he should become aware of criteria or principles of interpreting data which will permit him to avoid the pitfalls of
over-generalizing and other common errors. The kinds of
learning activities required for interpreting new data are
somewhat different from those implied for the first two

columns, since they include presentation of new information, opportunities to interpret this information, possibilities to discover the limitations implicit in interpretations, and the development of certain criteria for formulating interpretations. The fourth column--"ability to apply principles"-- adds a specification which permits the required learning activities to be planned. If the student is going to understand how to apply principles to concrete problems which he encounters in his personal life, he ought to learn how to solve new problems which cannot be resolved simply by reciting memorized formulas. The specified learning activities ought to underline the various possible ways of applying facts and principles as well as the diverse problems which may arise as a result of such application. The resulting problems-- product of this application--should also be evaluated in order to see in what manner the application was made. Thus, the "ability to apply principles" column adds specifications for developing the kinds of activities it is necessary to offer in this biology course.

The fifth column, "ability to study and report research results" suggests other specifications. What is desired here is that the student develop individual study habits as well as learn to prepare oral and written reports on specific studies. This requires that the teaching-learning process offer the student opportunities to carry out significant activities in the biological areas identified and that he be provided the opportunity to present oral or written reports of his work for evaluation by others.

It is important to underscore once again that specifying objectives in this way permits the establishment of the necessary kinds of learning activities and didactic methods. The sixth column, "wide and defined interests" implies still other specifications that ought to be considered in planning curricular activities. It indicates that it is not sufficient that the students understand, analyze, interpret and apply knowledge; they must encounter satisfaction in treating the various dimensions of the course. To select activities which will probably broaden student interests, it is necessary to know what their present interests are in order that these may serve as a base for nurturing them. It is obvious that the specification of these kinds of behavioral objectives is directly involved in the planning of learning activities.

The last column, "social attitudes, " also has a direct influence over curriculum planning. The suggestion that

students should develop attitudes in their study of biological
sciences which are more social than individual indicates that
the social effects of certain types of biological discoveries
should be considered.   It also indicates that students must
be helped in their analysis of the existing relations between
certain procedures applied by the biological sciences and
their implications in the social area.   The students should
come to realize that science is not a neutral process but
rather one that has public consequences and can contribute
to the general social welfare.   It should also awaken a desire to support those discoveries which contribute to the
general social welfare and to relate their own personal satisfactions and benefits with them.

Model Implementation

        The foregoing examples shed light on the way in which
the behavioral aspects of the objectives help to specify
more clearly the kind of curricular material, learning activities and methodological procedures which should be used.
As regards the content aspects of the objectives, it can be
seen how they aid in specifying more clearly the steps that
should be taken in the subsequent development of the curriculum.   The column headings in the chart indicate the content
categories to which the behavioral dimensions relate.   Moreover, they indicate the specific themes that ought to be developed in each category in relation to the behavioral traits.
Thus, under nutrition, it is necessary to identify important
facts and principles, work with reliable sources of information, give students new data to interpret, present problems
calling for the application of important facts and principles,
look for interesting materials, and discover the social implications which can be derived from studies in this area.   In
a similar way, each of the columns indicates the type of
content analysis which should be made.   Thus, putting together both dimensions of the objectives (content and activities) facilitates a more precise specification of the kinds of
desired behavioral changes as well as the materials, ideas
and specific classroom situations in which each of the behavioral traits stated in the objectives should be developed.

        In discussing the use of the bi-dimensional chart, the
following question is sometimes raised: are the proposed
items adequate objectives ?   The purpose of this particular
instrument is not to determine whether educational objectives
are appropriate or not.   It is assumed that these have al-

ready been analyzed and filtered in the steps previous to
their final selection and organization. The chart is simply
a scheme to present the formulated objectives in a clear
way to aid in planning learning activities which are more
evident than those which could be obtained with other schemes.

An individual teacher analyzing this chart might ask
why there is an objective concerning social attitudes in relation to energy but none which associates social attitudes with
evolution and development? It could be that in accordance
with the teacher's educational philosophy and consonant with
his knowledge about educational psychology, he would consider the second objective as worthy of being specified in the
chart as the first objective even though it had not been identified previously in the development of the objectives. This
is perfectly valid for there is no immaculate perception.

Thus, while the fundamental objective of this chart is
to assist in the development of a scheme for expressing educational objectives in the most convenient possible way, it
does not disregard the possibility that it may also serve to
suggest objectives that have perhaps been omitted.

Another problem which sometimes emerges concerns
the degree of generalization or specificity which should be
sought in the expression of the behavior and context aspects
of the objectives. With regard to the first, this depends
upon the degree desired as well as the limitations of what
is known in the field of educational psychology. In general,
broad objectives are more desirable than specific ones.
However, in order to identify adequate learning activities it
is most useful to clearly differentiate behaviors with dissimilar characteristics. In this way, it is possible to clearly differentiate a behavioral category, such as the acquisition of facts--which is largely memorization--and the ability
to apply principles to new problems, which involves the interpretation and use of facts and principles.

There are also intermediate categories. For example,
the understanding of important facts and principles calls for
memorization and yet is more than a simple recall of material in that it implies a certain ability ot indicate meaning
and suggest illustrations of these facts and principles. In
a limited sense it also implies the ability to apply them to
other situations. It is obvious that in spite of the fact that
some specific differences can be established, the formulation of behavioral categories is, in part, a question of cri-

teria. It is important, however, to point out the difficulty
which arises in differentiating a behavior in too much detail.
This is inconvenient for two reasons: because it is very difficult to carry out and because too many divisions make it
all the more difficult for the teacher to remember the types
of behaviors being pursued. Too many subcategories become
unmanageable as orienting objectives.

It is probably more satisfactory, therefore, to establish a list of behaviors fluctuating somewhere between seven
and 15. In the eight-year study in which it was necessary
to establish behavioral categories in order to determine what
should be evaluated, ten categories were used:

1. Acquisition of information
2. Maintaining physical health
3. Developing work and study habits
4. Developing methods of thinking
5. Developing social attitudes
6. Developing interests
7. Developing appreciations
8. Developing sensitivity
9. Developing social adaptability
10. Developing a personal philosophy

While this list may not be ideal, it does represent a
number of categories sufficient to permit separation but it is
also small enough to be easily remembered and used as a
guide in educational work.

The problem of general vs. specific objectives is also
inherent in the content categories. In general, it is desirable to formulate a sufficiently large enough number of categories to facilitate the distinction between the more important
content and the less important. Thus, in the example of the
natural sciences, if only three principle categories had been
used--functions of the human organism, utilization of vegetable and animal resources, and evolution and development--
it would still be possible to include a number of totally useless sub-categories. For example, in the category "functions
of the human organism, " it would have been possible to include content areas such as mechanical action, rest and rec-
reation, skin and protection. While these may have certain
relevance in other circumstances, they are excluded in this
scheme because they are not related to the objectives stated
in this specific course.

One of the basic functions of the sub-categories is to distinguish between the important, adequate content areas and those which are deemed not to be important. Another function is to unify reasonably homogeneous areas to be used in selecting specific content dimensions. The number of content categories will vary with circumstances. Nevertheless, as a general norm, ten to 16 are considered more useful than a smaller or larger number.

At this point a note of caution is necessary with respect to the use of this bi-dimensional chart. Each of the terms used to qualify behavioral and content categories must possess a precise and significant meaning which will truly serve the educational planner as a guide in the later steps of curriculum development. Objectives suggested by research concerning students and extra-curricular activities are generally sufficiently concrete since they are formulated in an inductive way and represent a variety of defined, specific materials that give meaning to the behavioral and content headings. Nevertheless, those objectives which subject specialists suggest or which arise from an analysis of the chart are not always afforded concrete meaning. In these instances the curriculum designer ought to study the possible meanings of the objectives suggested and examine them in different contexts until they are satisfactorily defined and useful in the following steps of the curriculum development process.

Among those objectives which may be cited to demonstrate a lack of concreteness are the following: "critical thinking," "social attitudes," "appreciations," "sensitivity," and "social adaptation." These forms are used frequently to indicate desired behavioral changes. Some educators have given them a concrete meaning; generally, however, they are used without any special meaning. An objective can be defined with sufficient clarity if it describes or illustrates the type of behavior that the student ought to acquire, in such a way that it may be recognized without major difficulties. For example, consider "critical thinking," which generally implies a certain type of mental operation related to facts and ideas, as opposed to the mere memorization of facts and ideas. This objective should be clearly defined in each specific case in order to express the behavior with greater precision. The secondary teachers who participated in the previously cited eight-year study defined "critical thinking" to include three types of mental behavior. The first included inductive thinking--that is, the interpretation of data, the establishment of generalizations from individual

facts or data. The second referred to deductive reasoning--
the ability to apply certain general principles already understood to concrete cases that, while novel for the students,
are appropriate examples of how the principles operate. The
third type of mental behavior indicated by the teachers was
logic--the ability to elaborate material with a dialectic content and to analyze it in such a way that it is possible to
identify and detect the important definitions, the basic hypo-
theses, the series of syllogisms, fallacies and inconsistencies.
Defining "critical thinking" in this way, the teachers were
able to transform a vague principle into a concrete concept
and provide a framework for understanding the possible implications which are present each time this expression is
used as a behavioral aspect of an educational objective.

        In general, the definition of the content categories for
a specific group of objectives presents no difficulty. The
tendency of specialists to generalize is less when they treat
content categories than when dealing with behavioral traits.
It may be necessary to indicate content sub-categories for
the sake of precision. Thus, in the illustrative chart, it
would be more convenient to define "evolution and development" more exactly by listing some sub-topics or indicating
aspects or materials which should be included in the category. In other cases, it may be useful to define the content categories by making a list of problems, generalizations
and individual situations in which the behavior ought to operate in order to avoid confusions and the inclusion of useless
aspects resulting from not having specified the content categories sufficiently.

        It is hoped that the examples cited are adequate to
indicate the problems involved in expressing educational objectives and that they may serve as useful guides in the work
of refining the later development of the curriculum. It ought
to be clear that a satisfactory expression of objectives--
which includes both behavioral and content aspects--provides
clear specifications as to what is involved in the educational
task. Having clearly defined the desired behavioral results,
the educational planner has a most useful tool to select content, to suggest learning activities and to decide upon the
methodology or methodologies to be used. In short, he has
the basis upon which to develop the strategy and tactics in
curriculum planning.

18. A MINISTER OF EDUCATION LOOKS BACKWARD AND
FORWARD
Guillermo Malavassi

After much contemplation, thought and study of various educational documents, I came to the conclusion, a little
before taking office, that the main problems which faced the
Costa Rican educational system were the following:

1. The system itself had deteriorated;
2. The Ministry of Education dedicated its greatest
    effort to the least important things;
3. Grave problems of desertion and repetition existed
    in all levels of the primary and secondary schools;
4. Primary school students were in school very few
    hours per week;
5. Teachers, especially those in primary, actually
    worked very few hours per week and days per
    year;
6. There was a shortage of secondary school teach-
    ers;
7. Teacher preparation was far from ideal;
8. The retirement system cut off one-fourth of the
    normal life time working span for all teachers;
9. There was a great shortage of educationl buildings;
10. There was a great shortage of educational teach-
    ing material;
11. The system of personnel selection needed improve-
    ment.

Two points in particular seemed most important to
me: (1) the need for the development of qualities in teachers
which would meet the needs of the country. These qualities
would develop a person who was cultured, wise, loved his
profession, loved his country, loved knowledge and understood the gravity of the task he had to do. (2) The necessity that the entire country participate as a public prosecu-
tor and as a teacher in the educational task and not expect
the government to do everything but that each community,
each home, each parent, each worker and each student do

his part.

I thought that these were the fundamental issues.
Everything else would come if we could find a way to accomplish these two points.   It would be difficult, but essential.
I thought of this: "It would be useless to make a detailed
reference to the difficult situation which exists in public education because the crisis is well known.   Abundant studies
have been published which reveal the weaknesses and warn
us of the crisis. If we remember the large number of students in the educational institutions and the constant building
of schools in all parts of the country as well as the shortage
of well-prepared teachers it is easy to see the fundamental
reasons for the crumbling of the educational system.   If
you add to this the parent's attitude toward the quality education you have a sad picture of the lack of vigor, of the
anemia in public education. "

As a result, it will be necessary to work with a renewed impetus in order to obtain the goals of the Constitution and the laws of Costa Rica in the area of education.
These desires deserve a further elaboration in order to
clearly see the direction which should be given this very
delicate situation.

The government offers education to all citizens.   The
main objectives are to develop citizens with a love of country who are conscious of their duties, rights and liberties
with a profound feeling for their responsibility, their respect
for human dignity, and their duty to conserve and to expand
their cultural heritage, especially in the history of man, the
great literary works and fundamental philosophical principles.
Costa Rican education would try to better the citizen and
enable him to develop intellectually, ethically, aesthetically
and religiously, giving him an appreciation of dignified family
life according to Christian traditions and the civic values of
Costa Rica, thus developing in him attitudes which correspond to his own personality and enable him to develop his
natural capacities.

While we have indicated the goals of the educational
system we should add that the country has not yet reached
these goals.   It could be said also that the country has not
yet reached these ideals.   It could be said that the system
has actually deteriorated in recent years as a result of the
forces which have pushed the idea of quantity.   Of course,
more teachers and buildings are needed and toward this goal

one should enthusiastically work. However, the essence of
the deterioration of public education does not come solely
from the problem of the number of persons who should be
educated, who should teach or in the number of classrooms
or textbooks. Today, the fundamental issue should be the
quality of what is done in education, the quality of teachers,
the quality of the man that our educational system develops.
In this respect it is important not to mistake what is the
principle, the collateral and the accessory. Therefore, it is
necessary to say what concept of man has guided the professional educational work.

In our western, Christian culture, whose imprint in
the development of the world has been so extraordinary, it
is possible to locate, thanks to the work of the most excep-
tional learned men of humanity, an idea of man, of the human being, that constitutes the most firm basis to state
justly any human subject. Particularly in education this becomes the guideline. This idea of man shows us as a person, as an individual with a rational nature who subsists for
his own right, who maintains his own entity as a characteristic of his own being. Man is irrevocably unique. From
this flows his grandeur, all his eminent dignity, his liberty of choice, his transcendent character. And in education
where the person is both the object and subject you can no-
tice a deep perspective which brings into consideration all
that is done. A base like this one may determine the theory
and the educational practice to dignify man, the main objective. Because human life historically flows continuously in
a formation and transformation of cultural benefits all that
can be done for education depends on the right approach and
esteem of the human being and the intelligent participation of
the cultural benefits.

With these ideas as a base you can understand the
necessity of reaching in education the fundamental objective:
to improve the human being in accordance with his nature.
However, even when stated in such a simple way, it implies
the immediate revision of the values of our educational system. It is disappointing to see the lack of a solid background in many teachers with respect to what should constitute the most serious matter of their lives. The most
precious resource of the nation--its children--is put in the
hands of the teachers. What idea of being human, of being
a person, have the teachers who will teach our future citizens to be human beings? What kind of an impression will
stay in their spirits? What cultural values will they trans-

mit to their pupils?

This presents the necessity of making extra efforts to count on the cultured, wise and prudent persons and leave in their hands the modeling of the youngsters' personalities. No one gives what he doesn't have; and if masters and teachers don't have much knowledge and the corresponding professional art, the teaching they give and the progress of the students will be mediocre. This will continue the break-down of the public education if the defects are not corrected as soon as possible.

It is prudent to remember criteria on the quality of those who are to be teachers:

"Our general low esteem for content as compared with method and our blind faith in the efficiency of mechanical formulas appears to be well documented in the number of required courses in the teacher training colleges as compared with the number of required courses in the liberal arts area. These future teachers come to understand how to teach any subject under the sun, but they teach very little concerning art, literature, history and of themselves. The teacher transmits to the student a small collection of misunderstood notions in a very detailed but uncomprehensable form. The considerations of 'the importance of using quotations in teaching' or 'the use of maps' take the place, in the normal schools, of the lesson from the historical texts. School boards give more importance to 30 hours of educational courses, where it is explained how to teach history or biology, than to the courses which teach the actual material. Future teachers, who traditionally come from poor homes, do not find anything in the school which makes up for these deficiencies. Nevertheless, we continue to depend on the individual teacher for the transmission of the rich contents of the scientific and literary tradition which we have today in our grasp. If we want to use these materials and enrich our culture, we should abandon our dependence on the individual teachers or better yet, give to them a more solid base during their years of preparation. If the teachers are to be the forefront of the civilization, it is necessary that they know how to feel and to understand this profoundly." (Margaret Mead.)

"We should work with the criteria that the 'leader'

in the educational area is not simply an organizer, but fundamentally an intellectual, a learned man, a man with ideas. This will represent a change in the tendency of the last thirty years but a change which we should make if we want the educational leadership at the level of ideas, left in the hands of professional groups.... The programs for the preparation of teachers and administrators, including those which give the doctorate in education, should include and 'require' a much larger portion of liberal art studies.

"A teacher with a superficial preparation cannot understand the potentiality of his teaching position to meet the challenges of the present. Nor can he understand the sciences, be enthused about art, do a work which is socially significant and much less stimulate in any lasting way of the spiritual growth.... We need capable teachers to lead us toward liberty and responsibility, toward significant work, toward creative thinking and dignified life. This class of teachers can only develop through a long, deep and high quality training program." (Rodrigo Facio.)

We should not feel afraid of the wide expansion of public education if we can count on excellent teachers. Each should permanently re-examine his values, his life, his preparation, if he wants to fully complete his important mission. An important reminder of the responsibility in education which falls to all men is that systematic or formal education is only one part of the total education of a person. The home, the theatre and the television, the magazines and the newspapers, the parents and the friends, the neighbors, the salesman--are all teachers. This shows on the one hand the need for acting righteously in every act of our lives, for in this way we contribute to form those who are near to us; and on the other hand, the conviction that one can't wait for perfection in what is related to the educational system, but consciously believe that this is a common work in which everyone must educate himself and others.

If we can really make better "educators," and educational work really is the fruit of the force of the entire country, like a common mission, then all the other educational problems could be solved at the same time. If once it is understood what is considered indispensable, there will be no reason to fear the natural growth of the student population, nor the consequent demand for teaching materials and services. It is graver to have many instruments and

no well-prepared teachers nor a national conscience of the
importance of the educational work.   If we once find the es-
sentials, it will not be difficult to develop the technical
methods or the reforms which should be done.   In my first
annual report I said the following in relation to these same
problems:

> "The country has never had institutions which could
> prepare in a satisfactory way secondary teachers as
> well as the special teachers of music, home economics,
> physical education, etc.   For this reason, but with the
> approval of the National School Board, I charged the
> Ministry with the responsibility of preparing special
> training plans for young teachers who aspired to these
> speciality areas.   During a period of nine months they
> were given a training course to better prepare them for
> the task, while still receiving full salary from their
> regular jobs.   Nevertheless, this alone did not resolve
> the problem.   It is necessary to create institutions
> which give a sound preparation and match the quantity
> need for special teachers in the country, especially
> secondary education.
>
> "It was necessary to look for a satisfactory solution
> to combat the fact that the secondary school doubled its
> enrollment every five years.   There were 2,210 second-
> ary teachers, but the University of Costa Rica (the only
> one in the country which trained secondary teachers)
> had prepared only 362 in 10 years.   In the next five
> years, considering the secondary school population
> growth and the number who will retire, about 2,000
> more teachers will be needed.   There is not one insti-
> tution which can meet this demand.   The Ministry is
> studying various possibilities, including the creation of a
> Normal School for training music teachers and a Normal
> School for training secondary teachers.   The consequences
> are very serious, if no action is taken.
>
> "We must replace the paternal administrative system
> in which each subordinate could solve his problems in
> private conversation with the Minister.   The growth of
> the school system no longer permits this.   To change it
> is very difficult because there is no model and because
> all the experience of all the people in the country has
> been with the paternal system.   Nevertheless, the Minis-
> try has started this process with the School Supervisors,
> with the possibility of complete delegation of authority
> and functions.   This will take time.   There remains a
> need for the adequate training of the supervisors in

these new functions. Plans are now in progress to do
this. However, this does not mean only changing a few
regulations, but changing ways of thinking in relation to
administration. "

I also commented in the report to the Legislative Assembly the following points concerning the development of the
educational system: "I reiterate the idea that our education
depends on the development of our fellow-citizens. For this
we should be careful of the budgetary and legal matters, of
the curriculum plans for the preparation of personnel and the
other elements, making sure that they are done in the best
order and to the highest perfection. "

No institution is separate from its environment. This
means that the function of whatever institution will be better
or worse because of the circumstances in which it is involved. It is not enough to consciously plan an institution;
the level in which it will develop will be the final and definite test of what it is able to make. Consequently, there is
an interrelation between level and institution. This is related to some commentary on our education that I want to
express. A certain weakness of our educational institutions
has been mentioned many times. Because it has been stated
many times does not make it less important or true. We
all want education to continue to be the most precious belonging. For this reason great expenditures are approved,
scholarships are given, study plans are developed, reforms
urged, etc. Nevertheless, any good idea rests upon two
basic items: the preparation of primary teachers and of
secondary teachers. We have reached a point at which teacher preparation for primary teachers provides neither liberally educated well-rounded minds nor a solid discipline-based
area of specialization. The situation with secondary teachers is still worse. I am referring not to all but to a number of them, for there exist many who are excellent in their
work.

This is caused by the slow but steady deterioration
of our teaching system, as if diseased, damaging, in the
long-term, all systems of teaching. A person not well prepared for primary teaching, will be unqualified for secondary
teaching. I'm trying to show that the solution for the problem is neither easy nor short-term, for it is very difficult
to make good institutions when they have suffered deficiencies
for a long time. Add to this the problem of opening more
than 100 new schools per year, creating new secondary

schools, facing well-intended but unclear changes, and it will indicate the damage to our system of teaching caused by gaps in personnel, planning, and materials. That is why it is urgent to attend to many things at the same time: to improve the skills of our teachers, to secure the preparation of professors in every subject, to improve the general status of primary, to improve the secondary teacher preparation, to regulate the maximum number of assignments and of hours for each teacher, to count on a good supervision, to better qualify the school directors, to have all programs and plans ready so as not to give the impression of a permanent experiment, and to have good, sufficient and cheap educational material.

This is enough to indicate that we should beware of the devilments in our education. These are many and should be exorcised at the same time. The success in solving these problems is related to the attitude of the whole country. It will not be a short-term solution, for it is impossible to perform miracles and the damage has been there for years. One hopes that solutions do not arrive too late: if the educational system is diseased, the principal resource of our nation is in crisis.

It was said in the 1967 report, "From March 1967 to March 1968 the Ministry of Education defined a policy regarding the preparation of teachers and professors: strengthened the existent curriculum plans and established others of great significance for the cultural development of the country." Inertia and the lack of planning are incompatible with the teaching function. With his inherent responsibility, the educator should constantly enrich himself with professional knowledge and knowledge of his culture. However, a good priority ranking of the opportunities for teachers was missing. The following 10 areas indicated the feelings of the Ministry in this regard.

1. Normal schools
Objective: An adequate training of the primary school teaching staff that is needed. Certify 450 teachers annually to fill the needs for personnel, increasing enrollments, retirements, desertions, death, etc.

2. Perez Zeledon Regional Center
Objective: To guide young graduates of far away areas into teaching so as to attend to the needs of the educational system of their own regions.

Train 50 teachers annually to attend to the schools that are in the southern part of the country.

3. Training of non-degree teachers in the areas of home-economics and music

To raise the level of general, specific and pedagogical training of the non-degree teachers, who work at the primary level in the areas of home-economics and music.

Train 133 non-degree teachers in service in the area of home-economics and 134 in the area of music.

4. Training for non-degree teachers in service through the professional teaching institute

To train 412 sixth-year non-degree teachers who are working in the Costa Rican primary schools.

5. Short-term in-service summer courses for teachers, offered jointly by the Ministry of Education and the University of Costa Rica

To train 100 non-degree secondary teachers through summer courses offered by the University of Costa Rica.

6. Training of non-degree secondary teachers of physical education

To train 40 non-degree teachers who teach physical education in the secondary schools in order to better fulfill the objectives.

7. Training of teachers and professors in education for family life

To train personnel needed for primary and secondary teaching of education for family life.

Graduate 40 primary teachers per year starting in 1968 and 40 secondary teachers starting in 1969.

8. In-service training for music professors

To train 50 non-degree secondary teachers of music education so they will be able to do their work in the best possible way.

9. Emergency in-service courses for teachers of physical education

To train 56 teachers of physical education for an efficient fulfillment of their work.

10. Training of teachers in secondary teaching

To train personnel that are urgently needed for second-

ary teaching.
    Train in a systematic plan of summer courses all
secondary teachers who lack adequate preparation.
    Train a number of competent secondary teachers for
the increasing needs through regular courses of 11 months.
    Train degree personnel for this work through periodical
courses and other means.

    To improve the work of the schools, it was necessary
to create a consciousness among the teachers of the great
importance of their work.   In 1967 I wrote about the educational associations as follows:

> "Teachers in Costa Rica enjoy the best conditions of
> work: good salary, long vacations, short working hours,
> early retirement allowance, illness insurance, attractive
> life insurance and three months before childbirth and
> one after with leave for every woman who works for the
> Ministry.   Compared with the rest of the people the
> teachers have an enviable situation.   And I have not
> cited all of the benefits.   In addition, they are joined
> together in a powerful association with adequate funds
> and much power.   These associations focus on a con-
> stant "defense" of their associates.   This is correct, but
> sometimes their intervention has a pitiful tone, as if
> teachers have no rights when the "truth" is just the oppo-
> site.   Besides, in certain cases, some of the leaders
> lived at a time when there was occasional bad treatment
> for the teachers and they have projected their pain and
> resentment of those days onto a present that is com-
> pletely changed.
> "Relations with the associations have always been
> good.   The only exception was more of a press show
> than a reality.   Nevertheless, the associations make
> one think that educators lack personalities for they are
> tied to a trade-union association which basically mis-
> shapes the facts.   The most serious thing is the mental
> deformation of the members.   They often judge things
> in a wrong way, only teachers' interests count, not
> those of the country.   It increases by a slow procedure
> their selfishness and they convert themselves into trade-
> unions.   And the education that these people can give
> might very well convert itself into a twisted and nega-
> tive education.   For this reason I believe that it is
> necessary, without forgetting the defense of the asso-
> ciates' rights, to meditate now and then about the coun-
> try, the teachers, and the great movements of education,

and a little less of the subjective rights.

"Individually, I always received kind consideration
on the part of the directors of the associations. We
worked together in various important programs (cultural
missions, Superior Normal School) and we talked frequently. Because of this, in what I have previously
said, I did not try to judge anyone without reason.

"Recently, the national Controller General said that
we Costa Ricans do not have common goals, that we
are without a "mystique." I agree with him. We have
lost the capacity to understand the common good, that
which is best for all. For each person to think only of
himself, or of his group, or of his party, or of his
school, or of his corporation, is to forget that there is
a homeland which needs the love of its citizens, for
which we should work, whose problems are our problems.
These demand sincere and daily attention, not just when
beautiful words are spoken on solemn occasions. Because of this I believe, in general, that the associations
have worked against the total directions of the country.
These are problems of balance and of education which
should be corrected."

After 40 months of work, I might summarize the following gains:

Modifications in All the Educational Cycles. We did
realize, with good results, changes from pre-primary to
the preparation of secondary school teachers at the Superior
Normal School. These changes included: (1) approval of
the laws which permitted the pre-primary institutions to
operate; (2) new primary school programs were started in
1969; (3) the secondary education reform was completed;
(4) the first cycle of the secondary school was revised;
(5) the differentiated cycle of the secondary school was more
clearly defined, with the application of novel plans and a
special stress on vocational education; (6) a commission reviewed the plans for the preparation of primary teachers
and presented their recommendations; and (7) the Superior
Normal School, offering summer and regular school training
for prospective secondary teachers, opened in January 1968.
While still not completed, never has such an extensive revision of all educational levels been undertaken in Costa Rica
as at that time. And all of these changes have been supported by numerous, well-defined regulations which precisely
specify the functions of advisors, supervisors and principles,
thus enabling each one to assume his obligations in a

Chart I. Primary school (including day, night, public and private) enrollments in the first month of each school year.

Year	Matriculation
1965	283, 210
1966	296, 058
1967	315, 424
1968	328, 166
1969	349, 117

The chart indicates a total primary school increase from 1965 to 1969 of 65, 907 students.

Chart II. Secondary school (including day, night, public, private, vocational and academic) enrollments in the first month of each school year.

Year	Matriculation
1965	44, 614
1966	51, 968
1967	57, 716
1968	62, 250
1969	69, 825

The chart indicates a total secondary school population increase from 1965 to 1969 of 25, 211 students.

In 1968 there were 30 public secondary schools in Costa Rica; in 1966, 61; in 1967, 64; in 1968, 70 and in 1969, 75.

It is quite evident from the above information that even under the most desirable conditions, it would be most difficult to include so many Costa Ricans within the school system.

---

responsible way.

Matriculation Information. The annual percentage of
population increase in Costa Rica is well-known. This puts
strong pressure upon many educational institutions to give
adequate attention to the thousands of persons who demand
these services. Naturally, this population increase produces
certain problems, especially in the area of the limited budgets, which the new dynamism of the times brings. It is
in this context that the accompanying matriculation figures,
Charts I and II, should be considered.

Educational Production. PRIMARY: In 1965 only 57
percent of the primary schools had classes from first through
sixth grades. By 1968 it had risen to 85 percent. The percentage of students who began first grade and completed sixth
grade in the 1945-50 period was just 16 percent of the total.
By 1951 it was 18 percent but by 1968 it had jumped to 48
percent. Thus, during the 18-year period, it rose 300 percent. The school promotion percentage, based on the final
matriculation figure, jumped from 79 to 83 percent in the
first grade and from 84 to 88 percent overall during the
1965 to 1968 period. SECONDARY: The development here
might be best indicated by comparing the results of the
"bachillerato" exams. In 1967 the pass percentage was just
44 percent. But in 1968, of the 4,340 students who took the
exam, 3,109 or 72 percent passed.

Diversified Secondary Programs. By law, students
may now select science, humanities, agriculture, industrial,
commercial and fine arts courses in the secondary diversified programs. This diversity of selection causes many administrative problems, but it does provide valuable preparation of opportunities to the young people of Costa Rica.

Superior Normal School. Created in the midst of
wide discussion, the Superior Normal School has come to
signify the only method for Costa Rica to train a sufficient
number of competent teachers. The 1969 enrollment was
1,875, including 1,020 in the full-year program and 855 in
summer training programs. This tremendous enrollment
figure, far beyond early estimates, still leaves the country
short of trained secondary teachers. Thus, the Superior
Normal School must expand its plant, to include laboratories,
more teaching materials, and a wider library selection, and
its program, to include the training of the educational leaders of the country.

School Libraries.   The Ministry of Education has begun an expansion of school libraries such as has never been
seen before.   A total of 1, 500 sets of 138 carefully selected
books have already arrived.   The National Institute of Spanish
Books helped in the selection process, the Spanish government paid for the transportation to the Costa Rican port and
each community will pay for the books and give a library
course to the teachers on their proper use.

Salary Raises for Teachers.   The most extraordinary
salary raise in the history of the country has been given to
teachers, professors, principals, and school administrators.
For example, a teacher in primary school, Group A category, had a 45 percent salary boost--not counting old com-
mitments for salary increase--between 1965 and 1969.   Even
though salary raises for teachers is a good and just cause,
it does create the grave situation where 95 percent of the
budget must be delegated to that one single item.   The remaining 5 percent must be used for everything else.   This
helps explain the lack of classrooms, didactic materials,
transportation for supervisors and officials, etc.   This budget imbalance remains as a great and serious problem.   The
professional teacher organizations should help intervene here.

1, 141 Classrooms Built in Three Years.   To meet
the quantity demands for education, "classrooms" have been
built via the community help plan and the work contract plan
as follows:

Chart III.   Cost of Classrooms built in Costa Rica, 1966-1968

Year		Classrooms	Cost (US$)
1965		442	$ 1, 200, 000
1967		365	1, 220, 000
1968		334	1, 110, 000
	Totals	1, 141	$ 3, 530, 000. 00

After much pressure and discussion in the Legislative
Assembly the new law for the construction of a large number
of the needed school buildings was passed.   Financed by
school bonds the new constructions began in November 1969.
However, the application of the law is slow and the financing
process complicated.   In 1969 there was a shortage of 3, 000
classrooms in primary schools alone.   The double-shift use
of schools makes it impossible to increase utilization.   Thus,
in the next decade it will be necessary for the Legislature
to pass laws and approve financing quickly in order to keep

up with the great increase in enrollment.

Readjustment of Teachers in the Schools.   A 1963
study indicated that there were more than 500 teachers appointed in the schools to positions which could not be justified or were unnecessary.   To correct this defect via the
administrative sector became a major goal of the Ministry.
To accomplish this it was necessary to re-evaluate the pupil-
teacher ratio, the size of the classrooms, the system of pay-
ment to teachers for "hours" worked and finally to readjust
the teachers themselves.   The goal was to apply all these
adjustments so that the teacher, on the average, would be
working with 35 students.   As difficult as this was to do, it
was accomplished.

The application of these adjustments resulted in long
discussions with ANDE (the National Education Association of
Costa Rica).   Representatives from the Association would
come daily to ask for exceptions, point out small errors or
problems or to plead for an end to the readjustments.   However, for the best use of the countries' resources and in
order to put method and order in the system, I continued
the application of the readjustments, where necessary.   The
guiding principle was that the schools exist for the children
and not for the teachers.

Increase in the Working Day in the Schools.   In 1967
the working time in the schools was increased by 33 percent.
The benefits of that change can now be seen.   However, the
children still must stay longer in school if education is to
have a real impact.   Yet, because of the lack of school
buildings, it is often necessary to run two shifts in the
same school building in the populated areas.   This is a big
impediment to the advancement of education.

A "Bachillerato" in Arts at the Conservatory.   It was
indispensable to give many young people with artistic talent
a chance to dedicate themselves to the development of these
aptitudes at the secondary level.   For this reason the National Education Board authorized a "bachillerato" in the
arts, but to be given only at a Conservatory named "Castel-
la. "   The program is similar to the others, except that
from the fourth year onward theoretical and practical studies
are added in theatre, music, ballet, literature, etc.   As a
result the student graduates with this artistic specialty.

Student Discipline.   Athletic competition, student

governments, the civic demonstrations during major national
holidays, and many other acts all demonstrate the strong internal student discipline at the secondary level. Of course
there are many negative influences: broken homes, alarming
news headlines, etc., which students must face, but culture,
wisdom, and respect are the chief tonics of the schools. It
is this style of life for the young which must be watched and
saved.

In view of the fact that the function of the teacher is more
difficult in the actual situation, that the preparation which he
now receives in the normal schools is insufficient and that
the country has no shortage of primary teachers, it is now
the hour to improve the quality of the preparation. The
plan to do this was presented to the National School Board
and they will study it before putting it into operation. The
changes stress a wider general studies program and a heavi-
er emphasis on science.

If one wants to open sources of work and better prepare individuals for their life, it is necessary to increase
the number of vocational schools. An occupational needs
study which had the technical support of the Inter-american
Development Bank, suggested the way in which the vocational
schools could meet this problem, the specialties which had
to be strengthened and the way in which an IDB loan might
solve the problem. The proposal included the preparation
of secondary teachers in vocational specialty areas, the construction of buildings, and the purchase of expensive but important equipment.

As a norm it might be said that the country has
reached an adequate balance when half of the secondary students are enrolled in the vocational areas. To reach that
point requires time, good intentions, perseverance and a
lot of patience. In addition, the project for the creation of
the National Technical Institute has been sent to the National
Education Board for their study.

In conclusion, I insist that there are two basic aspects essential to the improvement of education that still
have not been completed: (1) improve to the maximum the
training of teachers and administrators with constant opportunities for professional advancement (now being done by the
Upper Section of the Superior Normal School); and (2) insure
greater home and individual participation in the social control of education.

19. SOCIAL AND POLITICAL PROBLEMS
    IN LATIN AMERICAN EDUCATIONAL PLANNING
    Marshall Wolfe*

In a broad sense, educational planning or educational
policy expresses what a given society wants to be in the future. In this sense, education is more intimately related to
the structure and values of a society than any other sector
of social or economic activity. And just as war is said to
be too important a matter to be left to the generals, so is
education too important a matter to be left to the educators.
In any case, in a democratic society it will not be left to
them. Ideally, it is up to society itself, acting through its
elected representatives, through voluntary organizations, or
through the choices of its individual members, to give broad
policy directives to the planner, who must then find ways of
allocating the available resources as efficiently as possible
in conformity with the demands of society. In reality, the
Latin American planner must face up to a conflict between
social demand as expressed in public policy and social demand as expressed by the attitudes of the different strata of
society.

Public Policy and Social Attitudes

At the level of government policy, educational planners throughout Latin America have been given quite uniform
directives. These derived from two well-known sources:
first, the directives of Article 26 of the United Nations Universal Declaration of Human Rights, paralleled and elaborated upon in a series of regional declarations and national
laws; second, the directives originating in the concept of education as investment in human resources, as an essential

*Reprinted by permission of UNESCO from Raymond F. Ly-
ons, Problems and Strategies of Educational Planning; Lessons from Latin America, Paris: UNESCO, International Institute for Educational Planning, 1965.

element of economic and social advancement. To a certain extent, the "human rights" and the "human resources" concepts imply different priorities within an educational system, but for the most part they are compatible and complementary.

Thus the goal of universal six-year primary education can be considered as basic under either approach; and apparent conflicts at the secondary and higher education levels derive largely from too narrow interpretations of one concept or the other. An education aimed exclusively at satisfying the demand for special skills may not be the most effective way of securing the kind of human resources needed by a world undergoing continuous and rapid change; the function of social integration, which education can perform only if it gives due regard to the human rights concept, is indispensable if the human resources are not to be wasted or destroyed by the social and political conflicts that accompany the development process.

If this were all, the task of the planner, though hard enough in view of the ambitiousness of the targets and the scarcity of resources, would at least be straightforward. In reality, it is greatly complicated by official policy directives. All sectors of planning, of course, experience these contradictions, but in education the problem becomes particularly complex because of the role of education as a means by which society transmits its self-image and its aspirations to new generations. Moreover, in education, resistance to the publicly endorsed goals is relatively diffuse and who does not relate these decisions to national objectives? Hardly anyone objects to the principle of equality of opportunity and its corollary in the form of educational expansion, though the implementation of this principle would soon conflict with cherished prejudices and interpretations of self-interest. The political conflicts over education thus usually center on marginal questions with the opposition resorting to delaying tactics and techniques for distortion rather than systematic rejection of proclaimed policy. What then is to be the attitude of the planner?

He has the choice between two alternatives. He can dismiss the social and political factors as extraneous to planning, use his techniques to produce a consistent and feasible plan, and let the politicians and administrators do what they like with it. This has been the common solution in all sectors of planning in Latin America until now, and a good many of the plans thus elaborated have served no pur-

pose other than the adornment of ministerial bookcases. The
other alternative for the planner is to study the social ma-
neuvering for its adoption and implementation, and hope in
the long run to manipulate the society itself through guidance
of the educational system. It may be that an effective planner cannot, in the face of the conditions obtaining in Latin
America, avoid being something of a political lobbyist as
well as a sociologist, but he is himself a product of the society and of the educational system he is trying to influence,
and is not exempt from the prejudices and conflicts which
characterize that society. However, there is no reason to
believe that planners are either eager or qualified to undertake such a manipulative role.

It would rather seem that the social and political
requisites of educational or other planning are likely to
materialize as a consequence of a more enlightened public
opinion and of organized popular participation in policy-making, which in turn largely depend on advances in education.
This is one of the many vicious circles that complicate
planning for social and economic development. Present
trends in Latin America show, however, that social and political weaknesses need not prevent educational advances, although they cause considerable waste and deviation of educational content from that required by the objectives of public
policy. Also, a remarkable upsurge of educational initiative
can occur even among illiterate and culturally isolated rural
groups, once reforms in land tenure and changes in the
balance of local power make education meaningful to them.
The way in which the planner can contribute to the enlightenment of public opinion is by stressing the social and political prerequisites of planning, by explaining the issues to the
political leaders in terms they can understand, and by taking
an active part in the debate over these matters. There are
encouraging signs that planning institutions are becoming
aware of the need for assuming this role.

What then are the specific social and political factors
which have to be taken into account by the planners? In
singling out some of them, let us start by considering the
educational needs and demands of three broad groups that
have lately received a good deal of attention in analyses of
the region: the urban middle strata, the traditional rural
lower strata, and the newer, rapidly growing, and geographi-
cally mobile semi-urban strata frequently labelled "marginal." The first of these groups exerts a stronger pressure
for the allocation of more resources to education than any

other group in the national societies; the two other groups
exert pressures usually limited and ineffectual. It is probable that both the differences in the effectiveness of the
pressures exerted by these groups and the differences in
what they hope to get from education are powerful handicaps
to educational planning directed toward the twin goals of human rights and human resource development.

The Urban Middle Strata

The middle strata have grown with the degree of urbanization of the various countries. While definitions vary
and statistics are far from conclusive, it can be assumed
that their share in the national populations varies from about
one-half in the few most highly urbanized countries to less
than one-tenth in some of the overwhelmingly rural countries.
For present purposes, the middle strata can be considered
to include practically all urban occupational groups whose
jobs require the wearing of a coat and a tie and do not involve manual labor. They do not include the more skilled
and better organized urban workers in industry, transport,
power, etc., and the self-employed artisans, repairmen,
and like persons, whose incomes are often higher than those
of the salaried employees, but whose social status and typical outlook are quite different from those of the middle
strata.

A few years ago, some social scientists began to
point out that these middle strata were gradually displacing
the dominant tiny traditional upper class from their position
of power. Other social scientists stressed, however, that
these growing middle strata had very little in common with
the frugal, enterprising middle class who are supposed to
have contributed so much to the development of 19th-century
Europe; that they were aping the luxury consumption standards of the upper classes, relying on expansion of public
employment and on government protection against competition; and that they were failing to provide entrepreneurial
initiative or political and social leadership. It was pointed
out, in particular, that the three countries with a high proportion of population in the middle strata, Argentina, Chile
and Uruguay, had recently been economically the least dynamic in the region. These evaluations, first voiced by
social scientists, are now being repeated by influential
periodicals, which see the source of the increase in the
middle class in "the educational system, which leaves no

other field of activity than the liberal professions for a small
number and the search for an employer to serve for the majority. "[1]

The growth of the urban middle strata has undoubtedly
derived largely from the expansion of secondary and higher
education, and has in turn contributed to intensify the pressures for further expansion of education at these levels,
particularly at the secondary level. Between 1950 and 1960,
secondary enrollment in the region as a whole grew by nearly 10 percent annually, against 5 to 6 percent for primary
enrollment and 8 percent for enrollment in higher education.
But this growth at the secondary level, at first sight most
encouraging, seems to have been almost entirely unplanned
in terms of the needs of the region and contributed little or
nothing to a real equalization of educational opportunities.
What the urban middle class successfully pressed for was
the kind of secondary education that would lead, if possible,
to the university and a step up on the social ladder, or at
least to a certificate giving access to public or private
white-collar employment. In fact, Latin American secondary
and higher education, far from having a "humanistic" bias
as is often asserted, can be characterized more accurately
as narrowly "vocational"--in line with the vocations acceptable to their clientele.

The resulting difficulties for effective educational
planning are obvious. The character of demand for secondary education tends not only to limit it to the traditional
task of preparation for the university, but also to lower its
quality and to produce a lack of interest in the content of
education. The contradiction between what the customers
really want from education and what the planners expect
from it is a major obstacle to a policy for diversification of
secondary and higher education and for training of specialists
in line with national needs. If the families find admission
to traditional lines of education difficult and expensive and
admission to technical schools easy and cheap, some of
them will send their children to technical schools, but will
try to use them for the same purposes as those served by
the traditional schools and care little whether the training is
practical and up to date. The study of agriculture is a particularly good example; not only are enrollments very low in
relation to needs, but the overwhelming majority of the students come from the urban middle strata and seek urban
jobs after graduation, preferably in the Ministry of Agriculture.

Further, the children of the urban middle strata
leave very little room in the secondary schools for the children of the lower strata, and the few that gain admittance
have to pursue the kind of unproductive studies which the
schools foster. The better-off urban workers who are now
pressing for more education risk pushing their children into
the same pattern--the overcrowded ranks of the salaried employees. Under present conditions, any expansion of public
secondary education would benefit mainly the middle strata.
All this does not mean that the middle strata are consciously
and selfishly monopolizing educational opportunities. Their
position is difficult, particularly in countries in which they
are already numerous and where economic growth is lagging.
The burden of educating their children can be very heavy,
and the fruits of education are likely to be disappointing.
At present, they are encountering a particularly frustrating
bottleneck between the secondary school and the university,
as the universities have not expanded rapidly enough or have
thrown up their own barriers against the products of low
standard secondary schooling. The obvious unrest among
students at both secondary and higher levels, most of them
from middle strata families, may be attributed in part to a
conflict, conscious or unconscious, between a natural desire
to safeguard the privileges associated with their painfully acquired education in a highly stratified and class-conscious
society, and a more generous aspiration for a really democratic social order.

The characteristics of the urban middle strata set
limits for educational planning in another important respect:
their members staff the school system and inevitably impart
to it their own values and anxieties. The school system is
thus as subject as are other sources of livelihood monopo-
lized by the upper and middle strata to organized pressures
for protection of status, job security and expansion of employment. The planner finds that any reform remotely
threatening the interests of any group of teachers or officials will be resisted, usually through appeals to political
influence, and usually with success. His efforts to rationalize the expansion of the educational system will be
countered by continual pressures for special programs unrelated to priorities and contributing mainly to the creation
of new jobs. In fact, the planning agencies themselves
cannot claim to be exempt from this kind of pressure for
more bureaucratization.

There seems to be a fairly wide area of agreement

between policy-makers and educators on the kinds of reform
and diversification needed in secondary and higher education.
The problem is to find an effective strategy to "educate" the
most eager customers of education into accepting the reforms.
These problems can hardly be solved without major changes
in the social structure and a simultaneous broadening of economic opportunities. But the educational planner can contribute to their solution by stressing the implications of the
pressures now being exerted.

The Rural Strata

        Turning to the rural strata, one sees an educational
pattern apparently very remote from the one just described,
but in reality dominated by it. For, by and large, the rural
school has been an exotic and sickly import from the cities,
deriving from national policy rather than from local demands.
The small cultivator or rural worker might feel that literacy
would help his children to defend themselves against the
mysterious powers that landowners, officials, moneylenders
and shopkeepers derive from written documents, and he
might be willing to make sacrifices for this end; but, at
least until quite recently, he could exert almost no influence
on the supply of schooling or its content. Gradually, rural
schools expanded their geographical coverage but, lacking
any effective quality control from their customers, and with
the really effective demand for more education coming from
the cities, they remained pathetically ineffective copies of urban schools. Most of the rural children who attend them--
for one or two years--leave as illiterate as when they entered. Central attempts at planning and fixing of standards
were not effective, partly because of lack of resources to
back up the plans, partly because of remoteness, both geographical and cultural, of the educational authorities from
the rural people.

        In the capital, an educational bureaucracy--well in-
        tentioned, perhaps well trained, knowing exactly
        what is to be done and how to do it--gives orders
        in long reglamentos to teachers off in the jungle
        or in some mountain crevice and fills the air with
        sound of activity though with little meaning for
        those far distant from the capital. In periods of
        political instability ... the educational directors at
        the centre change with each government, the old
        plans are thrown out, new plans devised because

they are said to be better, and before these new
plans can really take effect, a change in government will bring a new minister of education, who
will have a newer and better plan that will also
fail of fulfillment. [2]

However, as peasant unions and other mass organizations begin to penetrate the countryside and as agrarian reform looms larger on the horizon, the educational planner
is beginning to encounter more insistent and specific rural
demands for education; and experimental rural school programs in many of the countries have at least contributed to
a better understanding of the practicability of alternative
strategies.   The planner faces a confusing mixture of static
backwardness and violent pressure for change, and needs
flexible and imaginative policies to take full advantage of
any nascent local initiative.   However, any solution of the
problems of educational planning for rural areas is dependent on economic and social reforms aimed at integrating
the rural masses into the national society.   The present
paper will not go into this complex subject, except for one
important aspect of it which seems to have been neglected--
the possible role of the small towns.

The Role of the Small Towns

While the opportunities of urban lower-class children
to advance beyond the primary school level are very small,
for rural children they are practically non-existent: most
of them do not have access to a school offering a complete
primary education, even if their parents are willing to dis-
pense with their labor for the required number of years.
This state of affairs might well turn the attention of the
planner to the role of the small towns, such as administrative centers of municipios, marketing centers, etc.   Ideally,
these small towns should function as specialized centers of
rural communities.   In a region in which most of the rural
population lives in tiny hamlets too small to support more
than a one-teacher primary school, one of the most important functions of the small towns could be to provide post-
primary schools as well as "complete" primary schools for
rural children.   The extension of roads and the consequent
possibility of using school buses make this a practical proposition for a rising proportion of the rural population.

Unfortunately, what evidence we have indicates that

such towns fill the role of community center either lethargi-
cally or oppressively; they monopolize whatever services are
available, exploit the surrounding rural people, and base
their feelings of self-esteem entirely on their superiority to
and detachment from anything rural. This divorce between
the small town and its rural hinterland is particularly pronounced in the large areas where the small town constitutes
a non-Indian island surrounded by Indian cultivators. In
fact, the small town is often just as divorced from the
rapidly changing realities of the large cities as it is from
the realities of rural life. It cannot serve effectively as an
educational center for rural people, not only because the
granting of equal educational opportunities to rural children
would conflict with its deepest prejudices, but also because
the kind of education its leading citizens want would be largely irrelevant either in a rural or in an urban setting.

I should like to quote from an anthropologist's description of a small town school system, no doubt an extreme
case. (In this town, called by the pseudonym "Aritama,"
the teachers are all women belonging to locally prominent
families, none of whom have themselves gone beyond primary school. While the teachers are appointed from a higher administrative level, the posts are important political
spoils, continually fought over by contending cliques of leading families, and the teachers change frequently. The national government provides a curriculum and textbooks that
emphasize practical matters and rural needs. The teachers,
however, "select from the curriculum only those subjects
that tend to affirm local values.")

> Teachers are very critical of the government pro-
> gramme and consider certain subjects quite useless
> or even offensive. Such government initiatives as
> reforestation or the establishment of kitchen gar-
> dens through rural schools are ridiculed and open-
> ly attacked. The teachers say: 'It seems that
> the government thinks we are a bunch of wild In-
> dians, asking us to make our children plant trees
> and vegetables.'[3]

In practice, the teachers usually ignore the government
texts and teach from their own "copybooks."

> These copybooks have been handed down from one
> teacher to another, from friends and relatives ...
> and contain a more or less complete outline of

subject matter arranged as questions and answers.
The method of teaching consists of having the
children copy, in the course of the year, all the
questions and answers and making them memorize
both. . . .

As these notebooks have been copied and recopied
for years and years, many errors have slipped into the transcription, and the children are taught
many quite meaningless or contradictory statements. . . .

Health education . . . is mainly oriented toward
teaching the child that all physical efforts should
be avoided. Great emphasis is placed upon the
dangers of over-exertion, explaining that movements
make the muscles tired, that reading is harmful for
the eyes and that thinking 'heats the head' and is
likely to cause dangerous diseases.

Children from the local lower class of cultivators,
who are considered Indian, although in this instance the
whole of the local population is Spanish-speaking, when they
attend school at all are ridiculed and discriminated against
by the teachers. The author concludes:

School creates . . . a world devoid of all reality.
It teaches the children . . . that their village is
the 'heart of the world' . . . and that the only
forces bent upon destroying this paradise are the
despised 'Indians' and the mistrusted 'government.'
They are taught that 'work' [trabajo] is to be
avoided, but that 'employment' [empleo] is to be
sought, as a sinecure well deserved by anyone who
has attended school.

The economists who are trying to calculate investment returns on educational expenditure might well meditate
on the returns from an education such as this. But the
significant point in relation to our present exploration of
social and political factors is that this kind of schooling and
this method of selecting teachers, although they do not usually take a form as exaggerated as in Aritama, correspond
to the desires of powerful elements in the local social structures. It will be harder to bring a worth-while content into
education in such towns than in the rural areas themselves,
where a positive value is attributed to hard work and where

the people usually make more realistic demands on the
schools.

It may be noted, however, that the small towns have
lately tended to lose whatever community functions they still
possessed.   As communications improve, local markets
dwindle in importance, and the youth from the upper and
middle strata migrate to the cities.   These migrants are
often replaced by families of landless agricultural workers
who drift in from the countryside and who contribute to the
"ruralization" of the small towns.   Policies for the selective
invigoration of the towns, so that they can become real
community centers, links rather than barriers between the
rural people and the national society, may well be among
the most important tasks of rural development planning.

Centralism versus Localism

The extreme case of Aritama shows that effective
planning requires a high degree of continuity and consistency
and, above all, transmission belts in good working order
between the central agency and the local bodies that actually
perform the services.   It also suggests that decentralized
local control of education, however desirable in principle,
is not a satisfactory alternative to centralized direction, unless it is accompanied by far-reaching reforms ending the
sterile monopoly of power by small urban cliques and giving
the rural people a voice in local government.

However, over-centralization tends to stimulate a reaction of intense localism, and local pressures, which can
be very effective, are hard to reconcile either with the fixing of priorities at the national level or with rational decentralization.   As educational systems have grown, they
have naturally attracted increased attention from the spokes-
men of localism, and the results have often been deplorable.
The national authorities are likely to yield half-way to the
pressure, permit the creation of an institution without any
thought to its staffing or the local availability of qualified
pupils, and then leave it too starved of funds to serve any
purpose in any case.   Sometimes the nationally influential
person responsible for pushing through the project loses his
influence and the project is stopped after important sums
have been spent on it.

Vigorous local pressures, however, may be on

balance a healthy phenomenon, if only to counteract the pressures for concentrating investments in the capital cities.
The role of the planner is to help the local authorities to
formulate rational and balanced demands, to explain the implications and associated requirements of the projects they
ask for, to induce them to commit local resources, and to
ensure that the national authorities understand the project
and accept the minimum future requirements for its functioning before committing resources to it. The technique for
accomplishing these purposes will presumably include the
organization of local planning committees representing the
different sectors of the public as well as local authorities,
and the provision of technical advisers to work with such
local committees.

The Marginal Groups

But perhaps the most troublesome social problem
with regard to educational planning arises in connection with
the growing marginal groups, rural as well as urban.   Millions of families that continue to depend on agricultural
work no longer fit into the traditional agricultural system
and have to depend on seasonal work.   They live in clusters
of improvised huts along the roadsides or on the outskirts of
the town, and since the men must follow the harvest, family
life is characteristically unstable.   As for the urban marginal groups, their present rapid growth is only too well
known.   So is their virtual isolation from the national society, their lack of opportunities and of purpose.   The application of educational planning to these rural and urban marginal groups deserves a study in itself.

The urban marginal groups are internally more varied
than the rural ones, are better organized, and have more
capacity to exert political pressure.   Undoubtedly, a good
many families trapped in them rely heavily on education as
a means of upward mobility and make desperate efforts to
keep their children at school.   But as such settlements grow
in size and become farther removed from the urban center,
the physical barriers between them and the rest of the urban population become harder to cross.   To the rest of the
city population they are almost a foreign country, ignored
or considered with a mixture of contempt and fear.

The tasks of the school in such an environment are
potentially of the highest importance, but it is questionable

how far a purely quantitative expansion of conventional schooling can be relevant. Meanwhile, the rapid growth of these
marginal groups combined with the more effective demand
for education on the part of other urban groups results in a
situation where the children of the marginal groups get only
a minimum of education in overcrowded schools. The real
opportunities of these children are only slightly better than
those of the rural groups.

The range of measures needed to deal with this problem will require, among other things, appropriate employment policies, regional and city planning, and housing and
social welfare programs, as well as educational programs.
The trouble is that all these measures are costly, and that
a diversion of resources to the marginal groups on a scale
that would enable them to overcome their marginality would
meet formidable obstacles, both economic and political.

The central problem of Latin America could hardly
be stated more vigorously than was done 12 years ago by
Alberto Lleras Camargo in his address in 1960 explaining
to the nation the bases of Colombia's ten-year development
plan:

> It would not be exaggerated to say that there are
> two sectors in which persist almost unchanged out-
> worn forms corresponding to social, political and
> economic systems that ... are going to disappear
> altogether in the course of a few years. One is
> agriculture; the other education. The anachronism
> of the second is the more harmful because it is
> transmitting false or sterile criteria to the new
> generations.

The major problems depend for their solution, first
on a real determination of the political leadership to solve
them and, second, on the willingness of the different sectors
of society to reconcile their educational aspirations for their
children with the requirements of economic development and
social justice. The planner, while contributing as fully as
he can to this reconciliation, must assume that society supports the directives he has been given.

Notes

1. El Mercurio (Santiago, Chile), 2 March 1964.

2. Frank Tannenbaum, Ten Keys to Latin America, New
    York: Knopf, 1962, p. 101.

3. Gerardo and Alicia Reichel-Dolmatoff, The People of
    Aritama. London: 1961.

20. EDUCATION FOR TODAY OR YESTERDAY?
Sylvain Lourié*

In recent years both Unesco and the OAS have carried out detailed studies on many aspects of Latin American education. These studies have made it possible to appreciate the efforts made to increase enrollments between 1950 and 1960, to obtain statistical information showing the framework within which this development took place, and to identify the obstacles to the effective working of the educational system. Indeed, the system does not yet appear capable of providing complete education for the entire seven- to 24-year-old age group or of meeting the needs for skilled manpower. This article will provide an overall survey and an analytic comparison of the problems involved in educational systems with the demands of developing societies in Latin America and with the efficiency with which public funds are used to maintain this system.

Primary Education

The outstanding feature of primary education in Latin America is the tremendous growth in enrollment, which far exceeds the demographic explosion. Between 1950 and 1960, the number of children in primary schools in the 20 countries rose from 15 million to 26 million, an increase of over 73 percent. Actually in six of the countries--Bolivia, Colombia, the Dominican Republic, El Salvador, Haiti and Venezuela--enrollments rose by over 100 percent. The enrollment ratio for the area rose from 72 percent in 1950 to 78.5 percent in 1960, [1] and should it continue to rise at the same rate, full enrollment would be reached by 1970.

This expansion equals 5.7 percent per annum, which

*Reprinted by permission of UNESCO from Raymond F. Lyons, Problems and Strategies of Educational Planning: Lessons from Latin America, Paris: UNESCO, International Institute for Educational Planning, 1965.

is twice the rate of expansion of the primary school age
group. [2] It reflects therefore not only the requirements of
an expanding population, but above all an increasing demand
for education.   This increase in demand is likely to continue
during the present decade, and it may be asked to what extent the rise in enrollments represents real education received by the relevant age group.

The compulsory schooling period varies, according to
country, between five and seven years in urban schools and
four to five years in rural schools.   However, an enrollment
ratio of 78. 5 percent in 1960 does not mean that that percentage of the five- to 14-year-old age group actually completed the full legal period.   In 16 Latin American countries,
the average length of education received by the population of
over 15 years of age amounted to 2. 2 years.   The explanation lies in the fact that, while a large number of children
are enrolled for the first year at primary school, an average
of 50 percent drop out after the first year.   Drop-out continues in the subsequent years, so that only 13. 5 percent
complete five years and 9. 5 percent, six years of education.

These figures may give an exaggerated picture of the
situation, as they are calculated by comparing the apex of
the primary school pyramid (fifth or sixth year) with the
base (first year) for the same year (1960).   A more accurate picture is given by the apparent retention rate, obtained
by following a cohort throughout the primary school period.
For countries where the enrollment ratio has been comparatively high in the last five or six years, the apparent retention rate gives the same results as the apex-base ratio; but
in countries where enrollment has expanded only recently,
the apparent retention rate after six years is nearer 12. 5
than 9. 5 percent.   This figure compares with a rate of 82
percent in the United States.   The average cost to the state
of a primary school-leaver is 1. 1 times the cost per pupil
of the educational cycle in the United States, but 4. 1 times
that cost in Latin America.

In the light of the existing legislation, the highest enrollment ratio should be at the age of seven.   However, in
eight countries the age at which the ratio was highest in
1960 was nine.   The average entrance age was between 8. 3
and 9. 2.   These figures reflect partly the high repeat rate
(about 20 percent), but mainly the relatively late age at
which rural children are enrolled--temporarily and irregu-
larly.   While they show that the rural population wants

(cont. p. 266)

EDUCATION FOR TODAY OR YESTERDAY; SYLVAIN LOURIÉ. STATISTICAL ANNEX

I. PRIMARY EDUCATION: TOTAL ENROLMENT AS A PERCENTAGE OF AGE GROUP 7-12 AND PRIVATE ENROLMENT

| | 1957 | | 1960 | | 1962 | | ENROLMENT AS PERCENTAGE OF AGE GROUP 7-12[a] | | | PRIVATE ENROLMENT[d] AS PERCENTAGE OF TOTAL | |
	THOUSANDS[d] ENROLLED	INDEX[e]	THOUSANDS[d] ENROLLED	INDEX[e] (1957=100)	THOUSANDS[d] ENROLLED	INDEX[e] (1957=100)	1957	1960	1962	1957	1962
Argentina	2 783	100	2 948	106	3 056	110	113	113	114	10[a]	12
Bolivia	317[a]	100	424	134	511[a]	161	60	76	87	15[a]	30[a]
Brazil	6 466	100	7 529	116	7 846	121	68	74	72	10[a]	11[a]
Chile	997	100	1 108	111	1 274	128	94	98	107	33	30
Colombia	1 381	100	1 674[a]	121	1 904	138	62	68	73	15	15
Costa Rica	168	100	198	118	222[a]	132	108	110	113	5	5[a]
Cuba	756	100	1 368	181	1 177[b]	156	83	141	116	16[a]	—
Dominican Repub.	462	100	499	108	487	105	108	105	96	4	5
Ecuador	502	100	595[a]	119	642[a]	128	80	86	87	20	19
El Salvador	237	100	290	122	354	149	71	80	89	8	4
Guatemala	250	100	297	119	335	134	45	46	47	19	19[a]
Haiti	200	100	238	119	260[a]	130	37	41	43	23	31[a]
Honduras	147	100	205	139	238	162	56	73	80	10	7
Mexico	3 826	100	4 807	126	5 620	147	74	84	92	9	8
Nicaragua	132	100	168	127	194[a]	147	65	75	78	9[a]	15[a]
Panama	143	100	162	113	180[a]	126	97	101	104	7	5[a]
Paraguay	287	100	305	106	323	113	117	117	120	7	8
Peru	1 202	100	1 433	119	1 562	120	78	86	88	9	15
Uruguay	302	100	322	107	343	114	104	107	112	18	21
Venezuela	694	100	1 095	158	1 277	184	71	101	109	19	12
TOTAL	21 249	100	25 664	121	27 804	131	75	84	86	12	—[c]

[a] Estimate.
[b] Public schools only.
[c] Not available.
[d] *Source:* Data kindly provided by Mr. Sebastián Ferrer Martín, Expert in Educational Statistics, Latin American Institute for Economic and Social Planning. Based on answers to questionnaires submitted in connection with the Report of the Intergovernmental Consultative Committee for the Unesco Major Project.
[e] *Source:* Indices and percentages calculated by the IIEP secretariat on the basis of data provided by Mr. Sebastián Ferrer Martín.

II. SECONDARY EDUCATION: TOTAL ENROLMENT AS A PERCENTAGE OF AGE GROUP 13-19 AND PRIVATE ENROLMENT

	1955		1960		1962		ENROLMENT AS PERCENTAGE OF AGE GROUP 13-19[c]		PRIVATE ENROLMENT AS PERCENTAGE OF TOTAL[c]
	THOUSANDS[a] ENROLLED	INDEX[c]	THOUSANDS[a] ENROLLED	INDEX[c] (1955=100)	THOUSANDS[b] ENROLLED	INDEX[c] (1955=100)	1960	1962	1962
Argentina	484	100	832	172	925	191	34	36	45
Bolivia	33	100	54	164	63	191	10	12	33
Brazil	766	100	1 308	171	1 464	191	14	15	64
Chile	166	100	230	139	286	172	22	26	42
Colombia	129	100	254	197	334	259	12	15	...
Costa Rica	18	100	34	189	37	206	21	22	32
Cuba	76	100	123	162	150	197	13	16	...
Dominican Republic	19	100	22	116	53	279	5	12	...
Ecuador	43	100	63	147	86	200	10	13	37
El Salvador	21	100	34	162	45	214	10	13	49
Guatemala	19	100	26	137	45	195	5	6	43
Haiti	15	100	19	127	23	153	4	4	...
Honduras	9	100	15	167	17	189	6	6	...
Mexico	179	100	390	218	593	331	8	11	35
Nicaragua	5	100	10	200	15	300	5	7	...
Panama	25	100	39	156	45	180	28	30	38
Paraguay	16	100	35	219	37	231	15	16	27
Peru	115	100	202	176	270	235	14	17	...
Uruguay	67	100	87	130	99	148	31	34	14
Venezuela	65	100	183	282	208	320	19	20	25
TOTAL	2 270	100	3 960	174	4 787	211	15	17	—[d]

a *Source:* Data kindly provided by Mr. Sylvain Lourié, member of the Institut d'étude du développement économique et social, Paris. Based on "Education in Latin America", a working document prepared for the OAS Special Committee on Education. Data for Cuba drawn from the *Unesco World Survey of Education, 1960*.

b *Source:* Data kindly provided by Mr. Sebastián Ferrer Martin. Based on data prepared by national Ministries of Education with the Unesco Major Project.

c *Source:* Indices and percentages calculated by the IIEP secretariat on the basis of data supplied by Mr. Sylvain Lourié and Mr. Sebastián Ferrer Martin.

d ... Not available.

EDUCATION FOR TODAY OR YESTERDAY; SYLVAIN LOURIÉ. STATISTICAL ANNEX

III. SECONDARY EDUCATION. ENROLMENT BY TYPE OF STUDY, 1962 (HUNDREDS)[d]

	ACADEMIC SECONDARY	TEACHER TRAINING	TECHNICAL INDUSTRIAL	COMMERCIAL	AGRICULTURAL	HOME ECONOMICS	OTHERS	TOTAL
Argentina	1 554	1 509	1 028	1 304	30	788	3 039	9 253
Bolivia	...	40	...	...	...	...	...	625
Brazil	10 748	1 138	366	2 320	72	—	...	14 644
Chile	1 979	76	228	368	35	178	—	2 864
Colombia	1 848	401	167	538	42	30	313	3 338
Costa Rica[a]	313	[b]	15	33	6	3	—	369
Cuba	967	86	149	201	...	...	55	1 497
Dominican Republic	321	3	35	46	—	12	113	531
Ecuador	492	93	...	278[c]	...	—	—	863
El Salvador	305	56	10	74	...	3	...	448
Guatemala	25	42	11	22	—	13	255	369
Haiti	...	2	...	...	...	...	...	228
Honduras	15	13	5	14	1	1	120	170
Mexico	4 626	388	...	777[c]	...	...	143	5 935
Nicaragua	95	29	5	21	1	—	3	154
Panama	...	9	...	...	...	...	...	453
Paraguay	44	81	8	12	2	24	199	370
Peru	2 006	65	207	214	46	164	—	2 703
Uruguay	760	27	...	204[c]	...	...	—	991
Venezuela	1 223	324	172	251	19	5	87	2 082
TOTAL	27 321	5 489	2 406	10 558[c]	254	1 221	4 327	47 887

... No available data.
— This type of study does not exist.
[a] Source: Data furnished by the Ministry of Education of Costa Rica in 1963.
[b] Teacher-training schools are at university level.
[c] Includes Technical, Industrial, Commercial, Agricultural and Home Economics studies.
[d] Source: Data kindly provided by Mr. Sebastián Ferrer Martín. Based on replies to questionnaires submitted in connection with the Report of the Intergovernmental Consultative Committee, Unesco Major Project.

EDUCATION FOR TODAY OR YESTERDAY; SYLVAIN LOURIÉ. STATISTICAL ANNEX

IV. HIGHER EDUCATION: TOTAL ENROLMENT AS A PERCENTAGE OF AGE GROUP 20-24. 1955, 1960, 1962

	1955[a]		1960[a]		1962[a]		ENROLMENT AS PERCENTAGE OF AGE GROUP 20-24[b]		
	THOUSANDS ENROLLED	INDEX[b]	THOUSANDS ENROLLED	INDEX[b] (1955=100)	THOUSANDS ENROLLED	INDEX[b] (1955=100)	1955	1960	1962
Argentina	149	100	166	111	192	129	9	10	11
Bolivia	4	100	8	200	...	...	2	3	...
Brazil	74	100	96	130	107	145	1	2	2
Chile	20	100	27	135	28	140	3	5	4
Colombia	13	100	23	177	29	223	1	2	2
Costa Rica	3	100	5	167	6	200	4	5	6
Cuba	17	100	12	71	...	...	3	2	...
Dominican Republic	3	100	5	167	4	133	1	2	1
Ecuador	6	100	9	150	11	183	2	3	3
El Salvador	1	100	2	200	3	300	1	1	1
Guatemala	3	100	4	133	7	233	1	1	2
Haiti	1	100	2	200	2	200	1	1	1
Honduras	1	100	2	200	2	200	1	1	1
Mexico	79	100	88	111	101	128	3	3	3
Nicaragua	1	100	1	100	2	200	1	1	1
Panama	2	100	4	200	5	250	3	5	5
Paraguay	2	100	3	150	4	200	2	2	3
Peru	17	100	29	171	38	224	1	3	4
Uruguay	15	100	21	140	...	...	7	10	...
Venezuela	8	100	24	300	32	400	2	4	5
TOTAL	419	100	530	126	573	137	3	3	3

... Data not available.

[a] *Source:* Data kindly provided by Mr. Sylvain Lourié, Member of the "Institut d'étude du développement économique et social", Paris. Based on "Education in Latin America", a working document prepared for the OAS Special Committee on Education. Data for Cuba drawn from the *Unesco World Survey of Education 1960.*

[b] *Source:* Indices and percentages calculated by the IIEP secretariat on the basis of data supplied by Mr. Sylvain Lourié and Mr. Sebastián Ferrer Martín.

[c] *Source:* Data kindly supplied by Mr. Sebastián Ferrer Martín. Based on answers to questionnaires submitted in connection with the Report of the Intergovernmental Consultative Committee, Unesco Major Project.

EDUCATION FOR TODAY OR YESTERDAY; SYLVAIN LOURIÉ. STATISTICAL ANNEX

V. HIGHER EDUCATION: TOTAL ENROLMENT BY TYPE OF STUDY, LATEST AVAILABLE DATA (HUNDREDS)[c]

	YEAR	AGRI-CULTURE	BEAUX ARTS	EXACT AND NATURAL SCIENCES	MEDICAL SCIENCES	SOCIAL SCIENCES	LAW	HUMAN-ITIES	ENGINEER-ING	EDUCATION	OTHERS	TOTAL
Argentina	1962	44	105	199	448	323	298	128	211	164	—	1 922
Bolivia	1961	...	...	...	...	...	...	...	...	...	...	1 000
Brazil	1962	42	...	—	200	116	235	223[a]	164	...	20	288
Chile	1961	12	7	2	45	30	29	3	72	79	9	269
Colombia	1962	20	—	5	46	26	44	15	82	10	23	48
Costa Rica[b]	1962	1	...	4	2	5	3	25	2	6	...	...
Cuba	...	...	...	...	...	...	...	...	...	...	...	41
Dominican Republic	1962	...	...	...	...	...	...	...	...	...	...	111
Ecuador	1962	...	...	3	4	5	7	5	6	...	...	30
El Salvador[b]	1962	1	...	4	10	11	15	5	10	3	...	59
Guatemala[b]	1962	4	2	1	4	4	6	—	1	...	...	16
Haiti	1962	...	...	1	2	4	3	5	2	...	6	17
Honduras[b]	1962	26	...	112	179	234	131	51	275	2	...	1 014
Mexico[b]	1962	...	...	...	5	4	2	16[a]	1	2	—	15
Nicaragua[b]	1962	1	2	8	1	7	2	3	5	1	—	40
Panama	1960	2	...	1	8	8	8	48	3	18	39	36
Paraguay	1962	...	2	6	39	39	30	11	39	—	—	268
Peru	1959	10	—	5	36	19	44	31	18	24	—	140
Uruguay	1961	6	—	7	58	60	55	31	68	...	5	316
Venezuela	1962	8	—									

... Data not available.

— Type of study does not exist.

a Includes teaching.

b Source: Data kindly supplied by Mr Carlos Tünnermann Bernheim, Secretary General, CSUCA.

c Source: Data kindly provided by Mr. Sebastián Ferrer Martín. Based on data prepared by national Ministries of Education in connection with the Unesco Major Project.

EDUCATION FOR TODAY OR YESTERDAY; SYLVAIN LOURIÉ. STATISTICAL ANNEX

VI. PUBLIC EXPENDITURE ON EDUCATION AS PERCENTAGE OF G.N.P. 1960

	G.P.N. IN NATIONAL CURRENCY (MILLIONS)	G.N.P. $ US (MILLIONS)	PUB. EXP. ON EDUCATION IN NATIONAL CURRENCY (MILLIONS)	PUB. EXP. ON EDUCATION $ US (MILLIONS)	PERCENTAGE PUB. EXP. G.N.P.	EXCHANGE RATE $ 1.00 US
Argentina (peso)	785 300.0	9 495	15.1	182.6	1.9	82.71
Bolivia (boliviano)	4 689.0	394	84.8	7.1	1.8	11.88
Brazil (cruzeiro)	2 454 000.0	11 963	51.4	250.5	2.1	205.14
Chile (escudo)	4 646.0	4 412	128.0	121.9	2.8	1.05
Colombia (peso)	26 200.0	3 618	492.0	68.0	1.9	7.23
Costa Rica (colon)	2 655.0	400	105.7	15.9	3.9	6.65
Cuba (peso)	2 400.0	2 400	110.2	110.2	4.6	1.00
Dominican Republic (peso)	708.0	708	10.6	10.6	1.5	1.00
Ecuador (sucre)	13 627.0	773	215.7	12.3	1.6	17.53
El Salvador (colon)	1 299.9	492	33.0	13.2	2.7	2.50
Guatemala (quetzal)	674.0	674	16.2	16.2	2.4	1.00
Haiti (gourde)	1 559.8	312	25.0	5.0	1.6	5.00
Honduras (lempira)	779.0	386	10.1	7.9	2.0	2.02
Mexico (peso)	134 400.0	10 760	2 593.0	207.6	1.9	12.89
Nicaragua (córdoba)	2 203.0	312	35.0	4.9	1.6	7.05
Panama (balboa)	423.0	423	16.6	16.6	3.9	1.00
Paraguay (guarabi)	25 035.0	232	440.0	3.5	1.5	126.00
Peru (sol)	53 400.0	1 995	1 387.0	51.9	2.6	26.76
Uruguay (peso)	12 020.0	1 089	272.0	24.7	2.3	11.03
Venezuela (bolivar)	22 900.0	6 899	635.0	189.5	2.7	3.35
TOTAL		57 737		1 320.0	2.3	

Source: Data provided by the "Institut d'étude du développement économique et social", Paris.

education for its children independently of the children's age,
they also illustrate the unsuitability of the system.

In the strict sense of the term, the pupils enrolled in
public primary schools in 1960 received free education. However, if free education is understood to mean that access to
education involves no discrimination based on financial means,
the mere fact that there are no school fees is not enough.
This is especially true for the vast majority of the pupils of
rural schools who must find the means to pay for clothing,
food, books, exercise books, pencils, etc., quite apart from
the fact that their attendance at school means one hand less
on the family plot. In fact, reality conforms to legislation
only in the traditional urban schools. Primary education is
still in its original form conceived to comply with the needs
of an urban society; it has not been adjusted to the rural environment either in nature and form (school-year unrelated
to the seasons of rural activity) or in content, in the sense
that it has not been adapted to a rural environment. Most
of the teachers without minimum qualifications, i.e., the
first or second cycle of secondary education, are to be found
in rural schools. In nine of the countries only 15 percent
of the rural teaching staff was qualified. In 1960, in the
19 countries (omitting Cuba) some 115,000 teachers out of a
total of 250,000 were unqualified.

Nor is the distribution of school facilities any more
satisfactory. Most studies recommend a more rational distribution of schools, particularly the establishment of single-
teacher schools. This appears justified by the fact that the
number of pupils per teacher, which is high in the lower
grades (up to 70) drops sharply in the upper grades (to
fewer than 10). Thus several upper grades might well be
looked after by the same teacher in a single class-room.

Secondary Education

In secondary education, the rate of growth in enrollments is far greater than in primary education, but the absolute figures are considerably lower, and full enrollment
cannot be expected to materialize even in the next 15 years.
Enrollments rose from 1,552,000 in 1950 to 3,960,000 in
1960, which represents a total increase of 155 percent and
an annual increase of 9.8 percent--i.e., 1.72 times the
rate of expansion in primary school enrollments. Yet in
1960, the enrollment ratio of the age group was only 15.5

percent, as compared with 7 percent in 1950.

If enrollments continue to expand at the same rate,
more than seven million pupils, or roughly 20 percent of the
age group, should be attending secondary schools in 1970.
However, because of the expansion in primary school enrollments, this figure is likely to be exceeded. According to a
survey of 19 Latin American countries (again excepting Cuba),
enrollments increased by 8.3 percent and secondary school
enrollments by 13.2 percent per annum between 1960 and
1962. Secondary school enrollments were thus likely to have
reached 10 million by 1970, [3] i.e., 30 percent of the age
group and 2.5 times the figure for 1960. Such an effort
would not be out of proportion to economic requirements,
since there is an increasing demand for medium-level staff
trained at technical and vocational secondary schools. This,
however, would imply a change in the present trend which
favors general secondary schools. It was seen as probable
that in eight countries--Argentina, Colombia, Costa Rica,
Cuba, El Salvador, Panama, Uruguay and Venezuela--the
enrollment ratio will exceed 40 percent, while in four coun-
tries--the Dominican Republic, Guatemala, Haiti and Nica-
ragua--it would still be below 10 percent in 1970.

As in the case of primary education, the main obstacle to such expansion is the high rate of drop-outs and,
consequently, the high cost of the matriculated pupil. Unfortunately, calculations based on the apparent retention rate
are available for only five countries. Output must therefore
be calculated by means of the apex-base ratio for the same
year, with all the reservations such calculation implies.
For the 19 countries as a whole, this ratio was 11.7 percent in 1960, as compared with 9.5 percent for primary
education. It may be mentioned that for the first cycle of
secondary education, the apex-base ratio is 44.5 percent,
which indicates a better output than for the corresponding
period of primary education, the ratio between the third and
first year being 36 percent. On the basis of these figures,
the cost of the matriculated pupil is four times the theoretical cost, i.e., the cost of the six-year cycle, while in the
United States the corresponding figure is 1.36. This fact
is of special importance for Latin America, as 50 percent
of the secondary school pupils attend private schools (70
percent in the case of general secondary schools).

As far as teaching staff is concerned, 70 percent of
the teachers are not qualified. Most of them are members

of liberal professions who teach, for only a few hours weekly, subjects not always related to their profession.   Trained
teachers often divide their time among several schools where
they are supposed to provide full-time teaching.   In 1960,
the pupil/teacher ratio was about 23:1.   It appears to have
increased slightly between 1957 and 1960, a fact which, far
from being discouraging, rather reflects an increased number of full-time teachers, each of whom does the work of
several part-time teachers.

In 1960, 64 percent of all the pupils were at general
secondary schools, which prepare pupils for higher education;
27 percent attended technical schools; and 9 percent, a great
majority of them girls, teacher-training schools.   Over half
of the pupils in technical schools studied commercial courses;
more than 40 percent, industrial techniques and women's
crafts; and 4 percent, agriculture.   The very small number
studying agriculture is quite inadequate to meet the needs,
especially as most of the pupils completing agricultural
schools end up in the civil service.   It is also worthy of
note that, with the exception of pupils at industrial technical
schools, who represent 9 percent of the total, all secondary
school-leavers enter the tertiary sector, i. e., liberal professions, commerce, administration, etc.

Not only are the structure and content of secondary
education out of line with modern economic requirements,
but the material conditions of education leave much to be
desired.   Facilities for practical work are inadequate and
there is a shortage of laboratories and libraries.

Analysis of the Educational System

As already mentioned, the rise in enrollments reflects not only an increase in population, but also an increase in the demand for education at all levels.   Does this
increase in demand correspond to the needs of the labor
market, and if not, what is the solution, and on what variables does it depend?   To answer this question, let us first
of all recapitulate the main features of Latin American educational development.   Between 1950 and 1960, the annual
average rates of increase in enrollments were 5. 7 percent
for primary education, 9. 8 percent for secondary education,
and 8. 4 percent for higher education.   In 1960, the enrollment ratios were as follows:

Primary education (7-12)   78. 5% (26 million pupils)
Secondary education (13-19)   15. 5% (3. 9 million pupils)
Higher education (20-24)   3. 1% (0. 54 million students).

The apex-base ratio per 1, 000 enrollments in 1960 was, in terms of sixth-year passes, 95 in primary education, 118 in secondary education, and 58 in higher education. For every 1, 000 pupils enrolled in the first year of primary school,

95 reach the last grade of primary school
15 reach the last grade of secondary school
 4 reach the fifth university year
 1 reaches the sixth university year.

In terms of total school enrollments, as distinct from the apex-base ratio, the proportion of school-leavers and graduates is 4 percent for primary education, 5 percent for secondary education, and 10 percent for higher education. Accepting the enrollment targets for 1970 as 100 percent for primary education, 30 percent for secondary education, and 5 percent for higher education, it was estimated that the expansion of education between 1960 and 1970 would produce

13. 5 million primary school-leavers
 3. 5 million secondary school-leavers
 1. 0 million higher education graduates.

The skilled manpower population (secondary school and university graduates or equivalent) in Latin America amounted to some 22. 5 million in 1960. Assuming a depletion rate of 25 percent over the period 1960-1970, the replacements required would amount to 5. 6 million. But the stock of secondary school and university graduates produced during this period were estimated to be 4. 5 million only, leaving out of account the needs for teachers: should these be taken into account, the figure of 4. 5 million would fall to 2. 2 million. In other words, the present educational system, should it continue to expand as planned, will not even be capable of meeting replacement requirements. Obviously, the assumption that all skilled personnel would have completed the full cycle of secondary education or of higher education is not realistic. Even so, the gap between supply and demand is spectacular enough to give an idea of the extent of the problem, especially if the educational system continues in the form in which it was conceived 150 years ago and if any changes in it are limited to the absorption of

a larger number of pupils.   It is clear that neither secondary
nor higher education is influenced by the requirements of the
labor market and, although specialized staff can be trained
outside the formal educational system, everything should be
done to adapt the formal educational system to the needs of
the economy.

One of the first steps would be the raising of the educational survival rate.   This might be brought about by obtaining qualified teachers.   If the apparent output of the system could be doubled, the number of teachers would not vary,
since it is based on the overall enrollment figures, but the
number of qualified personnel available to the economy would
rise correspondingly.

Another vital reform would consist of amending the
content of education with a view to increasing the number of
openings after three or four years of secondary school, or
two to three years of higher education.   This would considerably increase the supply of skilled personnel and high-level
technicians, and also increase the ratio of graduates to first-
year enrollments.   The remedy is to give freer access to
the various levels of education by abolishing the barriers
which hinder access at present.   One of these barriers is
the rural primary school which does not comply with entrance requirements of secondary schools.   Another is the
general secondary school cut off from technical or teacher-
training schools and designed exclusively to prepare pupils
for higher education.   Yet another barrier is the competi-
tive entrance examination at universities designed to eliminate applicants either because the secondary education has
been inadequate or because access to certain traditional professions has to be restricted.

Cost and Finance of Education

In establishing the cost per level, it was found advisable to express it in terms of the cost per primary school
pupil (C_p) rather than in terms of a standard monetary unit.
This shows that the cost of secondary education is on an
average 6.4 times the cost of primary education, and the
cost of higher education 27 times that of primary education.
With the present rate of educational wastage, the cost per
graduated pupil or student is as follows:

primary education: 4.125 times cost of 6-year education;
secondary education: 3.975 times cost of 6-year education;
higher education: 2.15 times cost of 5-year education.

The cost of complete education, expressed in terms
of the cost of primary education, would be given by the following equation, assuming that there is no wastage:

$$6C_p + 6(6.4C_p) + 5(27C_p) = 179.4C_p .$$

Wastage alters this equation as follows:

$$4.125x6Cp + 3.975x38.4Cp + 2.15x135Cp = 467.64Cp.$$

In other words, the complete educational cycle costs 2.6
times more per graduate than it would if there were no
wastage.

If we now examine the total budgets devoted to public
education, we find that primary education takes 53.8 percent,
secondary education, 30.5 percent, and higher education,
15.7 percent.[4] Neglecting other costs, such as administration and adult education, and subsidies to private education,
the total budget B_E would then be distributed as follows
among the three levels:

[Primary education] $B_F = 0.438 \ B_E$
[Secondary education] $B_S = 0.305 \ B_E$
[Higher education] $B_U = 0.157 \ B_E$

The proportion of the budget actually devoted to financing a
full education can be calculated as follows:

$$B_F \text{ graduates} = \frac{0.538 \ B_E}{4.125} = 0.1305.$$

$$B_S \text{ graduates} = \frac{0.305 \ B_E}{3.975} = 0.0768.$$

$$B_U \text{ graduates} = \frac{0.157 \ B_E}{2.15} = 0.0730.$$

$$\overline{B_E \text{ graduates}} = \overline{0.2803 \ B_E} \quad \text{i. e.,}$$

28 percent of B_E.

In other words, 72 percent of the budget is used to
pay for studies that are never completed. No doubt this is
not an absolute criterion, since even an incomplete education
has a definite value. It may be said, however, that 72 percent of the educational expenditure gives only a very small
return to society. An ideal system would yield a return
3. 5 times as high.

The total educational expenditures rose by almost 12
percent per year during the period 1955-1960, and by more
than 20 percent per year in Honduras, Chile and Venezuela.
In 1960, the arithmetic mean of public expenditures on education, expressed in local non-weighted currency, was 2. 5
percent of GNP. Expressed in U. S. dollars, the total was
1, 320 million--i. e., 2. 27 percent of a GNP evaluated at
57, 730 million. Taking into account private education, the
expenditure on which can be put roughly at 20 percent of
public expenditure, the total expenditure on education rises
to 1, 584 million--i. e., 2. 68 percent of GNP.

This proportion of 2. 68 percent compares with 4. 4
percent in the U. S. A., 3. 5 percent in France and the Bene-
lux countries, and 3. 74 percent in the U. S. S. R. It should
also be borne in mind that more than half of this expenditure
is devoted to primary education where, with an output of
only 10 percent, the cost of the school-leaver is over four
times the cost of the educational cycle. If the output could
be raised to 20 percent, the cost of the primary school-
leaver would be only 2. 5 times the cost of the educational
cycle, and the number of school-leavers would be doubled
with practically the same financial means. It can therefore
be concluded that the small returns on educational expenditure are due not to the small financial means provided, but
to the inefficiency of a system in which the available funds
are not properly used. The fact that this inefficiency is
barely beginning to be recognized as a result of budgetary
planning largely reflects the Latin American attitude to education, which is regarded as a social non-profitable activity,
and not as a factor of economic development which requires
rational administration in the framework of planning.

Notes

1.   Computed on the basis of 5/10, 6/10, or 7/10 of the
     ten-year age group (5-14), depending for each country
     on the legal duration of primary schooling, which

varies from five to seven years.

2. By primary school age group is meant the seven- to 12-
    year-old group taken as an average for the continent,
    and not the five to 14 demographic group often used
    as a basis for a global computation of enrollment
    ratios in primary education.

3. See OAS, Education in Latin America: Statistical Sur-
    vey, 1963 (Washington, D. C.).

4. Ibid.

21. EDUCATION FOR THE FUTURE: THE DILEMMA OF
      LATIN AMERICA
      Paul Hines*

Latin America is a land of potentially great wealth
but the area is now one marked by extreme poverty. While
there is a well-established upper class and a growing middle
class, ignorance coupled with poverty are the lot of those
living in the urban slums and in the vast undeveloped rural
areas. Millions of Latin Americans speak of themselves as
the abandonados, a people outside the national culture and
society.[1] The Latin America frequently envisioned by the
United States citizen is the Latin America of the travel
poster--Rio, Buenos Aires, and Acapulco. While these
beautiful vacation areas are indicative of a segment of Latin
American culture, they are not representative of the life
which most Latin Americans experience. In 1950, some 120
of the 200 million people from Mexico to Tierra del Fuego
lived directly or indirectly on primitive agriculture.[2] While
the urban population is growing much faster than the rural
population, the percentage of persons dependent upon primitive agriculture remains high.

After viewing the current literature available on Latin
America, there is no surprise at the misconceptions which
the general United States public has of Latin America. When
compared with most other cultural areas, the amount of peri-
odical information available on Latin America is not impressive. Secondary school world history textbooks give Latin
America scant coverage. One textbook widely used in the
United States limited its coverage of Latin America to nine
of 822 pages. Other chronologically oriented texts provide
similar coverage.[3] With the world situation so explosive
and with the increasingly prominent role Latin America
plays at the United Nations, more attention should be given

*Reprinted by permission of Ball State University and the
Indiana Social Studies Quarterly from Ind. Soc. Studies Q.,
vol. 22, no. 1 (Spring 1969), p. 32-43.

to this area.

Latin America is experiencing rapid change. In the field of education, the area is making significant progress. Still in no Latin American country do more than 27 percent of any age group get beyond the sixth grade. Yet no Latin American country spends less than 18 percent of its national budget on education. Some countries spend over 30 percent.[4] While these statistics may be viewed as both discouraging and encouraging, many authorities view the hope of Latin America as being the development of a universal education system.[5] They cite the example of the United States and its success in regard to universal education. But Latin America faces a number of complex problems which hamper its progress toward such a goal.

Latin America has one of the highest population growth rates of any geographic area in the world. The population of the continent has been increasing at the rate of 3 percent annually.[6] The result is a higher proportion of children in the population than would be usual. In Europe there are four adults to every child of school age, but in Latin America there are only two. Therefore, the educational costs borne by an individual in Latin America are twice as great as those borne by his more affluent counterpart in England or France. Coupled with this financial burden, the Latin American is frequently faced with the necessity of providing instruction in languages other than the expected Spanish or Portuguese. For example, at least one half the citizens of Bolivia, Ecuador, Guatemala, and Peru cannot speak the official language. The high population growth rate with its resulting financial burden and the numerous Indian dialects of the area make the establishment of a universal school system a difficult task.[7] Economic development has been unable to keep pace with the high population increase in Latin America. Per capita income has been increasing only at the rate of 1 percent per year. In some of the more advanced Latin American countries, the per capita income growth has been above 1 percent but in other areas the rate has actually been declining.[8]

In foreign trade, the situation has not improved. Prior to World War II, Latin America controlled 11 percent of the world market. By the 1950's this percentage had dropped to 9 percent, and by 1962, the share of the world market was only 6.5 percent. Part of the decline results from the fact that the raw materials which Latin America needs to trade are decreasing in value while the manufactured imports needed for continuation of the economy are increasing in price. The result is an unfavorable balance of trade and less foreign currency coming into Latin America. The need for foreign currency has forced many Latin American governments into heavy borrowing. In the period from 1951 to 1962, Latin America borrowed through public and private sources, medium-, short-, and long-term loans in the amount of eight billion dollars. During this same period, ten billion dollars in income was lost through decline in trade. In many Latin American countries, the proportion of earnings needed to service the foreign debt has risen to 22 percent, yet 15 percent is considered to be a high proportion of foreign exchange expended on servicing debts. At a time when more capital is a vital need of the area, the debt borrowing capacity is apparently at a saturation point. [9]

Economic conditions in Latin America seriously limit the ability to cope with the educational problems. The vast Latin American rural area's problems are evident--few schools, few teachers, inadequate transportation, and a lack of communications facilities. But the rural population is growing only at the rate of 1.5 percent per year. While the urban schools are superior to the rural ones, they also have serious problems. The population rate of increase here is from 4 to 5 percent. Caused in part by a migration of rural people into the cities as well as the high birthrate, the result is large slum areas or shanty towns and a breakdown in the educational facilities that exist. [10] Thus the urban schools are frequently overcrowded. Some elementary classes contain as many as 70 or 80 pupils. [11]

In spite of its obvious shortcomings, education is not new to Latin America. The National University of Mexico (1553) and the University of San Marcos (1551) long predate higher education in the United States. However, the same tradition of education was not established in Latin America which later developed in the United States. Although the early Latin American settlers came from homelands with rich cultural traditions, and with such great universities as Salamanca and Coimbra, Spain and Portugal did not consider educating their entire populace. The Franciscans and Jesuits who accompanied the Conquistadors felt a sense of responsibility toward education. Some pioneered schools in the area but they labored under great hardship. Such education as evolved received a major setback when the Jesuits who were the most active in the teaching field were expelled from the New World in the 1760's.

Traditionally, the well-to-do Latin American has
looked toward Europe for education.   Private schools, often
parochial, were established to give the transplanted European
the cultural background needed to return to Europe and, as
a second choice, to the United States for a higher education.[13]
There was no need to develop a public school system as there
was no intention for the masses to gain an education.

Most underdeveloped countries have gone through a
cycle whereby a number of factors determine the attention
which education receives.   Harold Benjamin in American Republics divides an underdeveloped nation's growth into five
stages.   Many countries have followed a similar development
pattern and every Latin American country may be placed at
a point on Benjamin's projected scale.   At the first stage or
in the least developed countries, a nation's chief concerns
are those dealing with the armed forces whose function is to
keep the current administration in power.   There is little if
any justice before the law.   Except for the small upper
class, the people exist on a bare subsistence economy--
housed in huts and clothed in rags.   The average lifespan is
usually between 20 and 30 years of age.   An elementary educational system is available for a few.   One in ten gets as
much as four years of education.   There are always a few
secondary schools and universities for the privileged classes.
The schooling which is usually private and often religious in
nature tends to be theoretical, traditional, and based on
memorizing facts.   There are a few countries in Latin America which are still in this stage of development although all
have been making efforts to improve conditions. [14]

At the second level of development attempts are made
to protect the rights of people.   A system of courts and a
police force are available both for protection against crimi-
nals as well as to suppress anti-administration agitation.
Constitutional recognition of the four freedoms is guaranteed
although they may be and frequently are abolished in times
of emergencies.   The executive branch of government decides
when these emergencies exist and for how long.   The economy is no longer on the subsistence level.   Large-scale
farming and mining operations are carried out, usually with
foreign capital and foreign management.   Cities begin to
grow and an influx of agricultural workers moves into the
cities where slum areas begin to develop.   While elementary
schools are usually found in cities and towns, 50 to 90 per-

cent of the children cannot attend because of inadequate or
complete lack of facilities and teachers. Stage two is where
the literacy campaigns which are designed to eliminate all
illiteracy among adults begin. The campaigns usually fail
but many Latin American countries continue to conduct them
at various intervals. [15]

On the third level of development, services designed
to provide security for the people are more formally organized. The executive is checked by judicial and legislative
restrictions. The police are supervised by the courts. The
economy is developing with increased use of domestic management and local capital. Elementary schooling is provided
for as many as 75 percent of children of school age. Some
secondary schools for children who do not intend to go to
college and vocational schools begin to appear. Approximately 30 persons per ten thousand of the total population
are given some form of post-secondary education. [16]

The fourth-level country may be identified by its increased concern for human rights. The rights of religious,
political, cultural, and racial minorities are safeguarded.
Health and social security services are available to most of
the population. The economy has a national, regional, and
local character and base. Banking, commerce, and most
industries are strictly regulated by the government, volunteer associations, or both. Over 80 percent of the children
attend schools for at least four years. Reading material,
television and cultural events are available for a high percentage of the population. As many as 100 persons per ten
thousand are given some post-secondary education. [17]

If the fifth and last stage of development, the progressive factors of law, public health, and other services,
are refined and strengthened. All facets of government are
available to guarantee the rights and freedom of citizens.
In a small country the national army is practically non-
existent. The economy is vigorous and flexible. All children of at least normal intelligence attend elementary school
for most of six years. At least one half of the children of
the country have some education on the secondary level.
From 100 to 200 persons per ten thousand of the general
population receive advanced training in some form of higher
education. [18]

It would be difficult to place each Latin American
country in its proper category on the five-point scale. How-

ever, the following list of post-secondary enrollment per ten
thousand provides some evidence as to the status of education
in the Latin American countries:

Argentina	93	Guatemala	27
Uruguay	48	Bolivia	23
Cuba	38	Paraguay	22
Chile	35	Dominican Rep.	17
Mexico	33	Costa Rica	14
Colombia	32	Nicaragua	9
Honduras	31	Venezuela	9
Peru	29	Brazil	8
Ecuador	28	Haiti	5
Panama	27	El Salvador	3

These figures may be compared with the United States which
had 201 per ten thousand in 1960 and which had over 300 per
ten thousand in 1970.[19]

Although a number of Latin American countries do
not have impressive statistics in higher education, there are
numerous forces present in the area which are promoting
change in all areas of Latin American life, including education.   While not an all-inclusive list, these influences include changing economic factors, the Alliance for Progress,
the Pan American Union, UNESCO, and the reaction to Fidel
Castro and his Cuban Revolution.

The economic crisis which has developed in Latin
America since World War II has been discussed earlier.
Traditionally Latin America has looked toward Europe for
cultural leadership.   The 20th century and World War II
have changed to a large extent the Latin American view of
the United States as being inferior to Europe.   The industri-
alism which has developed in the United States could be
cited as a guide which others could follow.   Figures can be
collected to illustrate the role which education has played
in making the United States economically successful.   A
1962 speech by José A. Mora, Secretary General of the Organization of American States, points out that the average
2 percent annual increase in the amount of education received by United States workers between 1929 and 1957 was
responsible for 23 percent of the growth of real national income over that period.[20]

Closely tied to economic motives is the Alliance for
Progress which was introduced by President Kennedy in

March 1961. The Alliance when adopted by the Organization
of American States later the same year became an inter-
American program. The central purpose of the Alliance as
stated in the Charter of Punta del Este was to increase the
rate of economic growth in Latin America and thereby raise
the living standards of the people. The need for social programs to accompany the economic development was understood and expressed in the Charter. In education, the goals
for elimination of adult illiteracy and provision of a minimum
of six years of elementary schooling for every child within
the region were established and plans were devised to meet
these goals within a ten-year period. According to the
Survey of International Development, VI, No. 7, page 5,
Secretary General of the United Nations, "Development policies and programs must be oriented toward steady improvement of living standards of the masses, and the goal of
balanced economic and social development, which is to serve
man, should, in fact, be at the heart of the Second Development Decade" [DOC E/4718]. Numerous United States universities, often through the auspices of the Agency of International Development (AID), have since that time assisted
various Latin American governments in an attempt to meet
the goals.[21] The United Nations and its subsidiary organization, UNESCO, have served to focus world public opinion
in needed reforms in all underdeveloped areas. Numerous
UNESCO teams work in Latin America and other undeveloped
areas of the world to improve educational standards. Through
publications, by providing trained consultants, and through
actual field contact the extreme urgency of educational reform has been proclaimed with some success.

Many aspects of Fidel Castro and the Cuban Revolution may be viewed negatively. His policy of exported revolution keeps many Latin American governments off balance
and his threat certainly may be viewed as reason for high
military expenditures. On the positive side the threat of
Castro has undoubtedly made several Latin American governments and even the United States much more receptive to
the immediate initiation of social reform in such areas as
education.

Cuban government press releases present an interesting array of educational statistics. While some authorities
would argue these figures are inaccurate, if accepted they
are impressive. In a speech delivered January 5, 1969, at
Cangre (Guines, Havana) the following statistical comparisons
of Cuba in 1959 and Cuba in 1969 were cited:

Education for the Future

	1959	1969
Number of schools	7, 567	14, 726
Number of teachers	17, 355	47, 876
Elementary education enrollment	717, 417	1, 444, 395
Junior and senior high teachers	2, 580	10, 499
Secondary students enrolled	63, 526	172, 144
Higher education instructors	1, 053	4, 449
University enrollment	25, 599	40, 147

Castro indicated there were 1, 702, 139 children and young
people enrolled in school. This figure represents a high
percentage of the total number of young people in the six-
to 12-year-old age group, which numbers 2, 182, 000. [22]
While the figures may be interpreted as propagands, if accurate they represent significant educational progress in
Cuba. In Cuba and all other areas of Latin America, the
focus on education is at the primary level. A Latin American elementary school may be a four-, five-, or six-year
program. Some studies show that over 90 percent of the
student enrollment in Latin America is in primary schools.[23]

While all Latin American school systems have different components, they are similar in many respects. Since
all the various systems cannot be examined in depth, the
Mexican schools may serve as an example for the entire
area. As late as 1911, only 20 percent of the Mexican population was literate. By the 1960's, this had improved to
55 percent (or 76 percent according to some authorities).
Either figure represents a concerted national effort toward
the improvement of literacy. [24] The school structure is administered through federal, state, or municipal authorities.
Private schools exist in all parts of the nation but they are
supervised by the government. The highest educational
authority is the Secretary of Public Education who is appointed by the President of Mexico. The Secretary of Public Education appoints a Director of Federal Education in
each state who is responsible for coordinating the federal,
state, and local programs and maintaining complete control
over federal schools. A Director General, responsible for
the state and municipal schools, is appointed by the state
governor. The state legislature decides the amount of state
income which is to be used for education. In recent years,
the amount has varied from 10 to 50 percent of the state
budget. [25]

Pre-elementary education in Mexico is usually found
only in large urban centers. Kindergartens began here as

early as 1904 but little expansion occurred until 1942. By
the early 1960's, there were 1,300 kindergartens with an enrollment of more than 200,000 between the ages of four and
six. In the urban areas, kindergarten lasts three years
with enrollment in primary school beginning at seven. In
the rural areas kindergarten is only one year with primary
school beginning at six. [26] As in all other Latin American
countries, Mexico emphasizes its primary school program.
Still the minimum standard of a universal sixth-grade education has not been obtained. Because of the large number of
elementary dropouts, the elementary school curriculum is
taught on a two-year cycle. When repeated, the curriculum
treats the same subjects but on a more intensified basis.
This philosophy is geared to provide as comprehensive an
education as possible to the students who drop out prior to
the sixth grade. The primary educational goals and subjects
are similar to those accepted in the United States. To be
eligible for promotion students must pass government examinations. [27]

Mexico has emphasized the establishment of rural
schools, which were virtually nonexistent prior to 1911.
These schools are often practical in nature with attempts to
gear the schools to the needs of the local area. Industrial
arts and crafts are prominent. Many rural areas are without elementary schools while others offer only two or three
grades. While inadequate in meeting the educational needs
of the rural area, the Mexican rural education program is
one of the most ambitious in Latin America. [28]

As usual in most Latin American countries, the
secondary education program begins at the end of the six-
year elementary school. The usual Mexican secondary
school is a three-year program followed by two years of a
separate pre-professional or vocational schooling. The
secondary schools are approximately half private and half
public. Recent changes in Mexican education planning indicates more emphasis on a type of high school designed to
meet the needs of all students whether or not they are planning to attend college. [29] Mexico has made slow but sus-
tained progress in post primary education since 1911. In
1958, there were over 193,000 pupils in the secondary
schools. Over 65,000 students were in the 21 Mexican universities and colleges. Although large numbers of students
are found in Mexican universities, there is a problem in
retaining students. Only 2,000 students graduated from the
National University of Mexico in the decade of the fifties. [30]

Higher education does not receive prominent attention in Mexico. While some excellent facilities do exist and the National University of Mexico has over 40,000 students enrolled, the educational focus is on primary and secondary education. The universities in Latin America have not played the same role as higher educational institutions in the United States. It is only recently that much attention has been given to the "leadership role" of Latin American higher education. [31]

Although faced with numerous economic and social obstacles, Latin America has made considerable progress in broadening the base of education. In 19 countries (Pan American Union members) the enrollment in all levels of education has increased from 16,230,000 in 1950 to 21,122,000 in 1955; and from 28,820,000 in 1960 to 32,207,900 in 1962. The average annual increase has been 6 percent from 1950 to 1955, 7.2 percent from 1955 to 1960, and 5 percent from 1960 to 1962. The rate of increase has been substantial in many of the undeveloped countries but less noticeable in the more developed countries such as Argentina, Uruguay, and Chile, which are nearing the point of providing some school facilities for the total population of school-age children. [32]

The increase in secondary education has been dramatic. From 1950 to 1955, the rate of increase was 15.2 percent; from 1955 to 1966, 9.5 percent; and from 1960 to 1962, 7.6 percent. Higher education while improving in numbers has not improved in its percentage relationship to the population. About 3 percent of the population receives some higher education. [33] The extent to which Latin America is supporting education may be determined by examining the percentage of the gross national product earmarked for education:

Argentina	1.9	Guatemala	2.4
Bolivia	1.8	Haiti	1.6
Brazil	2.1	Honduras	2.0
Chile	2.8	Mexico	1.9
Colombia	1.9	Nicaragua	1.6
Costa Rica	3.9	Panama	3.9
Cuba	4.6	Paraguay	1.5
Dominican Republic	1.5	Peru	2.6
Ecuador	1.6	Uruguay	2.3
El Salvador	2.7	Venezuela	2.7

The mean percentage expended is 2.3. While some of the
more affluent countries are able to function effectively below
the mean, many countries make outstanding efforts to improve the educational picture. [34]

Although today presents difficult problems for Latin
American education, the future holds even worse. The current school population of Latin America is expected to double
by 1980. The increase implies a budget allotment for the
area of nearly 11 billion dollars as compared to the current
budget of three billion dollars. Unless the economic pattern
described earlier is changed, continuing even the present
program will be difficult. [35]

Some authorities question the Latin American goal of
universal education. Ivan Illich, founder of the Centro Intercultural de Documentacion, indicates that universal education
is beyond the means of developing nations. His alternatives
to the universal education of the United States tradition include a suggestion for a massive adult-education program as
well as a program whereby industrial plants offer educational
training for their factory workers. [36] His thoughts are
echoed by Hla Myint in The Economics of the Developing
Countries. Myint points out that many developing nations
have tended to initiate crash programs in education beyond
the capacity of the limited number of teachers and the country's resources. [37] Other authorities express concern over
the direction of Latin American education. The systems appear to be becoming more Anglo-American and less Latin
American. The United States model may have many features
worth adopting but ultimately Latin America must evolve its
own system suited to its culture and stage of development. [38]

One possible direction Latin America might take is
regional cooperation. By cooperating in the use of teachers,
regional planning teams, technical facilities and finances,
problems that cannot be solved by an individual country may
be solved by several countries working together. The Central American Common Market for trade purposes and the
Higher Council of Central American Universities with its
plan for the regional integration of higher education in Central America are positive steps which other areas of Latin
America may follow. [39]

Even with the positive steps which are being taken
and with increased Alliance for Progress aid, the educational task remaining in Latin America is great. In a country

such as Ecuador, there are 2, 336, 100 children of school age,
but school enrollment is only 752, 000.[40] Here, as throughout Latin America, there is a severe teacher shortage.   Educational budgets are inadequate.   Low salaries are prevalent
for teaching personnel at all levels.   The political instability
in many of the countries makes it difficult to plan adequately
for educational reform.   The turbulent world situation is
working against the need for time to solve the area's educational problems.

    While progress is being made--in many instances re-
markably--economic and social reforms must change the entire society.   Land reform is desperately needed.   Human
rights, economic expansion, improved farm production, and
increased industrial output are other areas which must be
significantly improved in much of Latin America.   Education
can play a significant role in the development of Latin America but at this historical point, it is only one of the reforms
which must emerge for the area to enjoy the opportunities of
the twentieth century.

                            Notes

1.   "Latin America: The Rise of Education, " School and
        Society, 94 (March 19, 1966), 164.

2.   Ivan Illich, "The Futility of Schooling in Latin Ameri-
        ca, " Saturday Review, 51 (April 20, 1968), 57.

3.   Paul D. Hines, "The Growing Focus on World Cul-
        tures, " in C. Benjamin Cox and Byron Massialas,
        Social Studies in the United States: A Critical Ap-
        praisal, New York: Harcourt, Brace, and World,
        1967, p. 196-217.   Area studies texts such as
        Ethel Ewing, Our Widening World, Chicago: Rand
        McNally, 1965, provide better non-Western coverage.

4.   Illich, p. 59.   Cuban figures cited later indicate high-
        er percentages.

5.   Lincoln Gordon, New Deal for Latin America: The
        Alliance for Progress, Cambridge, Mass.:   Harvard
        University Press, 1963, p. 73.

6.   Raymond F. Lyons, Problems and Strategies of Educa-
        tional Planning: Lessons from Latin America,

Paris: UNESCO, 1965, p. 13.

7.   Frank Tannenbaum, Ten Keys to Latin America, New
     York: Knopf, 1962, p. 95-98.

8.   Lyons, p. 13.

9.   Ibid., p. 14.

10. Ibid., p. 17.

11. Rena Foy, The World of Education, New York: Mac-
     millan, 1968, p. 130.

12. Ibid., p. 209-210.

13. Mike Chiappetta, "Latin America: Education, the
     Baited Trap," Nation, 203 (October 3, 1966), p. 322.

14. Harold R. W. Benjamin, Higher Education in the Amer-
     ican Republics, New York: McGraw-Hill, 1965,
     p. 5.

15. Ibid., p. 7.

16. Ibid.

17. Ibid., p. 8.

18. Ibid., p. 9.

19. Ibid., p. 198.

20. Jose A. Mora in Challenges and Achievements of Edu-
     cation in Latin America, Reprot of the Eastern Re-
     gional Conference, Comparative Education Society,
     Pan American Union, 1964.   The study Mora cites
     was made by Edward Denison.

21. John C. Dreier, ed., The Alliance for Progress:
     Problems and Perspectives, Baltimore: Johns Hop-
     kins Press, 1962, p. xv-xvi.

22. Fidel Castro, Granma, January 12, 1969.

23. Foy, p. 131.

24. The 55 percent figure may be found in Harold Peterson,
     Latin America (Cultural Regions of the World Series),
     New York: Macmillan, 1966, p. 78. The percent-
     ages used here were obtained at the Center of Latin
     American Studies, University of California, Los
     Angeles. George Cressman and Harold Benda,
     Public Education in America, New York: Appleton-
     Century-Crofts, 1966, p. 401, estimate the literacy
     rate as 76 percent. The difficulty arises as to the
     definition of what is literacy. It is likely that many
     of the persons Latin American countries list as
     being literate are in fact functional illiterates. It is
     difficult for a person to be literate with only one or
     two years of schooling. While exact literacy figures
     may be difficult to secure, the statistics are con-
     stantly improving.

25. Cressman and Benda, p. 397.

26. Virgil G. Logan, "Mexico's Unified School System, "
     Journal of Educational Research, 47 (October 1953),
     p. 119.

27. Ibid., p. 120. See also Cressman and Benda, p. 400.

28. Cressman and Benda, p. 401.

29. Ibid.

30. Ibid., p. 403. See also Frank Brandenburg, The Mak-
     ing of Modern Mexico, Englewood Cliffs, N. J.:
     Prentice-Hall, 1964, p. 181.

31. Chiapetta, p. 322.

32. Francisco S. Cespedes, Challenges and Achievements
     of Education in Latin America, p. 44. Cespedes
     is Director, Department of Educational Affairs, Pan
     American Union.

33. Ibid.

34. Lyons, p. 41.

35. Yearbook of the United Nations, 1966, New York:
     United Nations Office of Information, 1968, p. 349.

36.   Illich, p. 74.

37.   Hla Myint, The Economics of the Developing Countries,
      New York: Praeger, 1965, p. 176.

38.   Chiappetta, p. 322.

39.   Lyons, p. 85.   See also Francisco S. Cespedes, "Edu-
      cation and Latin American Integration," Americas,
      19 (March 1967), bookcover.

40.   Patricia Appel, "UNICEF in the Andes," Americas,
      20 (June 1968), p. 17.

22. THE FUTILITY OF SCHOOLING IN LATIN AMERICA
Ivan Illich*

For the past two decades, demographic considerations
have colored all discussion about development in Latin America. In 1950, some 200 million people occupied the area
extending from Mexico to Chile. Of these, 120 million lived
directly or indirectly on primitive agriculture. Assuming
both effective population controls and the most favorable possible results from programs aimed at the increase of agriculture, 40, 000, 000 people will by 1985 produce most of the
food for a total population of 360 million. The remaining
320 million will be either marginal to the economy or will
have to be incorporated somehow into urban living and agricultural production.

During these same past 20 years, both Latin American governments and foreign technical assistance agencies
have come to rely increasingly on the capacity of grammar,
trade, and high schools to lead the non-rural majority out
of its marginality in shanty towns and subsistence farms into
the type of factory, market, and public forum which corresponds to modern technology. It was assumed that schooling
would eventually produce a broad middle class with values
resembling those of highly industrialized nations, despite
the economy of continued scarcity.

Accumulating evidence now indicates that schooling
does not and cannot produce the expected results. Seven
years ago the governments of the Americas joined in an Alliance for Progress, which has, in practice, served mainly
the progress of the middle classes in the Latin nations. In
most countries, the Alliance has encouraged the replacement
of a closed, feudal, hereditary elite by one which is sup-
posedly "meritocratic" and open to the few who manage to
finish school. Concomitantly, the urban service proletariat

*Reprinted by permission from Saturday Review, April 20,
1968. Copyright 1968 by Saturday Review, Inc.

has grown at several times the rate of the traditional landless rural mass and has replaced it in importance. The
marginal majority and the schooled minority grow ever further apart. One old feudal society has brought forth two
classes, separate and unequal.

This development has led to educational research focused on the improvement of the learning process in schools
and on the adaptations of schools themselves to the special
circumstances prevailing in underdeveloped societies. But
logic would seem to require that we do not stop with an effort to improve schools; rather, that we question the assumption on which the school system itself is based. We must
not exclude the possibility that the emerging nations cannot
be schooled; that schooling is not a viable answer to their
need for universal education. Perhaps this type of insight
is needed to clear the way for a futuristic scenario in which
schools as we know them today would disappear.

The social distance between the growing urban mass
and the new elite is a new phenomenon, unlike the traditional
forms of discrimination known in Latin America. This new
discrimination is not a transitory thing which can be overcome by schooling. On the contrary: I submit that one of
the reasons for the awakening frustration in the majorities
is the progressive acceptance of the "liberal myth, " the assumption that schooling is an assurance of social integration.
The solidarity of all citizens based on their common graduation from school has been an inalienable part of the modern,
Western self-image. Colonization has not succeeded in im-
planting this myth equally in all countries, but everywhere
schooling has become the prerequisite for membership in a
managerial middle class. The constitutional history of
Latin America since its independence has made the masses
of this continent particularly susceptible to the conviction
that all citizens have a right to enter--and, therefore, have
some possibility of entering--their society through the door
of a school.

More than elsewhere, in Latin America the teacher
as missionary for the school-gospel has found adherents at
the grassroots. Only a few years ago many of us were
happy when finally the Latin American school system was
singled out as the area of privileged investment for international assistance funds. In fact, during the past years,
both national budgets and private investment have been stimulated to increase educational allocations. But a second look

reveals that this school system has built a narrow bridge
across a widening social gap.   As the only legitimate passage to the middle class, the school restricts all unconventional crossings and leaves the under-achiever to bear the
blame for his marginality.   This statement is difficult for
Americans to understand.   In the United States, the 19th
century persuasion that free schooling insures all citizens
equality in the economy and effective participation in the society survives.   It is by no means certain that the result of
schooling ever measured up to this expectation, but the
schools certainly played a more prominent role in this process some hundred years ago.

   In the United States of the mid-19th century, six
years of schooling frequently made a young man the educational superior of his boss.   In a society largely dominated
by unschooled achievers, the little red schoolhouse was an
effective road to social equality.   A few years in school for
all brought most extremes together.   Those who achieved
power and money without schooling had to accept a degree
of equality with those who achieved literacy and did not strike
it rich.   Computers, television, and airplanes have changed
this.   Today in Latin America, in the midst of modern technology, three times as many years of schooling and 20
times as much money as was then spent on grammar schools
will not produce the same social result.   The dropout from
the sixth grade is unable to find a job even as a punchcard
operator or a railroad engineer.

   Contemporary Latin America needs school systems
no more than it needs railroad tracks.   Both--spanning con-
tinents--served to speed the now-rich and established nations
into the industrial age.   Both, if now handled with care, are
harmless heirlooms from the Victorian period.   But neither
is relevant to countries emerging from primitive agriculture
directly into the jet age.   Latin America cannot afford to
maintain outmoded social institutions amid modern technological processes.

   By "school," of course, I do not mean all organized
formal education.   I use the term "school" and "schooling"
here to designate a form of child-care and a rite de passage
which we take for granted.   We forget that this institution
and the corresponding creed appeared on the scene only with
the growth of the industrial state.   Comprehensive schooling
today involves year-round, obligatory, and universal classroom attendance in small groups for several hours each day.

It is imposed on all citizens for a period of ten to 18 years.
School divides life into two segments, which are increasingly
of comparable length. As much as anything else, schooling
implies custodial care for persons who are declared unde-
sirable elsewhere by the simple fact that a school has been
built to serve them. The school is supposed to take the
excess population from the street, the family, or the labor
force. Teachers are given the power to invent new criteria
according to which new segments of the population may be
committed to a school. This restraint on healthy, productive, and potentially independent human beings is performed
by schools with an economy which only labor camps could
rival.

Schooling also involves a process of accepted ritual
certification for all members of a "schooled" society.
Schools select those who are bound to succeed and send
them on their way with a badge marking them fit. Once universal schooling has been accepted as the hallmark for the
in-members of a society, fitness is measured by the amount
of time and money spent on formal education in youth rather
than by ability acquired independently from an "accredited"
curriculum.

A first important step toward radical educational reform in Latin America will be taken when the educational
system of the United States is accepted for what it is: a
recent, imaginative social invention perfected since World
War II and historically rooted in the American frontier.
The creation of the all-pervasive school establishment, tied
into industry, government, and the military, is an invention
no less original than the guild-centered apprenticeship of the
Middle Ages, or the doctrina de los indios and the Reducción
of Spanish missionaries in Mexico and Paraguay, respectively, or the lycée and the grandes écoles in France. Each
one of these systems was produced by its society to give
stability to an achievement; each has been heavily pervaded
by ritual to which society bowed; and each has been rationalized into an all-embracing persuasion, religion, or ideology. The United States is not the first nation which has
been willing to pay a high price to have its educational system exported by missionaries to all corners of the world.
The colonization of Latin America by the catechism is certainly a noteworthy precedent.

It is difficult now to challenge the school as a system
because we are so used to it. Our industrial categories

tend to define results as products of specialized institutions and instruments.   Armies produce defense for countries. Churches procure salvation in an afterlife.   Binet defined intelligence as that which his tests test.   Why not, then, conceive of education as the product of schools?   Once this tag has been accepted, unschooled education gives the impression of something spurious, illegitimate, and certainly unaccredited.

For some generations, education has been based on massive schooling, just as security was based on massive retaliation and, at least in the United States, transportation on the family car.   The United States, because it industrialized earlier, is rich enough to afford schools, the Strategic Air Command, and the car--no matter what the toll.   Most nations of the world are not that rich; they behave, however, as if they were.   The example of nations which "made it" leads Brazilians to pursue the ideal of the family car--just for a few.   It compels Peruvians to squander on Mirage bombers--just for a show.   And it drives every govenment in Latin America to spend up to two-fifths of its total budget on schools, and to do so unchallenged.

Let us insist, for a moment, on this analogy between the school system and the system of transportation based on the family car.   Ownership of a car is now rapidly becoming the ideal in Latin America--at least among those who have a voice in formulating national goals.   During the past 20 years, roads, parking facilities, and services for private automobiles have been immensely improved.   These improvements overwhelmingly benefit those who have their own cars--that is, a tiny percentage.   The bias of the budget allocated for transportation thus discriminates against the best transportation for the greatest number--and the huge capital investments in this area insure that this bias is here to stay.   In some countries, articulate minorities now challenge the family car as the fundamental unit of transportation in emerging societies.   But everywhere in Latin America it would be political suicide to advocate radical limitations on the multiplication of schools.   Opposition parties may challenge at times the need for super-highways or the need for weapons which will see active duty only in a parade.   But what man in his right mind would challenge the need to provide every child with a chance to go to high school?

Before poor nations could reach this point of universal schooling, however, their ability to educate would be

exhausted. Even ten or 12 years of schooling are beyond
85 percent of all men of our century if they happen to live
outside the tiny islands where capital accumulates. Nowhere
in Latin America do 27 percent of any age group get beyond
the sixth grade, nor do more than 1 percent graduate from
a university. Yet no government spends less than 18 percent of its budget on schools, and many spend more than
30 percent. Universal schooling, as this concept has been
defined recently in industrial societies, is obviously beyond
their means. The annual cost of schooling a United States
citizen between the ages of 12 and 24 costs as much as
most Latin American earn in two to three years.

Schools will stay beyond the means of the developing
nations: neither radical population control nor maximum re-
allocations of government budgets nor unprecedented foreign
aid would end the present unfeasibility of school systems
aimed at twelve years of schooling for all. Population control needs time to become effective when the total population is as young as that of tropical America. The percentage of the world's resources invested in schooling cannot be
raised beyond certain levels, nor can this budget grow beyond foreseeable maximal rates. Finally, foreign aid would
have to increase to 30 percent of the receiving nation's national budget to provide effectively for schooling, a goal not
to be anticipated. Furthermore, the percapita cost of
schooling itself is rising everywhere as schools accept those
who are difficult to teach, as retention rates rise, and as
the quality of schooling itself improves. This rise in cost
neutralizes much of the new investments. Schools do not
come cheaper by the dozen.

In view of all these factors, increases in school budgets must usually be defended by arguments which imply de-
fault. In fact, however, schools are untouchable because
they are vital to the status quo. Schools have the effect of
tempering the subversive potential of education in an alienated
society because, if education is confined to schools, only
those who have been schooled into compliance on a lower
grade are admitted to its higher reaches. In capital-starved
societies not rich enough to purchase unlimited schooling,
the majority is schooled not only into compliance but also
into subservience.

Since Latin American constitutions were written with
an eye on the United States, the ideal of universal schooling
was a creative utopia. It was a condition necessary to

create the Latin American 19th-century bourgeoisie. Without the pretense that every citizen has a right to go to school, the liberal bourgeoisie could never have developed; neither could the middle-class masses of present-day Europe and the United States (and Russia), nor the managerial middle elite of their cultural colonies in South America. But the same school which worked in the last century to overcome feudalism has now become an oppressive idol which protects those who are already schooled. Schools grade and, therefore, they degrade. They make the degraded accept his own submission. Social seniority is bestowed according to the level of schooling achieved. Everywhere in Latin America more money for schools means more privilege for a few at the cost of most and this patronage of an elite is explained as a political ideal. This ideal is written into laws which state the patently impossible: equal scholastic opportunities for all.

The number of satisfied clients who graduate from schools every year is much smaller than the number of frustrated dropouts who are conveniently graded by their failure for use in a marginal labor pool. The resulting steep educational pyramid defines a rationale for the corresponding levels of social status. Citizens are "schooled" into their places. This results in politically acceptable forms of discrimination which benefit the relatively few achievers.

The move from the farm to the city in Latin America still frequently means a move from a world where status is explained as a result of inheritance into a world where it is explained as a result of schooling. Schools allow a head start to be rationalized as an achievement. They give to privilege not only the appearance of equality but also of generosity: should somebody who missed out on early schooling be dissatisfied with the status he holds, he can always be referred to a night or trade school. If he does not take advantage of such recognized remedies, his exclusion from privilege can be explained as his own fault. Schools temper the frustrations they provoke. The school system also inculcates its own universal acceptance. Some schooling is not necessarily more educational than none, especially in a country where every year a few more people can get all the schooling they want while most people never complete the sixth grade. But much less than six years seems to be sufficient to inculcate in the child the acceptance of the ideology which goes with the school grade. The child

learns only about the superior status and unquestioned authority of those who have more schooling than he has.

Any discussion of radical alternatives to school-cen-
tered formal education upsets our notions of society. No
matter how inefficient schools are in educating a majority,
no matter how effective schools are in limiting the access to
the elite, no matter how liberally schools shower their non-
educational benefits on the members of this elite, schools
do increase the national income. They qualify their graduates for more economic production. In an economy on the
lower rungs of development toward United States-type industrialization, a school graduate is enormously more productive than a dropout. Schools are part and parcel of a society in which a minority is on the way to becoming so productive that the majority must be schooled into disciplined
consumption. Schooling therefore--under the best of circum-
stances--helps to divide society into two groups: those so
productive that their expectation of annual rise in personal
income lies far beyond the national average, and the overwhelming majority, whose income also rises, but at a rate
clearly below the former's. These rates, of course, are
compounded and lead the two groups further apart.

Radical innovation in formal education presupposes
radical political changes, radical changes in the organization
of production, and radical changes in man's image of himself as an animal which needs school. This is often forgotten when sweeping reforms of the schools are proposed
and fail because of the societal framework we accept. For
instance, the trade school is sometimes advocated as a
cure-all for mass schooling. Yet it is doubtful that the
products of trade schools would find employment in a continuously changing, ever more automated economy. Moreover, the capital and operating costs of trade schools, as
we know them today, are several times as high as those
for a standard school on the same grade. Also, trade
schools usually take in sixth graders, who, as we have
seen, are already the exception. They pretend to educate
by creating a spurious facsimile of the factory within a
school building.

Instead of the trade school, we should think of a
subsidized transformation of the industrial plant. It should
be possible to make it obligatory for factories to serve as
training centers during off hours, for managers to spend
part of their time planning and supervising this training,

and for the industrial process to be so redesigned that it has educational value.   If the expenditures for present schools were partly allocated to sponsor this kind of educational exploitation of existing resources, then the final results--both economic and educational--might be incomparably greater. If, further, such subsidized apprenticeship were offered to all who ask for it, irrespective of age, and not only to those who are destined to be employees in the particular plant, industry would have begun to assume an important role now played by school.   We would be on the way to disabuse ourselves of the idea that manpower qualification must precede employment, that schooling must precede productive work. There is no reason for us to continue the medieval tradition in which men are prepared for the "secular world" by incarceration in a sacred precinct, be it monastery, synagogue, or school.

A second, frequently discussed, remedy for the failure of schools is fundamental, or adult, education.   It has been proved by Paulo Freire in Brazil that those adults who can be interested in political issues of their community can be made literate within six weeks of evening classes.   The program teaching such reading and writing skills, of course, must be built around the emotion-loaded key words of their political vocabulary.   Understandably, this fact has gotten his program into trouble.   It has been equally suggested that the dollar-cost of ten separate months of adult education is equal to one year of early schooling, and can be incomparably more effective than schooling at its best.   Unfortunately, "adult education" now is conceived principally as a device to give the "underprivileged" a palliative for the schooling he lacks.   The situation would have to be reversed if we wanted to conceive of all education as an exercise in adulthood.   We should consider a radical reduction of the length of the formal, obligatory school sessions to only two months each year--but spread this type of formal schooling over the first 20 or 30 years of a man's life.

While various forms of in-service apprenticeship in factories and programed math and language teaching could assume a large proportion of what we have previously called "instruction, " two months a year of formal schooling should be considered ample time for what the Greeks meant by "schole"--leisure for the pursuit of insight.   No wonder we find it nearly impossible to conceive of comprehensive social changes in which the educational functions of schools would be thus redistributed in new patterns among institutions we

do not now envisage. We find it equally difficult to indicate
concrete ways in which the non-educational functions of a
vanishing school system would be redistributed. We do not
know what to do with those whom we now label "children"
or "students" and commit to school.

It is difficult to foresee the political consequences of
changes as fundamental as those proposed, not to mention
the international consequences. How should a school-reared
society coexist with one which has gone "off the school
standard, " and whose industry, commerce, advertising, and
participation in politics is different as a matter of principle?
Areas which develop outside the universal school standard
would lack the common language and criteria for respectful
coexistence with the schooled. Two such worlds, such as
China and the United States, might almost have to seal
themselves off from each other.

Rashly, the school-bred mind abhors the educational
devices available to these worlds. It is difficult mentally
to "accredit" Mao's party as an educational institution which
might prove more effective than the schools are at their
best--at least when it comes to inculcating citizenship.
Guerrilla warfare in Latin America is another educational
device much more frequently misused or misunderstood than
applied. Che Guevara, for instance, clearly saw it as a
last educational resort to teach a people about the illegiti-
macy of their political system. Especially in unschooled
countries, where the transistor radio has come to every
village, we must never underrate the educational functions
of great charismatic dissidents like Dom Helder Camara in
Brazil or Camilo Torres in Colombia; Castro described his
early charismatic harangues as teaching sessions.

The schooled mind perceives these processes exclusively as political indoctrination, and their educational purpose eludes its grasp. The legitimation of education by
schools tends to render all non-school education an accident,
if not an outright misdemeanor. And yet, it is surprising
with what difficulty the school-bred mind perceives the rigor
with which schools inculcate their own presumed necessity,
and with it the supposed inevitability of the system they
sponsor. Schools indoctrinate, the child into the acceptance
of the political system his teachers represent, despite the
claim that teaching is nonpolitical.

Ultimately, the cult of schooling will lead to violence.

The establishment of any religion has led to it.   To permit
the gospel of universal schooling to spread, the military's
ability to repress insurgency in Latin America must grow.
Only force will ultimately control the insurgency inspired by
the frustrated expectations which the propagation of the
school-myth enkindles.   The maintenance of the present
school system may turn out to be an important step on the
way to Latin American fascism.   Only fanaticism inspired
by idolatry of a system can ultimately rationalize the massive discrimination which will result from another 20 years
of grading a capital-starved society with school marks.

The time has come to recognize the real burden of
the schools in the emerging nations, so that we may become
free to envisage change in the social structure which now
makes schools a necessity.   I do not advocate a sweeping
utopia like the Chinese commune for Latin America.   But I
do suggest that we plunge our imagination into the construction of scenarios which would allow a bold reallocation of educational functions among industry, politics, short scholastic
retreats, and intensive preparation of parents for early
childhood education.   The cost of schools must be measured
not only in economic, social, and educational terms, but in
political terms as well.   Schools, in an economy of scarcity
invaded by automation, accentuate and rationalize the coexistence of two societies, one a colony of the other.

Once it is understood that the cost of schooling is not
inferior to the cost of chaos, we might be on the brink of
courageously costly compromise.   Today it is as dangerous
in Latin America to question the myth of social salvation
through schooling as it was dangerous 300 years ago to question the divine rights of the Catholic kings.

23. COOPERATIVE ACTION IN THE LATE 1960's*
Organization of American States

The major guidelines for inter-American cooperative action in the fields of education, science, and technology laid down by the Presidents of America in their famous Declaration of Punta del Este, April 14, 1967, needed a proper theoretical and practical formulation within the institutional framework of the Organization of American States; it was achieved a year later during the Fifth Meeting of the Inter-American Cultural Council, held in Maracay, Venezuela, prior to the entry into force of the Protocol of Reform of the OAS Charter, that is, before the new Inter-American Council for Education, Science, and Culture (CIECC) was established.

In Maracay, the Special Multilateral Fund (FEMCIECC) was set up to promote specific projects in the educational, scientific, and technological fields under two regional programs designed and proposed by ad hoc committees and groups of experts.

For the first time in the history of the Hemisphere, national and regional action was coordinated at the highest political and technical level for a clearly defined goal of mutual benefit.

The Protocol of Reform of the Charter entered into force on February 28, 1970, entailing a process of reorganization and adjustment of OAS organs and mechanisms in order to adapt them to the new needs and make their operation more flexible. The particular interests of education, science, and culture were entrusted to one main organ under the direct authority of the General Assembly. From the

---

*Reprinted by permission from Américas monthly magazine, April 1972, published by the General Secretariat of the Organization of American States, in English, Spanish, and Portuguese.

start of its activities, the new organ assumed responsibility for guiding and promoting the Regional Programs approved in Maracay. The status of directly representational organ assigned the Inter-American Council for Education, Science, and Culture, and its high government and technical standing is making a decisive contribution to ensuring the significance and effectiveness of its resolutions.

In addition, a Permanent Executive Committee (CEPCIECC) composed of a chairman and ten members elected by the Council itself is providing more effective program supervision, together with more direct identification with operations of the Special Fund.

The work done by the respective technical committees in developing each program is unquestionably an essential supplement to the functions of the Council. Both the Inter-American Committee on Education and the Inter-American Committee on Science and Technology are responsible for analysis of the projects and evaluation of their findings, as well as for various other operational aspects of the respective programs on which they make technical recommendations to the Permanent Executive Committee.

Although the Regional Programs differ in terms of the subject areas covered by their particular activities, they share a series of common features. Since they express the wishes of the Latin American countries, their orientation is consistent with the requirements of the countries themselves. Their activities are hemisphere wide in scope, inasmuch as they reflect the over-all interest of the region. Their projects, especially the multinational ones, are directed toward optimum use of the best institutions in each country to benefit the entire region. They are genuinely local, since their approach and technical structure derive exclusively from the efforts of the Latin American educational, scientific, and technological community, which played a very direct role in the preparatory work, while their implementation is the responsibility of that same educational, scientific, and technological community, for activities are carried out in Latin American institutions and directed with considerable independence by Latin American experts.

Channels of communication designated by the respective governments are available for planning program actions in each country. These channels are the ministries of education for the educational area and, in the main, the national

scientific and technological research councils or equivalent
agencies for the scientific and technological area. The centers in which program activities are carried out are national
institutions that are supported or assisted by the program,
but extend their action to the regional sphere without changing their makeup or national function.

The particular feature that distinguishes the activities
of the Special Multilateral Fund of the Inter-American Council for Education, Science, and Culture is undoubtedly its
realistic approach. Aimed at meeting urgent national needs,
each and every one of the projects is the result of an adaptation of available means and resources to the circumstances
of the aid request and to the type of need involved. Consequently the handling of problems varies from country to
country and in terms of opportunity for service, while the
goals sought are reviewed frequently and the results continually evaluated on both the national and international levels.

As a country learns more about its situation, new
problems are identified and changes inevitably occur in the
scale of national priorities. The Regional Programs could
not fail to reflect these changes within a continuing process
of accommodation and readjustment without losing their current and realistic character.

Only over the long range can we properly speak of
program goals, which identified as closely as possible with
the major program objectives established by the Presidents
of America at Punta del Este, could at present be defined
as follows: to strengthen the educational, scientific, and
technological intrastructure of Latin America; and to encourage and supplement national and multinational efforts in
the fields of education, science, and technology.

The efforts of CIECC during the first three years of
operation of the Regional Programs have been aimed in that
direction; the benefits secured to date are presented in
another section of this study. In the second stage, which is
believed imminent, the Regional Programs will gradually be
reoriented toward rapid utilization of national and inter-
American resources in terms of development goals. These
goals are: (1) to accelerate training of the manpower essential for attaining the socioeconomic development goals of the
region; (2) to promote the transfer and adaptation to the
Latin American countries of general know-how and technology
in other regions; and (3) to encourage Latin American coop-

eration and communication to accelerate progress in education, science, and technology in order to further regional
integration.

Program Strategy

Every ambitious aim includes the establishment of
goals, and the attainment of such goals inevitably entails a
need for standards of activity consistent with a plan of operations that can be termed strategic. Within the framework
of possibilities of CIECC, the cooperative action required is
in fact confined to the volume of resources allocated for the
Special Fund and to the inherent features of an international
program.

The basic hypothesis was that the various member
states in the exercise of their sovereignty were responsible
for determining their own needs for inter-American assistance and collaboration and for setting up the scale of priorities on which those needs could be satisfied.   The Inter-
American agency, acting through its representative bodies
and its technical instruments, would be responsible for
evaluating efforts and responding to national requests through
the formulation of specific short- and long-range plans designed to redistribute their benefits throughout the region.
The multinational projects and areas of concentration of efforts reflect that basic aim of maximum utilization of available resources and consolidation of their effects through
proper coordination of the related activities of the program.

For the achievement of its purposes, the regional
agency employs three fundamental means of action: multinational projects, designed to use some of the best institutions of Latin America as regional centers for training and
study of professional and technical personnel, as well as
providing direct technical assistance to institutions of other
countries; support actions, consisting of financial aid to
solve specific problems at the request of the countries; and
basic studies, designed to evaluate better the situation in
Latin America by collaborating with the governments in
order to provide adequate statistical studies.   Such collaboration can be utilized either independently, with a view to
satisfying specific high-priority national demands, or jointly,
to a greater or lesser extent, under integrated multinational
projects.

Reaction to Programs

The number and scope of the projects submitted for
consideration to the CIECC Inter-American Committees best
illustrates the interest evinced in these programs by the
Latin American countries. The educational and scientific
communities of those countries are now fully aware of the
importance of the cooperation they receive from the regional
organization for improvement of their institutions and adequate solution of the problems posed by development processes. The ministries of education in particular are taking
advantage of the Regional Educational Development Program
to supplement national efforts toward implementing urgently
needed changes in education plans and are taking an innovative approach to curriculums, procedures, and methods of
education. Indeed, pedagogical experimentation and research,
which were for many countries an academic aspiration beyond the reach of their resources, have been made possible
largely as a result of inter-American cooperation.

Although the problems of education in Latin America
call for quantitative and qualitative solutions, the former can
and should be achieved at the national level. Inter-American
cooperation and foreign aid in general are confined to the
solution of qualitative problems. This has been the view of
the member states that decided to establish for the Regional
Educational Development Program the following significant
areas of concentration of efforts: curriculum and educational technology; educational administration and planning; and
technical education, adult education, and educational research.

With regard to scientific activities in both pure and
applied technological research, more than 100 participating
Latin American institutions utilize the Regional Scientific and
Technological Development Program for, among other types
of collaboration, training of personnel, exchange of information, application of technologies developed, and improvement
of research instruments and laboratory equipment. A selected number of those scientific institutions function as regional centers responsible for multinational projects and the
remaining as centers participating in the benefits of technical assistance furnished through such projects.

Given the many problems posed by the scientific and
technological development of Latin America and the impossibility of contributing simultaneously to their solution, CIECC
resolved to divide the activities of the Regional Program into

four major areas of concentration of efforts: scientific infrastructure; technological infrastructure; technological development; scientific and technological planning.

No major reforms can be implemented without creating the objective and subjective conditions required for the proposed changes. In other words, Latin America was not prepared for reform, and its preparation entailed, in the view of the Council, improvement of its educational, scientific, and technological infrastructure in order to make available the material facilities and manpower essential to the success of this reformation.

Education: A High Priority Field

In Chapter V of their 1967 Declaration of Punta del Este, the Presidents of America acknowledged that during the past decade there was a development of educational services in Latin America unmatched in any other period of the history of their countries. They observed that nevertheless, to increase the effectiveness of national efforts in the field of education, it is imperative that educational systems be adjusted more adequately to meet the demands of economic, social, and cultural development, and that international cooperation in educational matters be rigorously strengthened. They agreed to improve educational administrative and planning systems, to raise the quality of education, to accelerate the expansion of educational systems at all levels, and to assign priority to a number of activities that the Organization of American States and the countries should carry out. The Action Program outlined by the Presidents in the belief that "education is a sector of high priority in the over-all development policy of Latin American nations" brings together the basic aspirations of the peoples of America in this important area, and opens the way for genuine and effective cooperation among the countries as seldom seen before in the hemisphere.

The implementation of the provisions on educational development set forth in this Action Program, because of their nature, importance and scope, required the adoption of a number of measures that could not be selected at random. There was need for thorough study of the situation, the possibilities of the countries, and the competent agencies of the inter-American system.

Aware of the responsibility facing them, the participants in the Second Special Meeting of the Inter-American
Cultural Council (Washington, D. C., May 1967), which was
convoked in part to approve the procedures necessary to begin the multinational efforts in education envisaged in the
Declaration of the Presidents of America, decided to create
an ad hoc committee composed of representatives of each
OAS member state; they entrusted the General Secretariat
of the Organization with making studies and recommendations
with respect to the topics that had been given priority by the
American Chiefs of State. One of the specific tasks assigned
to the ad hoc committee was to propose specific measures
that should be taken to fulfill the mandates of the Meeting of
Presidents, within the area of competence of the Inter-
American Cultural Council, on the basis of the studies prepared by the General Secretariat and the groups of experts.
The ad hoc committee, after exhaustive study of all the
background information and other documents placed at its
disposal, found that the Action Program of the Presidents
afforded a basis for the adoption of an education development
program at the inter-American level. As a result, and in
response to the educational development needs of the member
states of the Organization, it drew up an Inter-American
Educational Development Program to ensure a coherent and
comprehensive approach in the action plans.

At its Fifth Meeting (Maracay, February 1968), the
Inter-American Cultural Council took note of the report and
recommendations of the ad hoc committee, the multinational
projects prepared by the General Secretariat and 46 projects
presented by 11 Latin American governments. As a result
of its discussions, it established the Regional Educational
Development Program, thereby complementing the Regional
Scientific and Technological Development Program called for
in the Declaration of the Presidents of America.

The Regional Educational Development Program en-
compasses a number of suitably integrated activities, each
of which contributes to the fulfillment of the common objectives established. It is a multinational undertaking in which
various projects are implemented at the initiative of a single
state or with the cooperation of several or all of the member states; it serves the countries by strengthening national
services, institutions and programs that are fundamental to
the development of their educational systems.

The projects that make up the program are carried

out in national and regional public institutions that the governments have placed at its disposal, and in centers established
specifically for this purpose. Following the spirit of the
Declaration of the Presidents, the program has as its basic
objectives: to encourage and complement national and multinational efforts in the field of education; to promote research
and the introduction of modern methods in education and related fields; to foster inter-American cooperation in educational matters; and to promote Latin American integration
through education.

As may be seen, the objectives of the Regional Program have both a national and an inter-American aspect.
Its national objectives are to encourage and complement national efforts in raising the quality of education, accelerate
the expansion of educational systems at all levels, and to
improve educational administration and planning. The inter-
American objectives are directed at the integration and multinational cooperation of the member states.

To meet the far-reaching and ambitious goals of the
program, multinational projects are implemented to spur the
development of institutional resources in the education sector
by providing assistance for activities related to advanced
training in the field of education; educational research, planning, innovation, and experimentation; educational television
and other audio-visual methods; vocational and technical education; textbooks and teaching materials; adult education; and
educational and scientific journalism.

The program also provides for support actions which
help to strengthen the infrastructure of educational institutions in Latin America, assist in the development of national
programs to improve educational systems and services, and
cooperate in national plans for the basic and advanced training of teachers.

The Program is carrying on many different activities
in 54 institutions, through eight multinational projects in the
following: improvement of educational administration and
planning; improvement of curriculum, methods and teaching
materials; educational technology; development of school and
university libraries; technical education and vocational training; educational research; adult education; and production of
educational and scientific materials for the press. It also
has granted support actions in the fields of administration
and planning curriculum, technical education, adult education

and educational research.

While the activities undertaken by the program certainly have helped strengthen the countries' awareness of its importance, it is no less true that the increasing support given
to it is due to the fact that, through it, the member states
have found an added dimension of usefulness in many of their
institutions. Until quite recently, the activities and range of
these institutions had only a national aspect. But now they
are viewed in terms of the utility and benefit they bring to
the particular programs of other governments that, directly
or indirectly, have been associated with them through the
training and technical assistance activities they conduct within the Regional Program.

In fulfillment of the objectives of the program, and
bearing in mind the importance and influence of national institutions, the program has sought to make them its major
point of support. As it has strengthened their activities by
giving them an international field of action it has encouraged
special programs and activities that otherwise would have
been difficult for any one institution acting alone.

AREAS OF CONCENTRATION

The Regional Educational Development Program has
grouped its activities into the following areas of concentration: curriculum and educational technology; educational administration and planning; technical education, adult education, and educational research.

The purpose of adopting these areas of concentration
is to establish priority objectives for the development efforts
of the member states, so that the dimensions of the problem
will be matched by the availability of resources for the program, and that the action taken will involve primarily activities of direct service to the countries--without excluding,
of course, those that must be carried out at the regional
level because of their special nature. The following is a
summary of the principal activities carried out within these
areas and projects since the start of the program.

The Press

The Inter-American Center for the Production of Edu-

cational and Scientific Materials for the Press (CIMPEC), an
institution established by the Government of Colombia for
this purpose, is the executing agency of the Multinational
Project on Production of Educational and Scientific Materials
for Publication. The basic purpose of this project is to
provide the material that will allow the Latin American
press to contribute to the educational process in both on-
going education for adults and in systematic education taking
place in the fields of education, science and technology.

To meet the objectives of the project, CIMPEC and
the International Center for Advanced Studies in Journalism
for Latin America (CIESPAL), a cooperating agency with
headquarters in Quito, conducted a study on 78 daily newspapers in 20 Latin American countries to define the usefulness, content, meaning, and scope of the educational material that CIMPEC should develop. On the basis of that research, CIMPEC began in January 1971 to produce material
which has been published in 38 capital city newspapers and
65 provincial newspapers to date.

An over-all estimate of the acceptance of the first
24 packets sent to the Latin American press shows that this
material has occupied more than 21, 000 square inches in
those newspapers. Each packet usually consists of four
articles on various topics, with illustrations, and two sections entitled "News Briefs on Education, Science, and Technology" and "Something You May not Know. "

Likewise, implementing another objective of the report, CIESPAL has launched a program for professional
training of journalists through courses in educational and
scientific reporting. The first course was held in Quito in
March and April 1971, with the participation of 19 fellowship students from 13 OAS member countries, and 20 Ecuadorian students.

In addition, a meeting was held in Bogotá on "The
Dissemination of Scientific, Technological and Educational
Research in Latin America, " with the participation of 15
officials from scientific and educational research centers
and twelve journalists from ten OAS member countries.
The primary objective of this meeting was to establish the
required channels of communication and cooperation between
CIMPEC and the scientific and educational research centers
of Latin America, so that CIMPEC may be in better position to perform its mission: to utilize the press to report

on the most salient developments in educational and scientific research in Latin America.

Finally, a working group composed of staff members of CIMPEC, journalists, and two directors of schools of journalism in Colombia is conducting research that will serve as a basis for preparation of a handbook of educational and scientific journalism, thereby fulfilling another objective of the project.

Administration and Planning

The complexity of national educational systems, the number of persons serving in them, the diversity of educational centers, the resources required, and the changing approach in administration and planning have given rise in recent years to a serious concern both of ministers of education and of teaching personnel with the adoption of thoroughgoing reforms. The classical notion that educational administration meant a concentration of administrative functions in a single agency, with the technical aspects left to the personnel concerned, has fallen into disuse and a new approach has been introduced.

Fortunately, it is now evident that administration in its broad, functional, and dynamic sense must be reorganized in Latin America. The minimum elements of such a reorganization, to attain the desired goal, should include personnel training, specific orientation of administrative services and procedures, incorporation of planning as a function of administration, and up-to-date training of supervisors and directors of teaching centers and services.

Equal concern has been directed to the area of educational planning. The action of planning offices sometimes has been limited merely to performing one of the functions for which they were created: the preparation of national education plans. It has been forgotten that while this is truly an important activity, it is not enough, for the aim of planning is to help put into effect the principle of planned administration.

Planning as a tool of administration should be a useful instrument in the attainment of specific goals, and one that should analyze, clarify, and set goals in relation to the present and future needs of the countries.

It is no exaggeration to say that mistakes made in the field of education--for example, as a result of incorrect planning, improper administration, or poor management of the two elements--have an adverse effect on other aspects of development, since education is an important force for motivation and dynamism in society as a whole.

Thus, planning and administration are key elements in the area of education, since they serve to identify the strengths and weaknesses of the educational system, whatever its field of action.

Without objective planning and sound administration, it will be highly difficult to make adequate decisions on educational reforms, and the educational programs of the country will yield unsatisfactory results. Hence, the Regional Educational Development Program includes among its activities a Multinational Project on Educational Administration and Planning, and has made the various aspects of this project the major concern of one of its areas of concentration.

This project is carried out through a number of multinational activities that currently are under way in seven centers, as shown below:

Dr. Queiroz Filho Regional Center for Educational Research São Paulo, Brazil (To train highly skilled personnel for administration and supervision of school systems.)

National Center for Pedagogical Improvement, Experimentation and Research, Santiago, Chile (To train educational planners.)

University del Valle, Cali, Colombia (To train educational administrators at the graduate level.)

Central American Institute of Educational Administration and Supervision, Panama (To train educational administrators and supervisors.)

Advanced Center for Teacher Training, Lima, Peru (To train teachers and officials for executive functions in the administrative organization of educational systems.)

Inter-American Statistical Training Center (CIENES), Santiago, Chile (To provide technical training for the personnel of offices of educational statistics.)

Regional School Building Center for Latin America
(CONESCAL), Mexico (To provide refresher training for
architects, engineers, educators and economists in the planning, design, and evaluation of school buildings.)

In addition to these activities, support actions have
been granted to the Félix Fernando Bernasconi Institute,
Argentina (training of directors and supervisors); the National Office of Education Planning of the Ministry of Education,
Bolivia (training in techniques of school organization and administration); the Ministry of Education of Costa Rica (initiation of a comprehensive education plan); CONESCAL, Mexico (school construction); the Ministry of Education of Venezuela (development of a methodology for identification and
analysis of the input-output relationships of the educational
system); and the Central American Office of Educational
Planning, El Salvador (standardization and unification of educational statistics).

Among the principal activities of the project are
training courses in administration, planning, and statistics,
and the development of techniques for base studies to obtain
up-to-date, reliable data on the situation of education in
Latin America.

Two courses have been offered on educational administrators and supervisors, ten months each, at the Dr.
Queiroz Filho Regional Center for Educational Research,
Brazil, attended by 25 fellowship students of the program
and 20 students from the host country; two courses for the
master's degree in educational administration, 12 months
each, at the University del Valle, Cali, Colombia, with the
participation of 20 fellowship students of the program and
39 from the host country; two courses on educational planning, ten months' duration each, at the National Center for
Pedagogical Improvement, Experimentation, and Research,
Chile, with 33 fellowship students of the program and 35 from
the host country attending; two courses on educational administration and supervision, ten months each, at the Central
American Institute of Educational Administration and Supervision (ICASE) of the University of Panama, with the participation of 33 fellowship students from Central American
countries and 15 Panamanian officials; a course on educational administration, at Lima, Peru, with 12 fellowship
students of the program and 24 Peruvian students; a course
on educational statistics, held at the Inter-American Statistical Training Center, Santiago, Chile, with the participation

of 21 fellowship students of the program and two from the host country; and a course on school construction at the Regional School Building Center for Latin America (CONESCAL), Mexico, with the participation of Mexican professionals, eight special fellowship students from various countries of the region, and 21 fellowship students of the Regional Program.

A number of research projects have been carried out, in connection with these courses, including: "Analysis of the Position of Inspector of Secondary Education in São Paulo, " "Educational Sociology for Educational Administrators, " "Economics of Education for School Administrators, " "Philosophy of Education for School Administrators, " and "Human Organization and Behavior" (São Paulo); "Critical and Comparative Analysis of the Present Status of Educational Administration and Planning in Latin America" (Santiago, Chile); "Student Institution" and "Use of the Time of the Educational Administrator at the Secondary Level (Cali)"; "Study of Educational Output at the Primary Level" and "Comparative Analysis of the Objectives, Organization and Financing of Educational Systems in Latin America" (Lima) and "Manual of Procedures for Educational Statistics" and "Indicators of Educational Development" (CIENES).

With respect to the base studies for this area of concentration, a specialist contracted by the program prepared a proposed design which was analyzed by a group of experts from Argentina, Brazil, Colombia, Guatemala, Mexico, and the United States. The group made a number of recommendations that it incorporated in the proposal, which was published and distributed to the ministers of education and project directors of the Program. Procedures already have been started to contract the personnel that will carry out the activities outlined in this design. Concurrently, an English translation has been made of the survey form for study of the situation and requirements of educational statistics, and of the 31 headings of the tabulations for the Regional Program of Basic Statistics.

Curriculum Improvement

The design and preparation of educational content have become increasingly complex. In the past, many curriculum reforms were achieved because of the enthusiasm and inspiration of outstanding teachers working alone or in small groups. This deserving and unquestionably important task

is no longer effective and curriculum problems are currently
focused upon systematically and in an interdisciplinary manner.   New systems are needed, together with suitable adaptation to new values and provision for the many changes to
come.

Human knowledge has expanded so rapidly and social
life and relationships have become so complex that educational systems must devise coordinated and continuous institutional action programs for purposes of curriculum review and
development.   This work requires a variety of experts in
the related fields, and few countries are in a position to set
up curriculum centers with teams of this kind.   Accordingly,
it is essential to help develop a capability in Latin American
institutions for the study and formulation of criteria for curriculum preparation.

Furthermore, there is the problem of training enough
teachers.   It is generally recognized that the adequate expansion and qualitative improvement of education cannot be
achieved without a sufficient number of properly trained
teachers who constantly update their knowledge and skills to
keep abreast of the ever-changing needs of individuals and
of the society they serve.

The rapidity of social and technological change throughout the world means that teachers must be capable of adapting to such changes and of properly interpreting and making
them known to students; this capability is maintained by their
own education throughout their professional life.   The mission of keeping the teacher up-to-date--in relation to both his
understanding of human, social and technological development,
and the mastering of new teaching methods, skills, and
specialties--requires that special services be developed,
either through proper supervision and modern personnel administration or in the form of regular programs at institutions of higher education.   Accordingly, one area of concentration of the Regional Educational Development Program is
curriculum, which includes a Multinational Project on Improvement of Curricula and Teaching Methods and Materials,
the purpose of which is to assist the member states in curriculum improvement; this topic undoubtedly is a leading
concern of our time.

In fulfilling its goal, the project is carrying out a
number of multinational activities at the following eight centers:

Santa Maria Federal University, Rio Grande do Sul, Brazil (To train specialists in curriculum planning and development.)

Institute for Professional Improvement of Teachers, Caracas, Venezuela (To train primary school supervisors in technical and administrative methods related to curriculum.)

National Center for Pedagogical Improvement, Experimentation, and Investigation, Santiago, Chile (To train secondary school teachers.)

El Mácaro Teacher Training Center for Rural Education, Venezuela (To train personnel for preparation of textbooks and teaching materials in mathematics and science.)

Advanced Institute for Teacher Training, Montevideo, Uruguay (To train teachers in special education.)

National Institute for the Improvement of Science Teaching, Buenos Aires, Argentina (To train personnel for basic science teaching.)

Brazilian Foundation for the Development of Science Teaching, São Paulo, Brazil (To train leaders capable of organizing working groups in the countries to produce and adapt adequate materials for science teaching at the elementary level.)

Advanced Institute of Music of the National University of Rosario, Rosario, Argentina (To train professors of music education.)

In addition to the foregoing, support actions have been provided to the Francisco Morazán Superior School for secondary School Teachers of Honduras (advanced specialized training of secondary school teachers); the Institute of Education, University of the West Indies, Trinidad and Tobago (advanced training for secondary school teachers); the Ministry of Education of Ecuador (training of primary school teachers and diversification of secondary education); the Regional Institute for Textbooks for Central America and Panama (national seminars); the National Institute of Sciences, Paraguay (basic and advanced training of primary and secondary school teachers in science teaching); the Caro and Cuervo Institute of Colombia (master's degree program in linguistics); the Pedagogical Training Center, Normal, Vocational and Agricultural Education Service, Haiti (basic

and advanced training of personnel for rural schools); the
Superior Institute of Education, Ministry of Education, Asunción, Paraguay (basic and advanced training of primary and
secondary school teachers); and the Ministry of Education of
Panama (training of teachers and improvement of teaching
methods).

One of the most significant activities of the project
undoubtedly is its program of courses for the advanced training of teachers. The following have been held to date: two
courses on specialization in elementary school curricula, ten
months each, and two courses on training of advisory specialists for the first two grades of elementary school, four
months each, both at the Institute for the Professional Improvement of Teachers of Venezuela, attended by 62 fellowship students of the Program; two courses for specialized
training in intermediate level educational curricula, ten
months each, at the Santa Maria Federal University, Brazil,
with the participation of 22 fellowship students of the Program; three courses on improvement of science teaching,
two for six months and one for four months, at the National
Institute for the Improvement of Science Teaching (INEC) of
Argentina, attended by 58 fellowship students of the Program; two courses for teachers of children with learning
problems of psychological origin, 12 months each, and two
specialized courses for teachers of deaf children, also 12
months each, at the Advanced Institute for Teachers of Uruguay, with the participation of 35 fellowship students of the
program and 40 from the host country; two courses on preparation of textbooks and teaching materials for the elementary schools, five months each, at El Mácaro Teacher Training Center for Rural Education, Venezuela, with 27 fellowship students of the program attending; a course on production and use of audio-visual materials and methods, five
months, at the Dr. Queiroz Filho Regional Center for Educational Research of Brazil, with the participation of 16
fellowship students of the program; a course on study and
production of materials for science teaching at the elementary level, three months, at the Brazilian Foundation for
Development of Science Teaching, with 12 fellowship students
of the program; two courses on mathematics for secondary
school teachers, one course on improvement of social
sciences teaching at the secondary level, a course on native
languages and contemporary literature, a course on natural
sciences, and a course on educational evaluation and measurement, each lasting three months, at the National Center
for Pedagogical Improvement, Experimentation, and Research.

Santiago, Chile, with the participation of 98 fellowship students of the program.

Finally, it should be noted that the Regional Program sponsored a meeting in Buenos Aires on legal and institutional problems of Latin American integration, with the participation of 26 professors from eleven countries, and a round table on the same subject, in Caracas, with the participation of five professors from five countries.

Because of the importance of exchanges of personnel among the centers participating in the project in order to promote better communication and regional integration, it is worthwhile to note the sending of two fellowship students from Uruguay and three from Argentina who were studying at INEC, in Argentina on an observation visit to the Brazilian Foundation for the Development of Science Teaching, as well as the sending of a mission of three professors, also from INEC, to take part as consultants in a seminar on science teaching held in Ecuador.

Noteworthy among the actions taken within the program to help bring about the integration of our peoples is the study on "Harmonization of National Social Studies Programs with the Goals of Latin American Integration," prepared by five specialists from Chile, Costa Rica, Mexico, Panama, and Venezuela.

In view of the distinct value of this document CIECC, at its Second Meeting, recommended that the General Secretariat continue the study, in order to develop the model of harmonization programs proposed by the experts in their report. In compliance with this recommendation, the Secretariat has contracted the services of four specialists from Brazil, Chile, Colombia, and Panama; working with the staff members of the OAS Department of Educational Affairs, they will develop the requested model for harmonization programs.

Technology: Agent of Change

It is an indisputable fact that over the past decade Latin America has made a striking effort to expand its educational systems. Nonetheless, and even though school enrollment at all levels has risen at a faster rate than in the past, there are still tens of millions of illiterate adults in the region and a growing number of young people of school age who are being deprived of the opportunity of educational institutions.

This situation, aggravated by population growth-- which in quantitative terms has cost implications that already weigh heavily on national budgets--is complicated even further by the qualitative factor: the need for the educational system to afford students the possibility of developing attitudes and acquiring knowledge adequate to the needs of today, that is, directed more toward scientific and technical matter. This entails the need to modify study plans, teaching methods, and materials, and to bring this new approach to teachers already in service.

If this task is attempted with conventional methods, not only will it require massive resources that simply are unavailable, but it would take several decades to achieve the goals proposed. Thus, it is not only advisable but imperative to make use of the means offered by modern technology as an agent of change in the developing countries to provide a solution to these problems.

There are a number of technological developments, such as programmed education and the use of computers, which will come into play in this effort. However, television as a new technology for mass audio-visual communication is one of the most promising media; some of its uses, the effectiveness of which is a demonstrated fact, can be applied with great advantage in our countries. Aware of this, the ministers of education participating in the Sixth Meeting of the Inter-American Cultural Council resolved to approve a Multinational Project on Educational Television, which was given the primary objectives of developing, in each OAS member state, the capability to put technological resources to efficient use in the attainment of their educational objectives and of devising a cooperative multinational program.

To date, the activities of the project have been carried out at the following five institutions:

Ministry of Culture and Education, Buenos Aires, Argentina (Research and testing on the application of ETV and other audio-visual methods in the educational system.)

Regional Center for Educational Television, Bogotá, Colombia (To train teachers using television and producers of programs for ETV; to produce audio-visual materials; to study systems for the evaluation of ETV programs at the elementary level.)

University Television, Channel 11, Recife, Brazil (To extend the use of television to adult education programs; to train ETV producers for the secondary and university levels; to produce audio-visual materials.)

National Center for Pedagogical Improvement, Experimentation and Research, Santiago, Chile (To apply television and other audio-visual methods in the training of teachers; to produce audio-visual materials for science teaching.)

Regional Center for Educational Television, Mexico (To organize a service for the cataloging and distribution of information and materials related to educational television; to prepare, produce and distribute basic informational materials on educational technology to Latin American institutions.)

The more important activities carried out within this project include the holding of a three-month course on production of educational programs, at the INRAVISION Center of Colombia, with the participation of thirteen fellowship students of the program and four Colombians sent by educational institutions; a one-year course for specialized training in the field of educational television, at the General Office of Audio-visual Education, Mexico, with the participation of 18 fellowship students of the program; and a one-year graduate course on the application of educational technology to engineering, administration, economics, education, psychology, sociology and communications media at the Educational Technology Center of Florida State University, with 12 fellowship students of the program participating.

In addition, as part of inspection visits and exchanges of experience among personnel of the centers participating in this project, three staff members from the center in Colombia were sent to the center in Mexico, one from Chile went to Colombia, another from Chile went to Mexico, and one from the center at Recife, Brazil, went to the center in Argentina.

With respect to technical or advanced training missions, one staff member of the center in Colombia and another from Mexico went to the center at Recife, one from Recife went to the center in Argentina, two from Argentina went to Recife, and two from Recife went to Mexico.

        This account of the project's activities would be in-
complete without mention of the preparation of a design for
"research on the application of television and other audio-
visual methods to education in specific forms and areas, to
study the feasibility of such resources," prepared by a working group of three contract specialists and the staff members working in this area at headquarters. This design was
presented to the General Office of Education Techniques of
Argentina, which will be the host institution for the research
project.

The Library

        In general, the Latin American countries lack a policy
for library expansion. Plans aimed at activating library services have not been implemented, and library organization
and administration is frequently archaic, in the sense that
technical processes are too lengthy, restrictive practices
are followed for the sole purpose of keeping books from
being lost, and insufficient attention is paid to the attraction
of new readers.

        The need for libraries properly equipped with refe-
rence material and professional staffs is a categorical imperative for our countries, particularly those in which educational institutions lack sufficient textbooks and bibliographi-
cal materials.

        To cooperate in national efforts, the Regional Educa-
tional Development Program has in operation a Multinational
Project on School and University Libraries, which is carried
out by the Inter-American School of Library Science of the
University of Antioquia, Medellín, Colombia.

        This project, which is based on the concept that the
library is an essential element of the educational institution,
held a five-month course on professional training of university librarians, and a five-month course on professional
training of school librarians, at the project center mentioned
above, with the participation of 14 fellowship students of the
program.

Technical Education

The intensive process of industrialization underway in
Latin America, bolstered by scientific and technological
progress, requires a careful study and restatement of positions with respect to technical education as it now exists and
should be in the future. If our countries wish to remain in
a stage such as that of the "economy of commercial handi-
crafts," they can do so with a comparatively low level of
formal education, combined with training in small establishments. But if we wish to enjoy a higher standard of living,
we must have completely different types of technical training
and education. If the traditional methods are maintained, it
will be impossible to better our present living conditions.
An improved system of technical education is indispensible
if we are to take proper advantage of technological progress
and industrialization, and translate our earnest desire for a
better life into reality.

The role of technical education in this transformation
process is vitally important, so that it would be no exaggeration to say that if general education is fundamental in the
social and cultural development of peoples, technical education is crucial in their economic progress.

The comprehensive development of Latin America demands, on one hand, the training of technicians capable of
performing a variety of activities in specific areas, with
ready adaptability to the changes implied in this development;
on the other hand, it also requires that technical teachers
be trained in a systematic, organized, and directed manner,
as regards both scope and content, to meet the needs in
this area. The quality of technicians and workers undoubtedly will depend to a great extent on the level of training of
their teachers.

The efforts made in this connection by most of the
Latin American countries, while substantial in recent years,
have met only part of their quantitative and qualitative
needs. Thus, a reassessment of the problem within a new
context became essential, and the Inter-American Cultural
Council called for such action at its Sixth Meeting.

Considering that the implementation of a comprehensive plan in the area of technical education and vocational
training was of basic importance in economic, social and
educational development, the Council approved a Multination-

al Action Plan in this field, for the purpose of cooperating with the OAS member states in solving common problems that affect or limit the development of national systems of technical education and vocational training.

Three specific programs were selected to give concrete form to the plan: basic and advanced training of teachers, supervisors, technicians and administrators in the fields of technical education and vocational training; educational research, experimentation and innovation; and preparation of teaching materials.

In implementing the plan, the Multinational Project on Technical Education and Vocational Training, as a component of the Regional Educational and Development Program, has carried out multinational activities at the following centers:

Advanced National Institute for Technical Teachers, Buenos Aires, Argentina (To cooperate with the countries in implementing their technical education plans; training of personnel and adaptation of technical education and vocational training according to the demands of national development plans.)

Center for Technical Education, Labor University of Minas Gerais (UTRAMIG), Belo Horizonte, Brazil (To train researchers and planners in technical education; follow-up of the intensive program for training skilled workers; training of industrial technicians.)

General Office of Higher Education, Mexico City, Mexico (To establish, develop and test systems and methods for the planning and supervision of technological training; to design, test and construct prototypes for all classes of resources for technological education; to test new administrative and operating structures for technological centers; to provide advanced training for specialized personnel.)

Added to the above are the support actions provided to the General Office of Adult Education of Bolivia (basic and advanced training of adults in the technical field of their choice, training of workers in industry, improvement of worker productivity through supplementary technical-vocational training); the Pilot Center for Agricultural Education at Cañete, Peru (training in agricultural education, coordination of educational reform with agrarian reform, training intermediate level personnel and production workers

in the agricultural sector); and the Ecuadorian Service for
Professional Training (training of personnel for manpower
research, improvement of vocational training plans, programs, methods, and systems.)

The more important activities carried out within this
project include the following: two courses at the Advanced
Institute for Technical Teachers of Argentina on supervision
and administration of technical education, one lasting ten
months and the other lasting six months, with the participation of 38 fellowship students of the program; and the course
on training of supervisors for industry, ten months, at the
Technical Education Center of the Labor University of Minas
Gerais, Brazil, with the participation of six fellowship students of the program and 20 from the host country.

In addition, technical cooperation missions were sent
to Peru and Paraguay as part of the activities of the Advanced Institute for Technical Teachers of Argentina. The
first mission has five foreign technicians (Argentines and
Brazilians), two from the Inter-American Institute of Agricultural Sciences (Andean Zone) and two specialists from the
Department of Educational Affairs of the OAS; in the second
mission, eight advisors contracted by the program met with
63 national officials to make a thorough study of the reform
of technical education and vocational training in Paraguay,
which has been started by the authorities of the country.

Note should also be made of the research on the occupational structure of industrial manpower conducted in
Ecuador; research on effective measures for educational and
vocational guidance to be applied in general education, conducted in Brazil; research on personnel requirements for
the development of technical education in Argentina; and research on educational planning techniques, school organization, curriculum revision and methodology, which are to be
adopted in the technical education and vocational training system of São Paulo, with the participation of foreign specialists
as research associates.

Adult Education

Adult education unquestionably is a prerequisite to
the development of Latin American society. On one hand it
signifies implementation of the principles of justice, through
which society meets its responsibilities to those whom it

failed to provide with educational opportunities; on the other
hand, it is a factor of progress, for the adult population
that becomes part of economic life through education becomes
a more valuable source of manpower in the short run.

Some of the efforts of Latin American countries in
this area have been scattered, as institutions, plans, programs and methods have multiplied, and problems have been
approached without prior study. Without going into detail
regarding the areas that any systematic action in this field
should cover, it is worthwhile to note that a sound policy on
adult education will be incomplete if it does not include four
types of education as part of the plan, in their several
stages: a) a community education; b) vocational training;
c) literacy programs; and d) general education.

Recent years have seen the development of new ideas
for the orientation of adult education. They presuppose a
definite turn away from past concepts, since they call for
objective study of the political, social, economic, and cultural factors that have created the present educational situation, as well as a thorough revision of objectives and a
strengthening and reorganization of the institutions that carry
out programs in this field.

In line with these new concerns, the Inter-American
Council for Education, Science, and Culture, at its Second
Meeting, approved a Multinational Project on Adult Educa-
tion, which provides guidelines for the activities carried out
within this project by the Regional Educational Development
Program, at the following centers:

National Office of Adult Education, Buenos Aires, Argentina
(To analyze and evaluate adult education systems in Latin
America; to cooperate with the countries in preparing national projects on research, experimentation and innovation
in the field of adult education; to sponsor the basic and advanced training of high-level personnel in administration,
planning and research in the field of adult education.)

Regional Center for Adult Education (CREA), Caracas, Venezuela (To prepare, publish and disseminate materials related
to adult education; to train high and intermediate level personnel for the performance of technical functions in national
adult education programs; to promote and conduct technical
assistance missions in the field of adult education.)

In addition, support actions are being provided to the
Pilot Center for Adult Education for the Integral Development
of the Community of Lima, Peru (to promote research and the
adoption of modern methods in this field; to carry out tests
and introduce innovations in pilot centers in order to improve
the quality of adult education); the National Office for Literacy Programs and the Adult Education of Haiti (to provide
teaching materials to literacy centers and functional literacy
shops as required for the apprenticeship process; to prepare
demonstration materials for Community Action Councils); and
the Polivalent Center for Adult Education of Santiago, Chile
(to incorporate a unit of this type in the educational system
of the country on a pilot basis; to test a model of comprehensive education; training of personnel).

The more important activities carried out within this
project include the following: two advanced courses for officials and specialists of national adult education programs,
three months each, with the participation of 24 fellowship
students of the program, held at the Regional Center for
Adult Education, Caracas, Venezuela; and three courses and
study and observation visits, held in three stages (of four,
two and four months respectively), as part of the Multinational Experimental Plan for Adult Education of Argentina,
with 33 fellowship students of the Program participating.

Mention should also be made of the exchange visits
by project officials of Argentina, Venezuela, Chile, Peru and
Haiti to other Latin American and European countries, to
observe and study adult education programs, particularly as
regards the programming, organization and administration of
such programs; the support provided to the Literacy and
Adult Education Programs of the Dominican Republic and
Paraguay; the Workshops on Problems of Adult Education
held in Buenos Aires and four other cities of Argentina; and
the participation of five research associates from Chile,
Dominican Republic, Haiti, Paraguay, and Venezuela in the
National Direction of Adult Education of Argentina, and two
research associates from Argentina and Uruguay in CREA
of Venezuela.

Qualitative deficiencies in teaching practices have
been a major factor in preventing the efforts of countries
to improve their educational systems from yielding the desired benefits.

A glance at the past and a comparison of the expend-

itures made in education with the results obtained shows
that while a substantial number of new students have been
brought into the system, in most countries substantial
changes have yet to be made in the quality of teaching and
in the efficiency of procedures. For obvious reasons, this
situation makes it necessary to consider alternatives for
spending in education in order to improve its quality in the
future, naturally without neglecting the proper attention to
quantitative growth. The lack of background information required to form the basis of adequate educational policy is
partly responsible for the problems just mentioned. It has
meant that in many cases the authorities have not been able
to consider various courses of action, and have been obliged
to make decisions without a scientific basis.

All the countries, regardless of their level of development, need to conduct educational research on a systematic
and continuing basis. Those at an advanced level of development must review their objectives in the light of the new
conditions and problems that accompany progress, to make
the necessary adaptations and adjustments. Those that have
remained behind urgently require research to hasten the solution of their problems and meet the deficit at the lowest
cost in money, time and effort.

Thus, educational research is a basic and immediate
task, for which the Regional Educational Development Program has established a Multinational Plan for Educational
Research and Experimentation, approved by the Inter-American Cultural Council at its Sixth Meeting; this plan serves
as the frame of reference for the activities carried out within the Multinational Project on Research. The project has
multinational activities under way at the following centers:

National Center for Educational Research, Buenos Aires,
Argentina (To promote the basic and advanced training of
personnel of national and regional research centers and to
foster exchange through study missions and the participation
of research associates.)

National Center for Educational Research, San José, Costa
Rica (to promote the development of educational research in
all areas and at all levels.)

Department of Educational Research, Direction of Planning,
Caracas, Venezuela (To train intermediate and high level
specialists in the field of educational research; to encourage

the reform of the educational systems of Latin America on the basis of research.)

Support actions are being provided to the Division of Educational Planning, Panama (to aid the development of educational research through the preparation and implementation of comprehensive plans); the Education Unit of the Planning Department, Ministry of Education of Ecuador (to evaluate the results of the Ecuadorian education plan, in order to revise it as necessary; to evaluate the effects of reforms in progress at each level of education); to the General Office of Elementary Education, Secretariat of State for Education, Fine Arts, and Worship, Dominican Republic (to conduct psychopedagogical research in order to identify factors causing low return and productivity in this area and the high rate of school absenteeism; to apply teaching methods and techniques suitable for normal age groups or older groups); the Office of Education Planning and the National Center for Pedagogical Improvement Experimentation and Research, Santiago, Chile (to determine whether there are statistically significant relationships among the variations observed in factors that influence the education process and its results); the Ministry of Culture, Montevideo, Uruguay (to achieve the required coordination of education, with sufficient flexibility to prevent the lateral displacement of the student; to develop systems to evaluate and measure the efficiency of proposed solutions, and thereby to keep the educational system operating with maximum return); and the Colombian Institute of Pedagogy (ICOLPE), Bogotá, Colombia (to strengthen and supplement the activities of ICOLPE).

The principal activities carried out under this project include the work performed at the National Center for Educational Research of the Ministry of Culture and Education of Argentina by two groups of research associates including participants from Bolivia, Brazil, Chile, Colombia, Costa Rica, Ecuador, Guatemala, Mexico, Panama, Paraguay, Peru, Uruguay, and Venezuela. The purpose of this work was to assist in the advance training of these professionals through their active participation in the activities of the centers concerned.

Mention should be made of the study missions granted to a public official of Colombia to visit institutions in Venezuela and Mexico, and another to make a similar visit to Spain and France; to a specialist from Mexico to visit Chile, Colombia, and Uruguay; to eight professors from Uruguay to

go to Argentina, Brazil, Chile, Colombia, Ecuador, Mexico,
Paraguay, Peru, and Venezuela; to four officials of the Do-
minican Republic to observe centers in Brazil, Chile and
Venezuela; and to three specialists from Venezuela to carry
out a similar mission in Brazil, Chile, Mexico, and the
United States.

Finally, mention should be made of the assistance
rendered to the Project on Improvement of Educational Research and Statistics of Uruguay; of cooperation in the research activities of the projects "Study of Relationships Between the Elements and Results of the Educational Process"
in Chile, and "Basic Study of the Problems of Rural Education" conducted by the Inter-American Center for Rural Education (CIER) of Venezuela. In connection with the latter,
three Venezuelan specialists made fact-finding trips to Argentina, Bolivia, Chile, Colombia, Costa Rica, Ecuador,
Guatemala, Honduras, Nicaragua, Mexico, Peru, Trinidad
and Tobago and the United States.

Educational Research Program*

Development of a new approach to the training and up-
dating of educational research personnel in the Western
Hemisphere was implemented in the spring of 1971 in San
José, Costa Rica, where 24 participants from 16 of the member states of the Organization took part in the first Applied
Laboratory in Educational Research. This Laboratory dealt
with the Guttman Facet Theory and its application to attitude
measurement. Professor Louis Guttman, director of the
Israel Institute of Applied Social Research and the creator
of the Facet Theory, participated in the Laboratory and has
continued to cooperate with the program in the four research
projects which were developed in San Jose. The projects
are on attitudes toward educational change, the role of women, technical education, and the use of drugs. About 15
countries are participating in these cross-cultural research
projects; publication of the final reports is expected by early
fall of 1973. A second Applied Laboratory in Educational
Research dealing with inter-action analysis in the classroom,
i. e., the teaching-learning process, is planned for the spring
of 1973 at the Multinational Center in Venezuela.

---

*The director of the OAS Department of Educational Affairs
added this "updated information" while giving permission to
reprint the foregoing report.

The Multinational Center in Argentina is sponsoring a pilot project research study on school achievement and failures beginning in October 1972.   This project will bring together education technicians from Argentina, Bolivia, Colombia, Ecuador, Paraguay, and Uruguay in a unique experience combining training activities with field research, which will lead in turn to publication of a study on the subject of school achievement and failures and related matters.

Section IV

CURRENT PRECEDENT AND FUTURE PROSPECTS
Donald A. Lemke

The projects and plans in this volume are, in part, the Latin American education hopes and dreams of the decade just completed. In most cases, scientific models have been utilized to try to eliminate as much of the chance as the current usable technology permits. This has been the result, or perhaps the cause of a region-wide desire to "modernize." Its three-prong approach has included (1) short and long-range projections of educational goals, (2) extension of education opportunities to the masses, and (3) measurement and improvement of the qualitative aspects of education.

Both optimism and pessimism have been evident in the region and in the essays. Sometimes individual experiments or ideas have been presented as if they were the final solution to the problems by enthusiastic supporters of the change catalyst. In some instances, individuals have devoted their lives to the development of that change and its incorporation within the system. The best of these ideas have built large structures around them, becoming permanent entities within Ministries of Education or universities. It is partially for this reason that one sees the tremendous overlap of functions and services in many Latin American Ministries of Education today. The question of current utility is not always applied to programs which have had temporary successes, but have lived past their usefulness. And the bureaucratic structure mushrooms beyond the point of efficient use of human resources.

Many have viewed this burgeoning effect in a more negative fashion. Proposals to completely revamp the educational system have taken researchers back to the bases of the society itself. Often this has led to the presentation of a seemingly impossible situation, a type of self-destructive process which dooms that country, or the region as a

331

whole to a permanent state of underdevelopment. Sometimes ideas have been presented to completely reorganize the society, and the educational system with it, in order to create a more operant situation in which complete utilization of human resources becomes possible.

With few exceptions, however, the decade of the 1960's in Latin America has not fathered ideas which will bring about that type of change. Educational planners and theorists have been too involved in the daily numbers to step back and make sound, long-range projections. This need for introspection and projection is left as one of the first priority tasks for the decade of the 1970's. The decade just completed has also demonstrated a wide division between theory and practice, between planning and execution, and between financing and care of materials and equipment. Theoretical plans seldom are put into practice, even at the experimental level. This implies a problem of planning, but from the bottom up, not the top down. And it implies a problem of administration in the same order. This sticky problem of moving theory into practice looms as a second big challenge of the 1970's in Latin America.

One of the predispositions which has been most evident in the essays has been the desire to do everything with the modern conveniences which are available. These are, inevitably, expensive. This means that the best of the materials go no further than selected schools in the capital or the major cities. Restricted budgets will offer no relief to this problem for decades to come. Instead, a new realization of the need to better utilize what is available must be developed. To make rather than to buy ready-made educational materials must be the theme. Materials from the region must be brought into the school and the teacher must become a builder and organizer, rather than a distributor of materials. Only in this way can materials be spread to the great number of schools and children which exist in the region. This becomes a third challenge.

Certainly there are many other things which must be done in the 1970's to improve existing educational systems in the region. Some will evolve from discoveries not yet made in psychology, technology or education. Some will be left for the succeeding decades to realize. What will actually be done will depend heavily upon the shifts which are made in the way people look at fundamental bases of education. This philosophical movement is already in progress.

The basically conservative philosophy which gripped most of the major institutions in Latin America underwent a sharp reversal in the past decade. This was, in general, in keeping with the movement toward liberalism throughout the world. It has lifted the veil which sometimes sanctified the role of the business executive, the absentee landowner, the politician and the traditional educator and exposed each to public scrutiny. Almost invariably this has meant a re-ordering of goals by individuals and by institutions as the in-efficiencies of the previous system became evident.

This reordering has required a new look at the philo-sophical base of the institutions, of the society as a whole and of the individuals in particular. The previous structure strove, consciously or unconsciously, to maintain two socie-tal elements: the class structure as characterized by cheap labor, over-bureaucratization and high profits for the few, and the status quo of measuring out changes with eyedroppers. This approach led to the development of contrasts which any visitor notes almost everywhere in Latin America: huge mansions and cardboard shacks, high executive salaries and cheap labor, jet-line services for the few and crowded buses for the many, elegant restaurants and hotels for some, and for others, among the most unhealthy eating or sleeping facilities found anywhere, and a range of moral standards from chaperoning for the daughter to several mistresses for the father. This duplicity of standards has led to the de-velopment of strong private schools, of an exodus of the most affluent to foreign high schools and universities, of a curriculum based on past needs, of teaching through memor-ization, and of facilities and materials which were either too much or too little. Everywhere this had become the pattern for Latin American development with little real effort to change.

World changes, transportation improvements, tightened economic competition, improved communication techniques, new philosophical interpretations, and a variety of other fac-tors have gradually led Latin American leaders to see the need to move away from the existing structure. This is the process which is just now accelerating. It is one, how-ever, which cannot be slowed. The next decades are al-most certain to bring more and more institutions and indi-viduals moving away from traditional philosophical approaches into a new base which is more liberal and closer to the re-

alities of these institutions in the 20th century. Doubtless,
most educators will develop programs first and then look for
philosophical support. But, as Edmund J. King pointed out:
"What educators must look for is a philosophy with a future,
a philosophy that comes down to earth. All philosophies
should think of their words in terms of programmes" [World
Perspectives in Education, New York: Bobbs-Merrill, 1962,
p. 258-9]. Thus, if the two pull together in this decade
programs will more consistently reflect philosophies and
vice versa.

For purposes of parsimony, educational philosophies
are dichotomized into two main segments, traditional philosophies and those based upon scientific and/or historic experiences. The two main thrusts of the traditional philosophies, as seen in Latin America, have already been discussed. Precisely because these elements are changing in
Latin American societies, the traditional philosophies are
losing ground. The rising elements, somewhat different in
each country, will define the new programs and the new
philosophies. These will almost certainly include the following four characteristics:

First, a heavy stress upon the scientific process of
data collection, interpretation, analysis and application.
This mechanization may be used to make better projections,
better plans, better programs. Initially, countries may become overstaffed in the "hardware" aspects of data collection and understaffed in the more subtle steps of interpretation and application. Eventually this must be balanced.
But this use of modern mechanisms is certain to rise in the
1970's.

Second, a new interpretation of the historical heritage.
The youth of Latin America have already begun this interpretation, rejecting much of what their parents have held
sacred. This includes economic rules, personal values and
attitudes toward the value of education. As these youth ma-
ture they will seek to crystallize these attacks upon heritage
into a positive set of programs. This may move toward a
new interpretation of an existing philosophy (as has been
seen in Chile's experimentation with Marxism) or of the development of a whole new series of standards. Whichever,
it involves the re-interpretation of history and a syntheza-
tion of new goals.

Third, a heavy stress upon workable formulas seems

eminent.   This pragmatic view of institutions and their products will cut back much of the wastage of the 1960's as new programs evolve.   But experimentation will continue, seeking programs which work and not doing experimentation for its own sake.   This will include a great sharing of experiences at international conferences, seminars and meetings.   Inevitably, this will bring Latin American countries closer together philosophically as they apply similar tests of economic feasibility and pragmatic usefullness to programs.

Finally, new concern for the common man and his condition will lead to a reordering of governmental and institutional priorities.   Elite class privileges (exclusive shops, private clubs, private schools, etc.) will decline and more public facilities and products will develop.   This is almost certain to touch every aspect of the Latin American school life--entrance requirements, curriculum, teaching methods, facilities and all the rest.   It will lead to a wider spread of items of a lower quality.   It may lead to a certain decrease in the activity of things now considered as part of the quality life (art, music, high-grade furniture and houses) and an increase in such activities as large public performances, spectator athletics, public parks and other things which appeal to the great bulk of the people.

These four characteristics may not all be worked into programs at the same time or in the same countries. However, from these will develop the programs and eventually the philosophies that will replace traditional approaches. The first waves of what these programs and philosophies will include have been partially exposed in the essays. Some of these have been seen in the change catalysts and some in résumés of planning projects.   The second wave, that which will change these from separated experiments into system-wide programs, is likely to pass through important formative years in the 1970's.

In the development of nations, small groups often rise to power on the basis of a vacuum of leadership at the top or on the strength of a disciplined commitment to an idea in which they believe.   Sometimes this idea is unique to the country and sometimes it is part of a larger international network.   To achieve full power there must be an increase in support for the idea, presumably because more people see its value.   Gradually this becomes system-wide and is incorporated into the overall society.   The change agents described in this volume must follow a similar pat-

tern. As ideas are tested in practice, it is initially difficult to see if they will have long-range value. Much of this
depends upon the conditions which are prevelant at the time
the change is instituted. If, for example, the educational
system is ready for the use of television as a new media, a
well-planned program could receive immediate acceptance.
A few months in one direction or the other could make the
difference. If, however, conditions are not just right the
project may not get started.

        Even after its inauguration, there is no assurance
that an idea will be spread to the entire system. This is
the position in which most of the projects described in this
volume found themselves at the opening of the decade.
Which ones may rise to eventual influence depends, once
again, upon the conditions which exist in the country. It
seemed unlikely, for example, that the role of the private
school as an experimental center would flourish in Chile in
the 1970's while the government was placing such a heavy
emphasis upon the opening of public schools for the masses.
But it appeared more likely that the system-wide television-
based curriculum reform in El Salvador would transcend the
change of government.

        However, the future of experimentation seems to be
very much in doubt in Latin America. A general feeling
that tinkering with the system has not really solved the basic
problems seems to exist. The need for hardcore decisions
which will effect the entire system, not just isolated or privileged schools, is evident. Just what reaction this will
bring in the 1970's will depend partially upon the political
situations in each country. Those catalysts which are most
likely to continue to exist are those which:

        1.   Have a system-wide impact;
        2.   Reach groups not previously reached with funda-
mental programs;
        3.   Can be fit realistically into very tight budgets;
        4.   Can be implemented without greatly disturbing the
existing administrative organization,
        5.   Utilize personnel from within the country to fill
key slots;
        6.   Use modern techniques to create a wider effi-
ciency in the system and;
        7.   Stress the better utilization of human resources,
regardless of individual political connections, within the
country.

This is a very serious business at a very serious
moment in Latin America.   Educational systems are grinding
to a near halt under the weight of enrollment increases.

Planning mechanisms already exist in most Latin
American countries.   Often they structurally over-exist,
being stronger than their utility, providing more projections
and statistics than can be digested or used.   This might be
the result of their increasing sophistication (and the decreasing number of people who can understand their projections) or again it might be caused by the lack of contact between planning and policy-making.

Sophistication in educational planning is tied, at least
in part, to the computer revolution.   The ability, indeed the
necessity, of using mathematical models or symbols has
made available a quantity of information which the Ministry
is not always equipped to analyze and not always ready to
fit into current priorities, real or political.   The end result is a surplus of quantitative studies of the "how many"
type, but a surprising scarcity of "why" and "how" studies
in the educational area in Latin America.   These important
implementation steps have been left to the top administrators
with the thought that they could, somewhat as a magician,
take all the complicated plans and fit them into a program
of action for the system.   This points up one of the Latin
American educational planning needs of the 1970's.

Some shift toward "why" and "how" studies needs to
be made so that administrators can more fully interpret the
meaning of the data and bring it into policy-making decision.
This involves a much closer relationship between ministers
or sub-secretaries and planning offices.   This same movement has been more geared to the organization of long-range
studies, sometimes up to 30 years, than to those of the
short-range variety.   These long-term projections of student
population, of needs for teachers, of dropouts, of repeaters,
of school buildings or of budgets are usually based upon
some relatively recent reliable data, such as the census.
From that point, using mathematical formulas, projections
are made as to the needs of the future.   The trouble is that
almost all such projections have to be revised annually
when firm data become available.   But this type of study,
geared to long-range projections does not really fit the need
for short-range plans.   Thus a minister, bound as he is by
the same approximate budget as he had the previous year,
cannot effectively adjust his program to the actual yearly

fluctuations. He is locked in, with no studies to support
him in his confrontation with precedent.

A second need is for short-term planning and short-
term budgeting flexibility to enable a Ministry of Education
to adjust to the yearly changes. These are much more difficult studies to make because there is no time for data collection of any magnitude and little time for interpretation
and analysis. There are shelves of mimeographed studies
available on a great variety of educational topics in a great
variety of offices in Latin America. But seldom can one
find any one person who knows all of these studies or any
one center where they can all be found. Expatriot personnel
often initiate valuable studies, but then leave. And within
the national educational area there is a split between public
and private, between Ministry and universities and between
primary and secondary levels. Each jealously guards its
studies for its own purposes. The tremendous overlap and
duplication of human resources which develops has become
an accepted pattern.

Almost every country needs, thirdly, a documentation center for the coordination and interpretation of existing
educational planning studies. This could easily be a center
where researchers <u>must</u> go before starting their studies.
If all recent studies are available in this center, the researcher could make an ample review of what has been done
before starting his own research. This could serve as a
type of "data bank" for ministers, university officials and
other administrators to collect current information to make
pressing decisions.

A gap still exists between the planner and the decision-maker in Latin American education. The former is
usually an educator with specific training in a specific area--
educational planning. The latter is a generalist, sometimes
a politician, sometimes with a good global view of the place
of education in the overall society, but seldom with training
in educational planning. The logical thing happens when increasingly specialized studies pass from the planner to the
decision-maker and demands on his time makes it impossible
for him to give the plans the detailed study which would be
required for him to fully comprehend them.

A fourth desideratum is that planning office functions
must be expanded to include decision-making on certain
specific matters. These could include all types of counting

items, information which can be obtained and analyzed from objective data, as well as some policy matters. This should be a part of the decentralization of educational administration which is needed in most Latin American educational systems.

The planning essays included in this volume point toward these needs for the 1970's. But if any are to be effective, faster ways to collect data and change it into objective decisions must be found. If not, educational planning offices may find themselves incorporated into larger planning units or completely outside the central educational movement.

A Final Word

No summary can truly review the contents of a book, nor should it. That task is left to the individual reader to do in his own individual way. This is especially true in a book of readings which brings together a variety of viewpoints on a variety of topics by a variety of writers.

But a general feeling of urgency should have been conveyed by these readings. The problems presented and the approaches to solutions all stress this tendency. Situations exist which cannot be overlooked, which must be faced now. To overlook them is to create even greater problems later. As the masses become more fully incorporated into the political, economic and educational institutions, they will initially demand more. This could cause a stimulus to growth or it could create a revolutionary condition. Just which will prevail depends to a great degree on how it is handled by the individual governments.

While the purpose of this volume has been to present some representative Latin American educational movements, the fact that the region consists of individual countries with individual histories, economies and hopes is not overlooked. Regional tendencies are not yet strong enough to overcome nationalistic feelings. But if one could look back from 1980 to the decade of the 1970's, it would be likely that the educational systems of Latin America had made great advances, but that the tremendous variations from one country to another would still exist. From that vantage point the changes of the 1970's will take on a new meaning, one which could easily shape the educational directions in individual countries for decades to come.

NOTES ON CONTRIBUTORS

Co-editor Dr. Donald A. LEMKE, currently serving as a University of Indiana professor and resident educational consultant in Santiago, Chile, has previously worked as a resident consultant both to the Central American Textbook Program and to the Costa Rican Ministry of Education. Overall he has had more than a decade of experience in Central and South American educational development efforts. He is the author of numerous technical reports and Educational Systems of the Americas.

Co-editor Dr. Richard L. CUMMINGS, associate professor of comparative education in the School of Education, and associate director of the University of Wisconsin-Milwaukee Language and Area Studies Center for Latin America, has served as an educational advisor in the Brazilian National Ministry of Education and Culture as well as having lived and worked in both Panama and Colombia. He has enjoyed a total of over 15 years' experience in Latin America and Latin American Studies. He has written "Approaches to Manpower Planning" (International Review of Education, XVI/1970/2), the monograph Engineering Manpower and Development in Brazil: 1966-1970 and currently is a director of the Laboratory for International Research in Education, Inc.

Manuel A. ARCE is a Costa Rican, was graduated as an elementary school teacher in the normal school of his country. Later he attended the University of Kentucky and did his graduate work in education at Marshall University, Huntington, West Virginia. He has worked in international educational programs in several South and Central American countries. Since the organization of the Central American Textbook Project he has served as editor, coordinator, technical advisor and sub-director.

Rafael BARDALES B. is Minister of Education in Honduras and the man who has been chiefly responsible for the sweeping reform described in his article. A respected educator of considerable prominence inside and outside Honduras, he has himself been a teacher and writer for his entire life.   He is the author of the influential book, Nociones de Historia de la Educación.

Concepción E. CASTAÑEDA is currently a professor at Milliken University in Decatur, Illinois.   Dr. Castañeda lived in Cuba during the pre-Castro period and has kept close contact through the years with the methods employed in the educational system by the new socialist government. In her brief résumé in this book she stresses the strong influence and the heavy role which the Cuban youth played in the reformation of the educational system.   These changes are now well formulated and stand as the basis for the Cuban educational system of the 1970's.

Thomas N. CHIRIKOS and John R. SHEA are faculty associates, Center for Human Resource Research, Ohio State University.   Their essay is an offshoot of a human resource planning project which was sponsored by U.S.A.I.D. and the Government of Bolivia.   The final English language report of this project appeared as: Chirikos, T. N., ... Shea, J. R., et al., Human Resources in Bolivia, Problems Planning and Policy, Columbus: Center for Human Resource Research, Ohio State University, 1971, 382 p.

Charles Marden FITCH is an educational communications specialist who began teaching as a naturalist, then entered television and films while still in high school.   He later received a master's degree in educational communications from New York University.   Fitch has worked as producer-talent with television in the United States and as director-producer with educational television projects in Columbia and El Salvador, specializing in adult education and natural science programming.   He is a cinematographer, photographer, writer and teacher in both the natural sciences and communications.   Currently he is a TV-Film Coordinator with the Larchmont-Mamaroneck Public Schools and teaches courses in horticultural science, film and television. His book, Televisión Educativa was published in Spanish by the El Salvador Ministry of Education.

Paulo FREIRE is the author of Pedagogy of the Oppressed.   He initiated his methodology in literary work in the Brazilian Northeast and upon invitation by the Minister of Education coordinated Brazil's National Adult Literacy Plan from June 1963 until March 1964 at which time he

moved to Chile where he spent the following five years working in adult literacy programs. Currently a special consultant to the Educational Division of the World Council of
Churches in Geneva, Professor Freire also serves as a
fellow of the Center for the Study of Development and Social
Change at Harvard University.

Paul HINES: while maintaining an active interest in
Latin American studies, Dr. Hines is dean of instruction
and acting president at Barton County Community Junior College in Great Bend, Kansas.

Ivan ILLICH is a founder of the Centro Intercultural
de Documentación (CIDOC) in Cuernavaca, Mexico, an organization of scholars engaged in the study, analysis and
publication or socio-cultural information about Latin America. Monsignor Illich was formerly vice-president of the
Catholic University of Puerto Rico and on the Commonwealth
Board of Higher Education involved in educational planning
in Puerto Rico. He is the author of Celebration of Awareness.

Luis Arturo LEMUS and Dr. Peter C. WRIGHT:
Lic. Lemus, former director of the Planning Office and a
well-known writer in Latin America, is currently the director of the special project office responsible for over-
seeing the rural education reform (PEMEP) in Guatemala.
Dr. Wright has had many years on the front line of educational change in Guatemala. A former University of South
Florida administrator, Dr. Wright is currently the chief of
Human Resource Development for the Agency for International Development in Guatemala.

Mario LEYTON Soto and Ralph TYLER: Sr. Leyton
is a past Sub-Secretary of Education and one of Chile's
leading educators. He is currently the director of the National Center for Educational Experimentation and Investigation (CEEI). Dr. Ralph W. Tyler, senior consultant,
Science Research Associates, Inc., since 1967, had earlier
directed the Center for Advanced Study in the Behavioral
Sciences at Stanford, California for fourteen years after a
distinguished career as a University Professor from 1922
through 1953.

Sylvain LOURIE was a member of the Institute for
Economic and Social Development Studies in Paris at the
time he wrote this article. This essay was first published

by UNESCO's International Institute for Educational Planning
in Problems and Strategies of Educational Planning; Lessons
from Latin America and as such represents an example of
the state of the fast-moving planning art at that time.

Guillermo MALAVASSI, former philosophy professor
and administrator at the University of Costa Rica, was appointed Minister of Education in 1966 and remained in that
post until 1969.   In his article, written especially for this
book, Lic. Malavassi presents both a philosophical and a
practical look at what it is possible for a minister to
change.   He has now returned to his position at the University of Costa Rica.

Ministry of Education, Paraguay.   "The Expansion of
Complete Primary School to Rural Areas in Paraguay" was
first published in Boletín de Educación Paraguaya in 1969.
It has been revised in this English language version by the
editors, but with the approval of the Ministry of Education
and Culture, to fit the format of this book.

Eugene NUSS left his professorship at the University
of Bridgeport in 1968 to become the chief teacher education
advisor to the education reform program in El Salvador.   A
specialist in human growth and development, Dr. Nuss has
almost 20 years of experience at a variety of U.S. universities.

Rolland G. PAULSTON is a professor in the Inter-
national and Development Education Program, School of Edu-
cation, University of Pittsburgh, Pittsburgh, Pennsylvania.
He has worked for UNESCO, the Ford Foundation, AID, and
other agencies on problems of educational change in Latin
America.   His most recent books are Society, Schools, and
Progress in Peru (Pergamon Press, 1971), and Non-Formal
Education: An Annotated International Bibliography of the
Non-School Educational Sector (Praeger, 1972).

Ovidio SOTO BLANCO is a Costa Rican who has attended international conferences on three continents, has
been the head of educational planning units on national and
regional levels and has been a teacher, principal and university professor.   Recently the coordinator for the Central
American Planning Office, he has now returned to his own
country and is serving as chief education advisor to the
new Minister of Education.   He is the author of many articles published in international journals and in 1968 wrote

the book, Education in Central America, the first scientifically comparative study of education in these six countries.

Peter TOBIA is director of Human Resource Development for the Agency for International Development in Manag-
ua, Nicaragua. An old hand with AID, he finished his doctorate in Comparative Education at Ohio State University in
1968. His years of experience in Central America make
him particularly qualified to write this article on changes
which lead to educational development.

Herbert G. VAUGHAN has lived in Honduras, Guatemala and El Salvador and wrote his doctoral thesis at Michigan State on the American School in Guatemala. During the
past three years he and his Brazilian wife have been engaged in the Salvador educational reform project. He wrote
his article especially for this publication. Dr. Vaughan is
currently an assistant professor of education at Baldwin-
Wallace College.

Marshall WOLFE is acting chief, Division of Social
Affairs, Economic Commission for Latin America (ECLA).
His essay, originally published in 1965 along with Sylvain
Lourié's, also represents an example of educational practice,
at that time, and is not intended to reflect current thrusts
in the fast moving arena of educational planning.

America Mexico), 312, 313
Conference on Education and
Economic and Social De-
velopment in Latin America,
Santiago, Chile--March 5,
1962, 7
conquistadores, 52, 276
"Conscientization, " 137
Constitution of 1869 (Costa
Rica), 53
Constitutions of Ignatius Loyo-
la, 18
Consultive and Coordinating
Group of OCEPLAN, 203,
204
Controller General, Costa
Rica, 238
Costa Rica, 49, 51, 52, 53,
54, 228-43, 267
CREA (Regional Center for
Adult Education, Caracas,
Venezuela, 324, 325
CSUCA (Superior Council of
Central American Univer-
sities), 69, 203
Cuba, 145-177, 267, 280, 281
Cuban Revolution, 279, 280
Cultural and Educational Coun-
cil of ODECA, 202, 204
Czechoslovakia, 171

"Decade of Development" of
the United Nation, 24
Declaration of Punta del Este,
April 14, 1967; 300, 306,
307
decodification, 129, 130, f. n.
15, 142
Department of Basic Studies,
Univ. of San Carlos, 64
Department of Educational Research, Direction of Planning, Caracas, Venezuela,
326
Department of Educational (Instructional) Television, Ministry of Education (El Salvador), 86
Department of Jutiapa (Guatemala), 188, 196
Department of Psycho-pedagog-
ical Research in Paraguay,
181

Department of Santo Rosa
(Guatemala), 196
Department of Vocational Guid-
ance, American School of
Guatemala, 71
Descontes, Rene, 20
Dewey, John, 165
Directive Council, University of
Valle, 68, 69
Director General, Mexico, 281
Director of Federal Education,
Mexico, 281
Division of Educational Planning,
Panamá, 327
Division of Instructional Tele-
vision, El Salvador, 85
Dr. Mariano Galvaz, 69
Dr. Queiroz Filho Regional Cen-
ter for Educational Research,
São Paulo, Brazil, 311, 312,
316
Dominican Republic, 258, 267
Dominick, Saint, 17
Dwyer, Dr. Robert, 193

East Germany, 171
ECLA (Economic Commission of
Latin America), 25, 28, 31,
34, 36
Ecuador, 285, 317, 323
Ecuadorian Service for Profes-
sional Training, 323
Education Unit of the Planning
Department, Ministry of Edu-
cation of Ecuador, 327
Educational principles of unitary
schools in Paraguay, 179-80
Educational Reform Project of
El Salvador, 90-95
Educational services SCIDE (now
ACEN), Guatemala, 58
Educational Technology Center
of Florida State University,
319
Educational Testing Service,
Princeton, New Jersey (ETS),
69
Efficiency approach to educational
planning (Bolivia), 208, 211
Efficiency, Quality, Sufficiency,
85
Elligett, Mrs. Jane, 193, 194
El Mácaro Teacher Training

351

Jolbe, Richard, 163
Jóvenes Communistas (Young Communists), 146
Jóvenes Rebeldes (Young Rebels), Cuba, 146

Kalamazoo College, 69
Kandel, I. L., 54
Kellogg foundation, 58
Kennedy, President John F., 100, 279
King, Edmund J., 334

laboratory school (American school of Guatemala), 56-73
Laboratory School program, 60, 62
Lacerda, Carlos, 141, f.n. 5
Ladino pilot schools, Guatemala, 191, 192
laissez faire, 21, 22, 25
Lay council, 54
Lazo, Mario, 148
Legislative Assembly (Costa Rica), 234, 241
Lenin, 147
Leninist doctrine, 145
Liberalism, 9, 21
licenciature, 67
Lima, Peru, 312
Lipset, Seymour, 151
Literacy and Adult Education Programs of the Dominican Republic and Paraguay, 325
Locke, John, 20, 21
Loyola, Ignatius, 17, 18, 19, 20
Lyons, Raymond F., 244, 258

McKinley, President William, 152
McNamara, Robert, 205
Maldonado, Vincente, 20
manpower requirements approach to educational planning (Bolivia), 208, 209, 210
Maracay, Venezuela, 300
Marté, José, 146
Marx, 121
Marxism, 9, 22, 334
Marxism-Feminism, 163

Mauro, Dana G., 51, 52
Mead, Margaret, 231
Memphis Public Schools, 69
Mexican Ministry of Education, 193
Mexican rural education program, 282
Mexico, 125, 193, 281, 282
Michigan State University, 69
"minimal linguistic universe," 133
"Minimum Technician" program, 1962 (Cuba), 165
Minister of Education (Costa Rica), 54, 228
Ministers of Education and Finance (Guatemala), 190
Ministries of Education (six Central American states), 204
Ministry of Armed Forces (Cuba), 165
Ministry of Culture (Montevideo, Uruguay), 327
Ministry of Culture and Education, (Buenos Aires, Argentina), 318
Ministry of Education (Colombia), 75, 76
Ministry of Education (Costa Rica), 228, 233, 235, 236, 237, 241, 242, 312
Ministry of Education (Cuba), 160, 162, 171
Ministry of Education (Ecuador), 315
Ministry of Education (El Salvador), 85, 86, 90, 92, 93
Ministry of Education (Guatemala), 57, 58, 59, 61, 63, 64, 67, 70, 71, 72, 190
Ministry of Education (Nicaragua), 54
Ministry of Education (Panama), 316
Ministry of Education (Venezuela), 312
Ministry of Education and Culture, (Paraguay), 178
Ministry of Public Education (Honduras), 112, 116, 117, 118

352

165
University Television, Channel
11, Recife, Brazil, 319
Urban Reform Laws, Cuba,
145
Uruguay, 267
USAID (United States Agency
for International Development), 38, 92-93, 99, 101,
116, 188, 190, 280
U.S.S.R. (Union of Soviet Socialist Republics), 170, 171,
272
UTRAMIG (Center for Technical Education, Labor Uni-
versity of Minas Gerais,
Belo Horizonte, Brazil),
322

Varona, Enrique Jose, 153
Velasio, Juan de, 20
Velez, Claudio, 26
Venezuela, 125, 258, 267, 272
Vera, Oscar, 33
Verney, Luis Antonio, 21
Viver e Lutar, f.n. 5, 141

Wionczek, Miguel, 24
WNDT-13 TV, 78
Wood, General Leonard, 152
Worker, Peasant Preparatory
School, Cuba, 167, 170
Workshops on Problems of
Adult Education (Argentina),
325
World Bank, 205
World Bank report on Cuban
education, 157, 158, 161
World War I, 153
World War II, 25, 29, 56,
156, 275, 279, 292
Wyckoff, Dr. Donald, 194

"Year of Education" in 1961,
(Cuba), 164
You live as you can, 139
Yugoslavia, 171

Zeller, Frederick A., 207